*A Spell
in Wild France*

A Spell in Wild France

Bill and Laurel Cooper

Methuen

First published in Great Britain 1992
by Methuen London
Michelin House, 81 Fulham Road, London SW3 6RB

Copyright © 1992 Bill and Laurel Cooper
Illustrations copyright © 1992 Laurel Cooper

The authors have asserted their moral rights

A CIP catalogue record for this book
is available from the British Library
ISBN 0 413 66720 0

Photoset by Deltatype Limited, Ellesmere Port
Printed in Great Britain
by Clays Ltd, St. Ives PLC

Contents

List of
illustrations

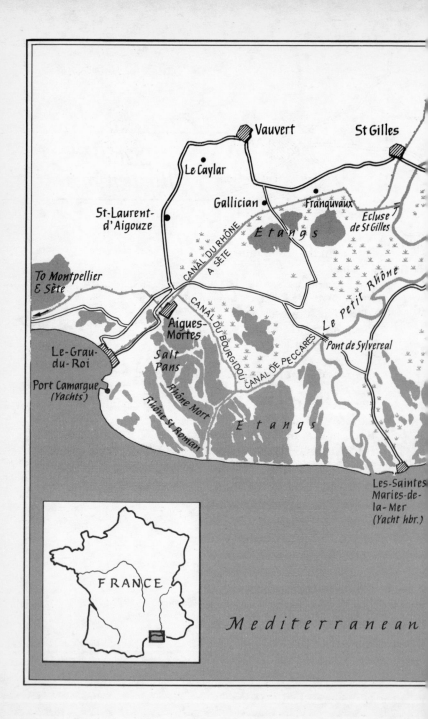

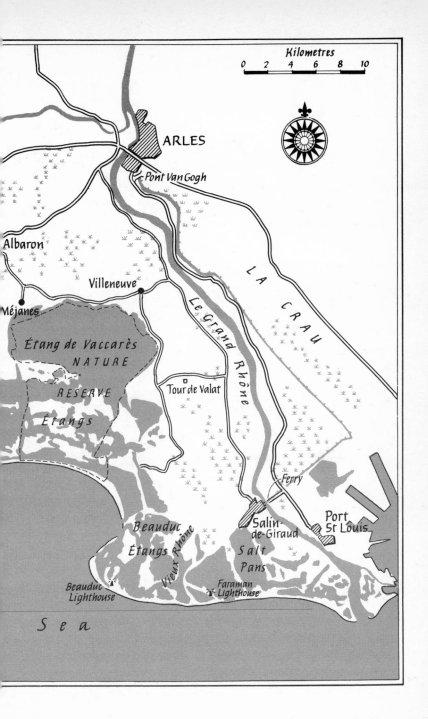

Authors' note

Epigraphs at the head of the chapters are from old Provençal sayings, except for four quotations from the works of Marquis Folco de Baroncelli-Javon, poet and *manadier* of the Camargue. All extracts were translated by Laurel Cooper.

1

Bull for beginners

'I am the Bull, who, since the Flood,
Has ruled, by Joy, by Art, by Blood.'
Marquis Folco de Baroncelli-Javon

'Here comes the eleven-o-clock cow,' Bill said looking up
from his copy of *Midi Libre*. Laurel looked at the church
clock.

'Right on time,' she said.

To live in the Camargue is to live with bulls, even if, as we
do, you live in a boat. Wild bulls driven through ancient
streets by mounted *gardians* on their way to or from the
stockade outside the ramparts of Aigues-Mortes, or bulls
let loose to keep the lads on their toes.

We were sitting in the Place St Louis outside the Express
Bar, the one with the pink chairs, and the town was *en fête*.
The ancient tradition of the *vache de onze heures*, the
eleven-o-clock cow, had been recently revived, and the
animal was let loose in the square just as in the old days, to
amuse the young till lunchtime. But the square had
changed considerably. A sepia photo we had seen in
Rancurel the photographer's window showed the square in
about 1898 with the statue of St Louis in the middle as now,
but at that time surrounded by stout railings. The buildings
round the square were simple, with wooden doors and
small shuttered windows, even the Epicerie Universelle
had no shop window. The church clock in the photo
showed ten past eleven, and there was the *vache de onze
heures*, loose in the square, trying creditably to horn a man
who was up a tree, a very small sapling plane tree. The

cautious had all joined St Louis, safe behind the railings, or were up on a farm cart in front of the sepia church.

Ninety years on, the plane trees had grown huge, far too big to climb. The railings round the statue of St Louis have gone (during the war, perhaps). The Epicerie Universelle has become a photographer's and a beauty shop. The square is surrounded by souvenir shops, bars and cafés all full of plate glass windows, and all of them spill into the centre with chairs and tables and parasols. The safest building would probably be the *mairie*, still with stout wooden doors and shuttered windows.

Someone, the municipal police or the *sapeurs-pompiers* maybe, had been spoilsport enough to insist on crowd barriers, so our visions of the bull in a china shop (well, in the Gallery Z, which sells wonderfully expensive crystal and glassware), or plunging through the parasols into the *panachés* and *pastis* of the punters, came to nought.

Assunta, the *patronne* of the Express Bar, said it was nice to see a bull in the square again: the last one she saw actually in the square and not just the adjoining streets where they are commonplace must have been . . . *voyons*, she mused, around 1940. But it was not quite the same as it had been ninety years ago. No one up a tree or leaping for a farmcart. Soon everyone drifted along to the Boulevard Gambetta to watch the real thing, the *abrivado*, a dozen *gardians* galloping on white Camargue horses surrounding three or four bulls, driving them from the meadows outside the town right through the ramparts, along Gambetta, out through the Porte de la Marine and into the stockade, with the youngsters trying to break the circle of horses and let the bulls escape. This is how the bulls were always brought to the arena for the bull games.

Cut off from the rest of France, practically and culturally, the Camargue has developed its own way of life to go with the wilderness of marshes and violent flooding rivers. The people are dour and introspective, though not humourless.

They are neither Provençal nor Languedoc. The Camargue is an island of little economic importance, and its people have been largely ignored.

Existence is concerned with the land and the water, the wild white horses, and black bulls which are the basis of the Camarguais culture. The Camargue proper is peopled mainly by a few wardens and natural historians of the Nature Reserve, plus the *gardians*, who tend their gods: the Bulls, with their acolytes, the Horses.

The rest of the Camarguais live on the perimeter and in the Petite Camargue, where the dolorous toil of generations has hacked and coaxed some kind of living from the harsh land, whether it was the white piles of sea salt, or the thin wines, or mulberry leaves to feed the silkworms which furnished the spinners and weavers at Alès and Nîmes.

Drainage and tourism have brought some prosperity to the area. The *mas* or farmsteads now have more fertile soil for crops, and the improved vines make better wine. Better flood control further up the Rhône has meant irrigation for the Camargue, and rice can now be grown where the soil is not salty. The *manades* or ranches continue to breed the elegant black bulls of the Camargue.

It is probable that this virus of prosperity will sooner or later kill the Camargue. Tourists eventually change and destroy the very things they come to see, just as evolving agriculture alters the land irrevocably, and the land here is like no other part of France, even of Europe. It is the diversity of the place which makes it unique. Not just wetland, but fresh and saltwater lakes, and every gradation of brackish in between, deep and shallow pools, dry land, water-laden marsh, land partly and intermittently flooded, providing a rich variety of habitats for fussy, difficult, and therefore rare birds.

The Camargue is still one of the deserts of France. It is almost unknown even to the French; part of it is a nature reserve and may help to save it now tourism is beginning to make an impact on the terrain and the people. The French Green Guide still apologises for it as 'not one of the most beautiful regions of France, but one of marked originality,' and says that tourists will experience profound feelings of strangeness and solitude. To us, it is as beautiful as the wetlands, flat meadows, and huge skies of our native Norfolk Broads, but harsher and wilder. Tourists mostly mass themselves round its boundaries, at Arles, Les-Saintes-Maries-de-la-Mer and Aigues-Mortes, and if they visit the Camargue proper it is usually by field trips, on horseback or bicycles, or on foot, though there is an alarming growth of four-wheel-drive cars to take marauding tourists into what should remain inaccessible. The Petite Camargue can be explored in one of the growing fleet of small cruising boats (with bicycles) for hire.

The Camargue is effectively a triangle, the marshy delta of the River Rhône, enclosed by two arms: the Rhône itself, and the Petit Rhône, which branches off the main Rhône just above Arles, and flows into the sea forty kilometres to the westward. The Petite Camargue lies to the west,

between the Petit Rhône and the Canal du Rhône à Sète.
The pebble desert of the Crau lies to the east of the Rhône,
and stretches nearly to Marseille.

The whole delta is a wild flat country of wetlands, salt
lakes, and seagrass prairies, much of it below sea level. The
absence of motor roads (none at all through to the seacoast
between the Saintes-Maries and the mouth of the Rhône, a
distance of about twenty miles; long may this continue)
means pure air and pure sound, a wealth of flora, and a
benison of birds.

2

Agues and ampères

'Jou neissen, fred couyen.'
. . . .
'Daylight pipping, frost nipping.'

From our home, the barge *Hosanna*, moored in the Canal du Rhône à Sète, a kilometre north of the medieval walls of Aigues-Mortes, we could see the Camargue in its cloak of winter.

The reeds that edged the saltpools were bleached and brittle from the heat of last summer, and the wind that swept across the seamarsh stirred them to a dry insistent rustle.

Some winter days were wet and grey, and the market traders along the ramparts of the old town grumbled or stayed at home, and so did the customers.

Some days were crisp and clear, making the breath of the wild white horses steam, feathery in the cold air, as they stamped and snorted by the canalside; and the grasses were rimed with frost in the early morning until the sun was high enough to warm the ground, and the day turned, blessedly, from winter to spring. When the sun set the cold returned.

Some January days seemed like a waft from Africa; the wind was soft and balmy, the sun was warm early, a benison to the bones of the old men sitting in the massive shelter of the main gate, the Porte de la Gardette. By lunchtime on such a day we could eat out of doors.

Some days the mistral blew, sweeping the sky clear of the last few shreds of cloud, whisking up leaves and twigs and paper scraps, and blowing the earth off the fields. We

looked for our windcheaters, scarves and gloves, and walked with our backs to the north-west to keep the grit out of our eyes. The market traders, wrapped for the Arctic, cursed and tussled with their canvas awnings, and weighted their merchandise down with ancient stones; and the old men did not sit down, they shuffled and stamped, and told each other how important it was to keep the kidneys warm.

The two of us, longstanding boat-livers, were for the time being moored in the canal not far from the ramparts of Aigues-Mortes, alongside the peninsula which divides the old Canal du Bourgidou (now no longer navigable) from the main Canal that leads from the River Rhône along the coast to the port of Sète.

Other boat dwellers lived here too, some only in summer, some stopping for the winter. Most were members of the Association for the Defence and Protection of the Patrimony and Tourism of the Canal du Midi, which we will call the Association.

In spite of this resounding name we were not regarded as very respectable. The *mairie* would not empty our dustbins, though Electricité de France (EDF) consented to supply the peninsula with power.

The Association had a concession to moor boats on the peninsula at Le Bourgidou and provide amenities for them. Forming an association, preferably to protect something, is the first thing you must do in France if you wish to be allowed to do anything. You then go ahead and do it till someone stops you, and then you can argue from a stronger position. So the members of the Association had water and power (intermittently), two fig trees, two very solid picnic tables on the bank, rather less solid bollards (*Hosanna*'s was pulling out of the ground at the rate of one centimetre every time a really big Rhône barge went past), and some beautiful rubbish bins which the *mairie* would not empty as we paid no local tax. We were in fact not allowed to pay the local tax because we did not live in a house. This problem is not soluble given the French addiction to bureaucracy, which is both a word and a concept that they originated. Bins were provided for passing tourists, but on the peninsula we were not strictly tourists nor were we passing. So it irritated us to read in the local paper that there would be a '*ramassage de déchets encombrants*' ('collection of large items of domestic refuse') such as old furniture, mattresses, cooking stoves, and large packing cases, at a town too far away for us to use this useful service. It would have to be a journey to the town dump again.

Our boat was not yet finished, so any time was building time, and we put in a big spurt on the galley. We like our food, and although there was a sink with taps, a cooker, a mixed hob (gas and electricity) and even a microwave oven, these luxuries sat in makeshift timber frames, held in place, as Laurel once complained, by paper clips (she meant G-clamps).

The galley was open to the saloon, and underneath the appliances all stores were in cardboard boxes, some of them very difficult to get at. There were no shelves and no cupboards, and the drawers, though they had been constructed on the journey down the canals, had not been fitted.

Laurel embarked on a period of total chaos quite cheerfully, given the end in view. Bill always did the woodwork, she did the varnishing, painting, and cooking, and tried not to mix them all up. (All yachts know of diesel pudding, which is merely one that fell on the floor. Toast and varnish is another delicacy to be avoided, as is sawdust in the sauce. The real difficulty is to avoid absent-mindedly dipping the paintbrush in the coffee pot.)

A proper carcase was made for each side of the galley, and underneath the worktops that housed the hob and sink there would be nothing but drawers. Laurel had watched her mother and aunt, valiant ladies well into their eighties, battling on their knees to find an object at the back of a floor-level cupboard. She observed them gradually give up the struggle, and she sensibly put all the things they regularly needed in drawers, or on accessible shelves between thigh and shoulder height. Laurel would have nothing in the galley that was not easy to get at, and she was lucky that Bill was an obliging sort of husband.

Between the galley and the saloon, above the sink and drainer, appeared stowages for china and mugs, and an ingenious plate rack (one cannot have crockery moving about at sea). A hatch was made through to the dining end of the saloon, and an inconspicuous door under this hatch gave onto a well which contained the things one needs to reach from both table and galley: salt, sugar, marmalade, pickles and so on.

Gradually order came to the galley as varnish and paint dried sufficiently for stores to be put in their proper places. Rows of jars with comforting contents, rice and brown sugar, oats and flour, smiled fatly down from the shelves. Beneath them were smaller shelves for spices and herbs. Suddenly it became much easier to cook, since it was now a simple matter to put one's hand on a pan or an ingredient, or a favourite implement.

It was also far easier to clean. The galley began to look very good, its new window frame gleamed with varnish, and Laurel felt she could now wave proudly from her domain to the passing barges, most of which she recognised from the pattern of the lace curtains in their living quarters: if it was cat, lamp-post and crescent moon, it was *Port Navalo*, cats and a birdcage was *Surcoing*, the barge *Suffren* fancied roses. *Scirocco* (flowers and a scalloped edge) was a relative of Bernard of *Massabielle*, our neighbour in the next barge upstream, alongside which he would often stop for the night, while the huge *Vaccarès* had a procession of swimming ducks.

On fine Sunday mornings, after visiting the market, it was our habit to sit in the Place St Louis, at the Express Bar. We would enjoy the sunshine, and watch the world go by (not a lot of it in winter), watch the smartly dressed sheep coming out of Church, and the heathen goats checking their lottery tickets or dashing out for the bread.

We would order our coffee from the waiter Serge, who would greet us with '*Ah! Les Brittaniques!*'. His little brown bitch, curled up under a table, watched him with bright eyes. One of her hind legs was missing. We asked him how the accident had occurred. 'She was in a circus,' he said, as if that was a full and complete explanation. We sometimes invented reasons for the missing leg. A tiger bit it off? She got into the same box as the lady sawn in half? The knife thrower had an off-day? We never found out.

We would also pass the time of day with the *patronne* of the Express Bar, Assunta. Her hennaed hair was strained back from her grave old face and twisted into a bun, Spanish style, and you could tell the weather from the number of cardigans she wore. If it was three she would not be seen out on the terrace at all, but remain in the cosy, smoky, greasy warmth inside.

Anyone with any sense did the same in winter when the mistral (the dreaded wind that howls down the Rhône Valley from the north) blew hard and strong. At such times it was good in our barge *Hosanna* to contemplate the woodfire burning in the stove, and relish the scent of beans simmering on the hob with a chunk of *petit salé*, a trotter and some sausage, all with a touch of rosemary and wood-smoke to sharpen a winter appetite. (We were thankful that we were not at sea in this weather.) However, for every pro there is a con, and a wood stove is as hungry as it is comforting, and must be fed. Yesterday Bill ricked his back bringing the log basket down the companionway. He had a bad night, and his movements the following morning were cautious.

The electricity failed the next night, so we started the generator to cook breakfast. Bill, his back improved, went along to give a hand with patching the cable. He returned to announce that everyone was coughing and sneezing, and to demand vitamin C tablets to boost his resistance to germs.

With power restored we were able to print out a couple of magazine articles. Writing occurs when we are not finishing the interior of the barge, cruising, or just wandering about the countryside. Laurel took the articles down to *la poste* in town, and bought her bread. Every street rang with coughing, the Aigues-Mortais were having the first of their annual plagues, *la grippe*. In the short interval between hacks and splutters you could hear the whistle and wheeze of straining lungs, and every other phrase was *'A tes souhaits!'* as someone delivered yet another mighty sneeze. Who would think that here in the Midi the pharmacy's window back in November urged inoculation against the 'flu, and was now full of remedies for *bronchite*, *grippe*, coughs and colds, and the newspaper was rapping un-inoculated knuckles and pointing out gleefully that it was now too late for precautions – *la grippe* was HERE. The only question was now which foreigners to blame: was it Spanish 'flu, Chinese or Russian? It could not possibly be French.

Best wishes for the New Year were exchanged in all the streets and shops as a preliminary to any other transaction, and the *'Bonne Année's'* and *'Boueno Annado's'* were followed by *'Surtout pour la santé'* (above all health) and the agreement *'Oui, pardi,* after all, that is what counts', but the fervent wish for health in the coming year was nullified by the usual three (or sometimes four) kisses bestowed on alternate cheeks of your *proches* which ensured an even spread of your cold round *tout* Aigues-Mortes.

Back at the barge Bill was trying to start the central heating, but there were a few snags as he had only recently installed the system. There were one or two leaks. The boiler kept going out. He was spending a good deal of time on his knees in the engine room which houses the boiler and coming up filthy, both in his person and his temper. The first leak was a bad one, pints of water spraying into the after bathroom, causing a red alert for buckets. A pipe connector had not been tightened sufficiently. Thereafter the bilges into which the water had cascaded had to be mopped and sponged and dried, as no boat-liver likes to think of even a tiny puddle of water lurking down there, rusting things, growing mould, dirty, a sheen of oil on it, charged with fluff and crumbs, dead insects and old screws. *Beurk!* is the appropriate French expression of disgust.

The leak was all the more annoying because we were extremely short of water at the time, and could not afford to waste it, no baths were to be taken, and minimum washing up, seagoing style. The *cabane* containing the communal tap was locked; Mario (our President) had gone to Dunkerque for Christmas taking the key with him, and the spare key that he left with Daniel (Boubou, our Secretary) on the barge *Escaut* was accidentally dropped in the canal on New Year's Eve in the course of some entirely natural celebration. We all awaited Mario's return with some impatience.

After a few days the electricity failed again. This was not an uncommon event on our little peninsula. We were connected to the very efficient network of EDF via a main cable that passed under the water and across to the point of the peninsula where it climbed a pole and then hung in a slack catenary over to the *cabane* which housed all the meters and fuse-boards.

Inside the Association's *cabane*, as well as the water tap, there was a switchboard, makeshift, but quite soundly done. A sheet of plywood was fixed to one wall on which was screwed a meter for each boat. From there a spider's web of smaller cables carried the power to the individual boats. The main supply cable brought in three-phase alternating current of 380 volts. At the *cabane* the four wires were arranged in various confusing patterns by Jean-Claude, the Association's Treasurer and electrician (once a Communications Officer of the French Navy, and reputed to understand these things), as a result of which each boat received single phase electricity of 220 volts except when Mario was welding something: it then dropped to 190. We were all quite happy. Or we would have been if it had worked all the time.

Jean-Claude was retired and lived in a house close by. He was very respectable, paid his taxes and got his rubbish collected.

Boubou once tried to put his rubbish in Jean-Claude's elegant bin, standing temptingly in the road, and received a severe telling off:

'You pay no tax, you have not the right!' said the Treasurer to the Secretary.

Jean-Claude's boat, *Monfranc*, was not one of the more handsome boats on the peninsula. It was parked in the disused Canal du Bourgidou. He seldom used it, and it looked neglected. Jean-Claude was like the drawing of M. Dupont in one's school French book, round of face, slightly balding, and with a little moustache. His wife Nise was tiny, smiling, angular, and a little powdery. She demanded at least four kisses at all encounters.

Jean-Claude knew a lot about radio and electronics. Where Mario was good with welding and hammer work, Jean-Claude could mend tiny things with a soldering iron. At the time he was working on our auto pilot.

The main electric supply cable to the peninsula had seen better days. None of us knew exactly its condition under the water because no one dared to try to bring it to the surface for examination. It must, however, have been occasionally rasped by the keels of passing boats engaged in nautical agriculture (ploughing through the mud because the water is not deep enough, or more logically, because the boats are too deep for the water). Its delicate state could be inferred by the forty or so metres which then hung above ground between two ancient and expropriated barge masts planted in the soft earth. In the visible overhead parts there were some fifty or so joins, mostly cocooned in mastic to try to stop the rain getting in, a precaution only partially successful. Laurel, observing that the cocoons looked like an air grafting diagram in a gardening book, suggested that they were trying to grow an electricity plant.

'Current bushes,' said Bill, 'in magnetic fields.'

The mends were a forlorn effort, for the wires swooped at their lowest to about two and a half metres above the ground where a manoeuvring lorry or van, or even a man with a ladder on his shoulder, could touch them and precipitate yet another blackout on the peninsula.

Last month one of the wires under the water failed completely, and there was much anxious talk of renewal. 'It is,' said one Associate, 'made up of more joints than cable.' The trouble was that we would need 120 metres of very large 100 amp four-core cable and that cost a lot of *balles*. So Jean-Claude did something very clever with the wiring, identifying which one of the four had failed and isolating it, then connecting us all up to the other three in differing ways. At first our meter went backwards, but after a cunningly delicate adjustment by Jean-Claude (he thumped it) to everyone's surprise and joy it went round the right way and we once more had power. A loose end was left dangling from one of the poles outside, but no one seemed to worry about it, and we all assumed it was not alive. Jean-Claude's thump was of considerable reassurance to Bill who has always maintained that a craftsman is someone who knows exactly where to thump inanimate objects in order to knock sense into them.

Electricity failures were, as we have seen, frequent, and

only a few could be blamed on EDF, usually those which occurred during heavy thunderstorms, and here in the Camargue they could sometimes be very heavy. If we could see a thunder-black sky over towards Nîmes the storm almost always came to Le Bourgidou.

Usually the blue-overalled gentlemen of EDF could be observed in the locality afterwards, climbing poles or dashing through huge puddles in their vans and the supply was swiftly re-connected. But more often the cuts were due to defects in our material or in our collective selves, as when Boubou severed his cable with the grass cutter when mowing the 'lawn' beside his barge. He was unwise enough to pick up the severed cable to inspect it which gave him a sharp dose of electro-convulsive therapy and cured him of curiosity. Usually the cable was to blame for the breakdowns.

Some boats, the Swiss and the Germans, empty for the winter, used little power, so the three major users had a wire each to balance things. When the supply failed it was usually necessary to wait until the exposed bit of wire dried out, and then climb a ladder and remake the overhead joints where the aluminium conductors had corroded. More often than not the problem was simply an overload. The system was capable of bearing a good sixty ampères in theory, but that was when the cables were new. Now common sense had led two of our number to impose on themselves a limit of fifteen ampères each (or 3,000 watts).

Unfortunately the third boat was in the hands of a young couple who were very competent with computers and hi-fis, but could not add up. They touchingly believed that their immersion heater used less than 3,000 watts and that they could switch other things on at the same time. There was also something wrong with their main fuse, if they had one at all. Instead of blowing when they had an overload, as it should have done, every main fuse on the peninsula blew (and for all we knew, half the neighbourhood too). This is electrically impossible but the special little god of Le

Bourgidou – the power that IS – seems to be able to arrange it. When this happened there was a general meeting at the *cabane* to reset the circuit-breakers. This time there was no one about with a key to the *cabane*. The *cabane* was stone built without windows, and with a two-inch thick oak door. We mentally planned to get our own key cut as soon as all the *fêtes* were over and shopping was back to normal.

In the early part of the month we managed to get our barge connected to the French telephone system. We had been to Nîmes two weeks before to ask for this, and were shown, bemused, into a designer waiting area with thick carpets, soothing muzak and comfortable chairs. When our turn came, a smart young lady attempted to put our long address on a computer (which bad-temperedly bit off the end and reduced it to six lines: there is no room for more, it snapped). We hoped any communication would still find the communal post box which all the boat-dwellers of the Association use. The computer then printed out a card with our new number on, and (through its mouthpiece the smart young lady) asked if next Thursday would be convenient for the installation, and which of these elegant *postes de téléphone* would we like? To be connected a week from our first enquiry was a pleasant surprise, though it took an extra week when the engineer discovered we lived in a boat; he explained that he would have to return with a *poteau* (a pole) to carry the line down to the canal bank from the nearest source up there on the bridge.

Now we were on the phone.

No longer would we have to go round all the phoneboxes in town (we knew the position of all of them) looking for one that was in order.

No longer would we fry in the heat of a glass box almost always placed in the full glare of the Midi sun, Laurel complaining that it felt as if one were being microwaved.

At least the days of carrying with us a weighty bag of five-franc pieces that rapidly wore through our pockets were long over, and for some time we had been using the little plastic phone-card which works only two times out of three. (The third provokes flashing messages on the screen telling us that the *appareil* is now out of order and only emergency calls can be connected, the tartness of the tone implying that it is ALL OUR FAULT).

No longer would Laurel get trapped in our nearest box, the one with the door that sticks, and have to shout to an astonished man on a bicycle to assist her to emerge.

No longer (perhaps regrettably) would our neighbours be involved in our affairs, births, deaths, and marriages, by passing on intriguing messages from family or editors that demanded a glass of rosé and lengthy explanation of their meaning.

We rang up all our relatives in England, and wished them a Happy New Year. They all said the same thing: 'You sound as if you were just next door.' French telephones have come a long way since the days when even calling someone in the next street entailed an underwater dialogue as of irritated porpoises, with deafening rushing noises, then clicks and hoots, peppered with shouts of '*Quoi*?' and '*Comment*?', and finally ending with 'I can't hear a word, come round to the house.'

Twelfth Night is not known as such in France, but here in the Midi the twelve days between Christmas and Epiphany are studied carefully, and the weather on each day is tabulated. They believe each day corresponds with the coming months and foretells what the weather will be. Thus if December 26th is frosty, that will be the weather for the whole of January.

On Twelfth Night Mario came back. Power was on again, and we were all in the queue for the waterhose.

His mother in Dunkerque had fed him Christmas pudding, he said in disgust. English Christmas pudding? we asked.

'No, my mother's recipe is from Calais, but also full of suet. It is revolting, but *traditionel*.' Laurel feels rather the same about the English variety.

Mario was the Association's President, as was right, since he was the instigator and the dynamo. He hoped to build a slipway here one day. Mario: ex-*batelier*, boat-builder, handyman, and cook. A *dur*. A tough guy.

Mario had to go to Nîmes quite often, as he was having a financial wrangle with his ex-wife. She claimed, very simply, everything he was possessed of. Said Mario: 'There is no point in making money, the court takes it all.'

His beloved restaurant boat, the *Isles de Stel*, built with his own hands (and those of his ex-wife, it must be said), laid idle in escrow next to his *péniche*. He lived fifty yards from us, in a caravan next to the stone *cabane*, with Martine, whom he had lured away from her husband and teenage children with promises of romance and adventure. He tried to look as if he was a *chômeur*, unemployed, but he worked like a maniac: there was always someone on the peninsula who needed a bit of welding, or some steelwork or painting, and Mario was a hard worker. Money, however, must never be seen to change hands.

Mario was also a caveman.

'He came back for me twice,' Martine told us with modest pride. 'I went back to Jean-Pierre, my husband, but Mario came after me again. He was determined and romantic, and Jean-Pierre was so timid, and I was bored. Now,' she sighed, 'I wonder if I need a man whose *caractère* is somewhere between the two. But I do not think Mario will give me the chance to look for one.'

Nor do we. Mario, we have said, is a *dur*.

Martine was born in a *péniche*, child and grandchild of *bateliers*. She had her permit as a *marinière*, and was missing the barge life still led by her ex-husband. The caravan was '*pas terrible*' (not marvellous), and Mario's restaurant boat that might have kept her occupied was laid up pending the court decision. Her bubbling spirits sometimes got a bit low.

'But at least,' she shrugged, 'life with Mario is not dull.'

Indeed not. They both shouted at each other a great deal,

and sometimes after a particularly loud and virulent session, accompanied by the barking of Martine's alsation, inappropriately named Dinky, Martine could be seen in tears putting her dog and her suitcase into her little red car (they filled it) and driving off.

Just for a while. 'If you lose five sous and your woman,' says the local proverb, 'pity about the money.'

The Secretary of our Association was Daniel, known as Boubou. He was the only one of us who was fairly fully employed, the rest of us were retired, *en chômage*, or worked only in the tourist season. He was a publicist, and on his barge *Escaut* he had a dark room and a desktop publishing computer. He had our affection as well as our respect, as he was the kindest of men.

His wife Francine was his brother's ex-wife, so his stepchildren were also his nephew and niece. This did not seem to confuse the French at all. Francine was a *gamine*. Twists and spirals of blond hair escaped in all directions from under her bakerboy beret. Long thin legs emerged from very short skirts, or were clad in colourful tights. Her face was pale, pixie-like, and her teeth were small and white, and disarmingly crooked. Every winter she died, like pansies in a child's garden, the legs were padded almost to normal by thick black tights, and the little face was wrapped in scarves. She called almost every day to ask if we needed bread, an immense help if we were busy.

'Half a *gros pain*, as always?' her gentle voice would ask. We liked the big loaf, as it was fatter than a baguette, and made better toast the next morning.

'It goes well? Me, I am not well today. I am *pas terrible*.' It was the eyes, the skin, the neck, the head, the disc, the *bronchite*, or a *crise de nerfs*. She was sensitive and emotional, and took things hard. She worried about her children. Her daughter Cathy travelled adventurously, and was in India at that time, with her little *copain*.

'Him I do not trust,' said Francine. 'I told him before the

départ, if anything happens to Cathy I shall kill him.' The thought was the more striking for being expressed in such a gentle voice. Her son Nicholas was a fruitful source of agitation. A quiet and pleasant youngster, he was nevertheless accident-prone. He spent all last summer recovering from a broken thigh acquired in his second car smash. As it was Francine's car he wrecked, she was on a bicycle at the moment.

Francine, Cathy, and Nicholas loved the *péniche Escaut*, and they all loved Boubou. (Cathy is saving up for a barge of her own.) Boubou did not always love *Escaut*. On discovering after a damp winter that some of his boxes of books had got mould on them he told us: 'I nearly wept. But I tell myself, *c'est ça, la vie du bateau*.'

He is the Professor of the peninsula of Le Bourgidou. He is the one we all go to when we have a knotty point to discuss, or a difficult letter to write. He is educated, he possesses books, even dictionaries, he speaks and writes good French, and we suspect he knows more English than he lets on. He looks the part of a professor, he has the grey hair and beard and the abstracted look, and he is less prone to DIY than the rest of us. He leaves that to his family. 'They do it so much better,' he says contentedly.

We were busy attacking the wheelhouse ceiling. This meant clearing everything out (we eat our lunch there in winter) and cutting back the insulating foam which coats the steel roof. This was done either with a kitchen knife, which is slow (but the resulting pieces are easy to clean up) or with a wire brush on the electric drill, fast but drastic, our noses protected from the invasive polythene dust. When Francine called by with the bread we loomed out of the smog overalled and face-masked like moonmen.

'Always working?' she said. 'Don't kill yourselves!' Now at the end of the week the dreadful dust had either been sucked into the hoover, or settled into impossible cracks and corners whence it would emerge in wreaths and puffs next time we started the generator or the engine.

Jean-Claude, refusing payment, had mended the tiny broken wires on the auto-pilot, whose power supply could then be run behind the tongue-and-groove ceiling boards, which were now in place, and had had three coats of paint. The ceiling looked magnificent, we moved everything back again, polished the chart table and replaced the geraniums upon it.

> Entre san Antoni e san Bastian
> Se fa mai de fre qu'en tout l'an
>
> Twixt Saints Anton and Sebastian
> It's colder than all winter gone

Frosts on the 18th and the 20th were very sharp indeed. We continued to have morning frosts for several days, but even in the midst of them we were able at least once to eat lunch out of doors on a day that was sunny with no wind.

Near the end of January a policeman called. He was very polite and wanted to see the ship's papers. All was in order, he said, and were we staying long? We explained that the boat was a long way from being finished, and that this was a good place to do the work. He nodded, smiling, and wished us a good stay.

The tremendous gales which hit Britain in the last days of January dislodged the anticyclone that had given us cold bright weather for a whole month, and it became warmer and damp. The first rain fell since mid December. The last Sunday market of the month was windy, wet and warm, and Bill spent the very last day of January in a cupboard, as the electricity had failed again.

3

Carnival and cowboys

'*Carnaval senso luno*
De cent fremo se n'en sauva mas uno.'
. . . .
'No moon when Carnival is come
Of a hundred women you'll save but
one.'

Candlemas, February 2nd, was the birthday of a much
loved member of our family, and we lit candles for dinner in
memory. Feeling the Provençal influence, we ate our
pancakes then, rather than on Mardi Gras (Pancake
Tuesday) but ended up eating them on both occasions
because we like pancakes, either French or English style.

February in most Mediterranean countries means
Carnival. On the Côte d'Azur at Nice this intense tourist
attraction takes place on at least two weekends before Lent
begins, and as it is much too lucrative to stop on Mardi
Gras, just as the weather is nearly always improving, it
goes on well into Lent. Christianity gives way to tourism.

Here in the Camargue, Carnival is on a more modest
scale but well celebrated nonetheless. Old ladies, telling
you their age, may well say 'I've seventy *carnavals* on my
back,' as they might admit to seventy summers. In mid
January the market cloth stall was already stocked with the
theatrical gold and silver lamé, the multicoloured
diamonds for Harlequin, the crazy clown prints, the stiff
tarletan for ballet skirts, and cheap satin in a rainbow of
colours. Mothers are poring over the Burda Catalogue of
Carnival Costumes. A prince this year, or a pirate? A
milkmaid or an odalisque? You can bet your Texas boots it

will not be a cowboy or girl, since round here that is perfectly normal dress; any fine Sunday sees the high boots, the colourful Camargue shirts, worn with jeans or tiered skirts in Provençal print, the neckerchief and the black *gardian*'s hat, worn by much of the population.

Mme Poitavin, dark and vivacious, wife of the *patissier*, was an indefatigable window dresser, between serving customers she was tying bows, decorating baskets of confectionery, and arranging mouth-watering trays of marzipan. Her carnival window showed a suspended crescent moon, with a tearful pierrot sitting on it.

There are two carnival processions in Aigues-Mortes, on the two consecutive Sundays prior to Mardi Gras. They are organised by rival hunting societies. One of these is the Cercle des Chasseurs Sous-Marins, which in spite of its title has nothing to do with underwater activities, it seems more likely that the origin of the name is a joke; that they are '*saoul-marins*', the society of the drunken sailors. The *chasseurs* make an effigy, *un caramantran*, representing some special subject of current antipathy for hunters, perhaps an environmentalist or the director of a chemical company, and then they suspend it from the Tour de Constance. All the society, in their dozens, take their guns and riddle the effigy with shot and shell and then drown it in the canal. After that they have a very convivial lunch which goes on for a long time. The Aigues-Mortais are hot on tradition. There is a somewhat similar ceremony of *caramantran* at Marseilles, where the effigy is hung all Mardi Gras from the yard of a ship, then on Ash Wednesday is judged, and burnt or thrown into the sea.

A strong mistral arrived in mid February and blew for three days. The old rhyme goes:

> Mistral qui lève le nuit
> Ne dure qu'aujordhui,
> Mistral qui lève le jour

Dure trois, six, ou neuf jours.

Should mistral rise ere night is done
T'will last but till the setting sun,
But if it rise when sun do shine
T'will last days three or six, or nine.

In February, they say, the mistral is king. This wind, when it blows, changes your life. The temperature plummets, the puddles dry or freeze as you watch them, and the topsoil, accompanied by dried twigs, small bushes, flying plastic, and anything weighing less than a ton that has not been tied down goes screaming off towards Africa. Howling like the trumpets of Jericho, the mistral flattens everything in its path, and is reputed in the Camargue to blow the horns off the bulls. No woman of child-bearing age should stand with her back to it.

The *mariniers* get into difficulty. Not those in the loaded barges, which are deep in the water and are not much affected by the wind, but crews of unladen *péniches* with three quarters of their hulls above the water fear weather like this. When the wind is blowing across the canal the boats are under control only when they are going fast. We too, being moored on the leeward side of the waterway, are uneasy in these conditions, and so is our neighbour the barge *Escaut*, for our berths are between two pairs of stone knuckles which once carried lock gates, and now narrow the width of the canal to barely more than that of a big barge. It is the front of an unladen barge that is the most affected by the cross wind because its steering gear is at the stern, making it crab along pointing about fifteen degrees into the wind. To negotiate a narrow gap it has to parallel itself with the canal for a couple of boats' lengths and hope for the best before it can recommence steering, and this has to be done at speed. An empty barge is as redoubtable as a wind-blown furniture van on the Severn bridge.

We are moored behind the knuckle, thank the Lord, but

every now and then a '*vide*' (unladen barge) hits us a glancing blow (the knuckle also gets its share judging by its disordered stonework). The task of the *mariniers* is not made easier by the barges' cocked-up bows preventing vision ahead from the wheelhouse, and one of the crew of two has either to go forward or out to one side and direct the man (or woman, for it is often the *marinière* handling the barge) at the wheel. Bill has asked a *batelier* why they do not have ballast tanks forward to bring the bows down, and was told that many of them do, but that bringing the bows down inevitably causes the stern to go up and the screw is further out of the water than ever, which wastes fuel.

Some of the smaller Freycinet barges (those built to fit the locks on the smaller canals) have bow rudders that they can lower when the barges are light. This helps, but it involves one of the crew being out in the deep midwinter for longish periods. There is an unavoidable tendency for the frozen one to nip back to the wheelhouse for a quick warm-up, and it is then that collision with *Hosanna* seems most likely.

The laden barges are more controllable. They go much slower and the larger ones, loaded to two metres or more draught, plough through the muddy bottom at times and one can hear the occasional clunk as their screws hit some piece of debris that has been thrown into the canal by a local resident. These barges push a positive wall of water ahead of them and a well of suction alongside their hulls which sends moored boats like ourselves surging fore and aft as they pass. We are moored with nylon ropes and they can stretch as much as twenty-five percent. Old bargemen use wire ropes which do not stretch, but they rust and break strands to cut your hands. Nothing about boats is ever perfect.

We know the crews of most of the barges which pass regularly, working on a contract to carry sand or paper. Some pass slowly and cause us few problems; others are inconsiderate and pass at full power upsetting moored craft all along the canal. The occasional barges, strangers picking up a one-off cargo from Sète and bound a long way up country, perhaps even to Holland, are not familiar with the waters and are more cautious. The biggest barges in our canal are the *citernes*, tankers carrying up to a thousand tonnes of products from the refinery at Frontignan. They are so big that in order to navigate this canal they are only two-thirds loaded.

There is a project under way to construct a canal by-pass, (or *déviation*) round Aigues-Mortes, thus avoiding a sharp turn and a narrow railway swing bridge. When this is complete the whole canal will be deepened and widened. Already the road bridges to cross the projected *déviation* are built and stand forlorn amid the alien fields, waiting for the excavators to dig out the new length of canal.

The ecologists, greens, and other disaffected folk are campaigning to have the project abandoned as a blot on the landscape, death to the lesser crested piptit, and upsetting the habitat of the bonesetting caterpillar. They are joined by the *chasseurs*, or hunters, unlikely bedfellows, who fear that the bulldozers will scare away the rabbits or whatever living thing they wish to destroy there. The protest is futile for the bridges are there already; and it is they that are the eyesores, standing six metres above the ground. The canal itself will be virtually invisible from ground level (and there is no other level in the Camargue). But where will all the excavating material go? Aye, there's the rub. It will be used, say horrified ecologists, to fill in the *étangs*, to enable landowners to reclaim land and convert it from unproductive marsh to agricultural use, or worse still, for someone to sow villa seeds, the most lucrative crop a farmer can plant. Opposers of any project always seem to suspect a conspiracy; they are probably right.

As foreigners we are outside the argument except that when the canal is completed the old, abandoned section through Aigues-Mortes, in which we are moored, will pass out of the control of Voies Navigables de France, an administration of good-natured pragmatic civil engineers, tolerant and always approachable, to be administered by local politicians, who, we have observed, know nothing about canals, and talk only to other politicians and pressure groups.

This causes dismay among our Association. Nobody could call us a pressure group. All our concessions will automatically expire. One might expect normally to have to renegotiate, which would be troublesome but ought not to be impossible. But with the coming in the last two decades of tourism to the Camargue, and its present exponential growth rate, the old canal is seen as a gold mine for whoever can get their hands on it. The in-fighting has already begun. One commune has put forward a proposal for a huge new marina with a thousand holiday flats and berths for four thousand boats. (In the Petite Camargue!) The prospect of even ten percent of those boats trying to get in or out of that marina during a summer weekend would daunt a London taxi driver. It would be intolerable to the commercial barges for whom the canals exist. However, the bargees being unorganised, their case will almost certainly go by default.

Given all the different communes competing with their independent and grandiose schemes (except Aigues-Mortes, which is behaving with the quiet dignity becoming an ancient city), it is likely that the whole affair will be called in by the Chamber of Commerce at Nîmes, known locally as Le Mafia du Gard, who will see that the *pots de vin* and other benefits are divided among the big-wigs in the departmental capital and exclude the local folk.

And we, we will anyway be on the move, our boat finished and our eyes on new waters. We are, as seamen, denied the cliché 'pastures new'. Except that our seas are populated in English by white horses, and in French by white sheep.

Our Association, finding it had thirty-three members and a surplus of money, held an AGM. We usually try to avoid such things, but the matters under discussion touched us closely and it turned out to be one of the most enjoyable we had ever been to, since the spare money was used to give all who attended (about twenty of us) a good dinner at Les Quatre Vents Restaurant. It also helped to sweeten certain officers of the Navigation Authority, who were invited to join us after the meeting.

Mario presiding got the business over at reasonable speed. There was no written agenda. The *vin rosé* circulated, so did the *pastis*. We re-elected our officers, and decided that Boubou our Secretary should again write to the Mayor on our behalf. Bill suggested that we might try and get the media interested in the *Gaulois* – the ancient wooden barge in the pond under the bridge, the last on the Canal and of great historical interest, so Mario claimed. Mario was polite but doubtful – he had obviously been that route himself, without success. We decided that we should plant some trees, and do something about the electricity cable.

And that was it, the meeting over, the gathering continued with great good humour as the food began to arrive. It was a good example of how the French profit by using their restaurants to advantage, for few of the dishes served in the private room to the rear were on the standard menu, and we suspect most of them were the favourite dishes of the committee, there being by coincidence as many courses as there were members. It was a large committee. We recall among other things a delicious crab mousse, roast guinea-fowl, and *clafouti*, or cherry batter pudding. We staggered back to our boat extremely late, extremely full, wafted home (we believe) by the final brandy, since we do not recall the journey.

Our friend Jeannot owned the Mas Rancier which borders on our mooring and grew vines and asparagus. The Mas was managed by his brother-in-law Serge, because Jeannot is drummer for a well-known group playing syncopated Bach, which has been touring all over the world since the sixties. As soon as the cold relents at the end of February the vines are pruned to check them just before they spurt into growth. Different varieties seem to do this at different times, for we noticed vineyards side by side, in one of which the vines were neatly pruned, while in the other the vines were still wearing their winter whiskers, sometimes well into March. One was sharply aware of the seasons in the Camargue. Everywhere one looked the signs changed daily, in the vineyards, in the sky, in the kitchen gardens, and down on the Réserve de Vaccarès, the great brackish lake at the sea's edge that is a meeting place for birds of every continent, particularly waterfowl. Here the water birds began to pair off, beginning with the majestic purple heron and the mallards.

At the warmer end of the month spring's harbingers were the buds on ash and willow, and a veil of green in the pastures, no longer inundated by the winter water table, to the great relief of the *manadiers* (ranchers) and *gardians*.

One can imagine with what joy these signs of spring were greeted in the old days by a *gardian* who had spent a harsh and sometimes glacial winter out of doors, tending the bulls, following the herd as it found what meagre pasture it could in the waterlogged marshes. He risked death by cold or famine, or a fall into a frozen *roubine* (ditch), risks run by both man and beast. From the accounts of the day there was little cowboy glamour; they were ill fed, except when at the Mas itself, poorly clad, and ill housed in the *cabanes* that were their shelter at night.

A *cabane* nowadays makes an attractive little weekend fishing hut or seaside cabin, whitewashed, thatched, rounded at the north-western end so that the roof did not blow off in a mistral. A sloping kingpost formed the top of this cone, which was made into a cross above the thatch by adding a transverse piece of wood, or a bull's horn, to keep the thunder away. The door (and window if there was one) were at the opposite end, which was more often sheltered. In the old days, however, it was rough shelter.

An old *gardian* wrote: 'My lodging was precarious. The

cabane which served as my home provided no comfort. The floor of beaten earth became slippery when torrential rain flooded the land. Planks and a straw mattress served as a bed. No running water, of course, my morning toilet was made in a basinful of brackish water from a *roubine*. The only heating was from a wide fireplace where the mistral blew in with violence, and the only light in this simple room was a small oil lamp.'

There is little doubt that the *gardians* are the predecessors of the wild-west cowboys. Herding the Camargue bulls goes back way beyond the creation of the USA.

It is high time to introduce the Lord of the Camargue, the black bull, still called wild, the *taureau sauvage*. The locals call him Toro, and dignify him with a capital T.

He has been here certainly since Roman times. The Roman soldiers brought with them the cult of Mithras, who was personified by a bull. Other legends said that he escaped from the herd stolen by Hercules from Geryon. His ancient bones have been found in the arena at Nîmes, where he faced the gladiators under the eyes of Franks and Visigoths.

Now it seems his presence in Provence goes back much further. A cave has recently been discovered near Cassis, the Grotte Croquier, in which there are paintings to equal those of Lascaux, dating back over 12,000 years and showing a black bull with the characteristic horns of the Camargue bull, lyre shaped and up-rising. There is some doubt at the moment whether the paintings are genuine. The experts are still arguing.

In the old days not all the bulls were black. A fifteenth-century document at St Gilles records the sale of five wild bulls: two black, one red, and two pied.

For centuries, even millenia, the bulls existed pre-cariously in the wild delta of the Rhône, browsing on the salt flats in winter, on *salicornes* and everlastings, and feasting on the young reed shoots in spring. They were hunted, as the wild boars were, by the few local inhabitants, all of whose second, if not main, occupation was poaching.

Most authorities agree that about two hundred years ago, the herds became 'privatised' instead of being completely wild, and for the last century or so the bulls have been raised on *manades* or ranches. Their herdsmen are the *gardians* of the Camargue, the 'cowboys'.

Around 1890 some *manades* strengthened the breed by crossing with Spanish Corrida bulls. It made them meatier to eat, and more ill-tempered for the Courses, that game, the passion of the Camargue, which has nothing to do with bullfighting (the Corrida), and may go back long before the Romans to the bull-dancing of Theseus and his companions, depicted in the frescoes of Knossos in Crete. In these paintings slim young men dance with the bulls and somersault over the horns, and we have seen just such a feat in a village arena in the Camargue.

Some *manades* refused to countenance crossing, and stuck to the old black breed, and in the first decades of this century, under the fierce persuasion of Marquis Folco de Baroncelli-Javon (Lou Marquès) – poet, *manadier*, and founder of tradition in the Camargue – selective breeding brought back the pure race of the Camargue bull, black, wiry and very fast on his feet.

February is too early for the Courses; better weather is needed, both for players and spectators. Over the winter months the Camarguais gets lonely without his bulls, so to remind everyone who is King, there are *encierros*, that is to say a few bulls loose in the streets for no reason at all except that it has always been so, a street without bulls is not quite dressed; it seems right to have them there, and the boys can practise, and the horsemen perfect their skills.

A square, or a few streets of the village are barricaded off more or less effectively according to whether the barriers are modern portable crowd-controllers, or a couple of old farm carts, which are less bull-proof, but have the advantage of acting as grandstands. Then half a dozen bulls are let into the enclosure, where the young men cry 'Toro! Toro!', whistle and shout, flex their muscles, flap their anoraks, and perform doughty deeds to impress the girls, leaping for safety when a bull gets too close.

The older *gardians* mostly came from the surrounding villages, Le Caylar and Vauvert for example, where the bulls were pastured in the summer. The young boys were recruited as *gardianons*, to watch the herds and to see they did not stray into cultivated land, for there were no fences. As the lads were on foot and armed only with a stick, they soon learnt a lot about bulls.

They were given each one a horse, but they were forbidden to use it for controlling the bulls. It was usually a very old horse, no saddle, and it was to carry them to and from the village where they lived. One old *gardian* says they were beaten if they rode the horse for any other reason – it was purely for use as a bicycle.

When they were older they would be allowed to ride a more lively horse and to help herd the cattle. They would be given now the least popular horse, and they would learn a lot about awkward horses, and particularly how to stay in the saddle when the horse wished otherwise.

The famous Camargue white horse is really a present day reconstruction, and is indebted to some very skilful breeding by devotees. Years ago the breed's purity was weakened by being crossed with both Breton and Arab horses; people were not so obsessed by the concept of purity as by efficacy. Later on, between the wars, the French Army was keen to buy good horses of a certain type, and many local people used the Camargue horse crossbred to satisfy the Army's specification. The Army paid well, and in those days there was no tourism.

When our young *gardianon* had grown he would try for a job as a *gardian*, and would go off to live in the *mas*, a sprawling cluster of farm buildings, often in very uncomfortable conditions. One retired *gardian* recalls that their worst problems were the fleas with which the straw mattresses in the old bunk-houses were infested. The single sheet they were given was washed only once a month. Conditions were rough.

The *gardian* had a close relationship with his horse, when he finally got one. He would break it in, train it, and keep it for all its life. It was not his property, it belonged to the proprietor of the *mas*, but traditionally no one other than the *gardian* interfered with it. One sometimes hears that the horses were better at sorting out bulls (the *triage*) than the men, and in rough terrain it occasionally paid to let the horse get on with it. Nowadays the horse is more a sort of professional status symbol, and the old men joke that instead of working on his *cheval*, the modern *gardian* uses a *deux-chevaux*, or '*deuch*', as the extraordinarily ugly but very common little Citroëns are called.

There are fewer *gardians* nowadays for the same number of bulls. When things are busy, for *abrivados* or *bandidos* (which is the same as an *abrivado*, but in the reverse direction, going home to the *manade*), there are always plenty of amateur riders ready to help out.

The Spanish words used in talking about the bulls should cause no surprise, many of them are local dialect, but their origin is probably due to the large numbers of people of Spanish descent who settled here. Spanish names such as Pons, Lopez, and Burgos abound: there has been a strong Spanish connection going back many generations. In Victorian times the tunny was fished from Grau-du-Roi by Italian and Spanish fishermen, and many of them settled. There were also a number of refugees from the Spanish Civil War in the thirties.

We were not keen on *encierros*. Not being in there with the bulls, keeping warm with sheer fright, we found it often as cold as football on a winter's day in England, and decided we could pass up on bulls till the weather was warmer.

4

The Easter ferrade

'Quan Mars tona
L'amendo es bona.'
. . . .
'March thunder makes the almonds a
wonder.'

With the warmer weather the Mayor blossomed into a
mimosa yellow waistcoast, matching the mimosa in Mme
Poitavin's Easter window, and the holiday brought Aigues-
Mortes' second plague: the tourists.

They are an essential plague, a sickness that must be
endured until the autumn, since the town makes most of its
money out of them, but there is no doubt that it suffers from
the syndrome that they bring:

A headache of overcrowding in a small town of 4,000
inhabitants suddenly grown at lunchtime to five times that
number.

A rash of cars and coaches parked outside the gates.

Eyesores in the form of gimcrack souvenir shops that are
closed and ugly all winter, their windows whitewashed or
curtained with yellowing newspaper, and open and even
uglier all summer.

Plague spots: insensitive fast food establishments blott-
ing a nice old street with stainless steel robots that spit out
chemical icecreams, or pancakes, or obscenely pink hot
dogs, and this just inside the most stupendous medieval
gateway, the Port de la Gardette. If such things are
essential, and it seems that for the kind of tourism that the
town expects and caters for, and therefore gets, they are,
then they could, and should be done in a manner more

appropriate to the ancient setting. The municipality are working on it.

On the bright side, no *commerce* could quite ruin the tree-lined Place St Louis, which is very attractive, gay even, particularly the waiters. The square is dominated by the statue of St Louis, whose pedestal includes two ends of a *nef* (or medieval ship) and dolphins spouting into a pool, irresistible to climbing children, photographers and dogs.

Now Easter was here, the season had begun, and tables from every establishment surrounding the square surged into the middle, under the plane trees, areas carefully delineated by the colour of the chairs and parasols, and occasionally by tubs of trees and flowers. If you sat at a green table you were at the Minos, brown for the Voyageurs, and bright pink for our local, the Express Bar. (In spite of the colour of its decor the Express was *not* gay, just happy.) The waiters at the Minos all wore spring green aprons to match the tablecloths, except for the head waiter, who had an inexhaustible and colourful wardrobe of shirts; we do not remember ever seeing him wear the same shirt twice.

So here they were, the tourists, spilling into the square with their cameras and camcorders. What did they do while they were here? They made a quick tour, filmed the gates, bought a couple of postcards, and climbed the ramparts and the Tower of Constance. They went round the outside of the ramparts in the little train (with commentary). They looked at the shops, which did not take long. They had lunch, some of them in the town, but many departed to have lunch somewhere where the coach could park near a large, impersonal restaurant that would not serve them *sèiches à la rouille* (cuttlefish in a hot, spicey sauce) or *pâté de grives* (thrush pâté), for example, which the tourist might find odd, indigestible, or even culturally inedible.

Then they got in their cars or their coaches and went somewhere else. Perhaps to the Feria at Arles or Nîmes, passing on the way the cherry orchards round Arles; the

orchards that in full bloom lifted the heavy heart of Van Gogh, who had arrived in the long-looked-for sunny Midi in a March snowstorm.

Sometimes the happy holidaymakers spend the day at a *ferrade*, which also begin at Easter, and mark the start of the bull season here in the Camargue.

The *ferrade*, or branding, was originally to sort out the new animals and mark them, traditionally by branding, though this nearly died out at one time, being replaced by ear-marking. The *ferrade* was typically an excuse for the *manade* and their friends to have a party, and the young lads were given their first serious chance to prove their growing manhood by handling the bulls, and promising boys would be noted for schooling in the art of the Courses Camarguaises, which are to the Camargue what rugby used to be to Wales. The *bistournage* furnished the same opportunity, when the young bulls were castrated to prevent the fights that would have been inevitable to establish the pecking order in big herds. This latter event is not usually attended by tourists.

Nowadays the *ferrade* has become a commercial affair. They start with the arrival of better weather and (alas) the tourists. They are held for this or that Club Taurin, for the Electricity Employees, for the Camping des Tamaris, or any group that cares to bespeak one. There is a great deal to eat, and even more *pastis* to drink at trestle tables in the open air, and the bulls are not driven at the spectators as they once were, though there is always a young bull with its horn points covered (*emboulé*) for the amateurs to sport with.

The Easter Feria at Arles is more Spanish than French; there are parades of horsemen with their Arlésiennes in costume up side-saddle behind them, reminiscent of Seville; and Corridas with the huge heavy bulls specially brought from Spain to meet their destiny: the *mise à mort*. It was the start of the season's bullfighting.

Just as it would be impossible to write about the

Camargue without going into the relationship between the Camarguais and his bulls, so it is difficult to write about bulls without considering in some detail the difference between the Courses Camarguaises (the traditional bull games of the Camargue) and the Corrida or Spanish type of bullfighting.

The difficulty is due to the existence of both types side by side in those towns surrounding the Camargue proper. The cult of the Courses (bull games) is called La Bouvine, the cult of the Corrida is known as La Tauromachie. Both are written up separately in the local press. They are more different than Association and Rugby football.

In times past the Courses were closely connected with local *fêtes*; there were no formal arenas and the games were held in the village squares inside a ring of farm carts on which the spectators sat, though in the wealthier places such as Aigues-Mortes, temporary stockades were erected and these were surrounded by little wooden 'grandstands' called *théâtres*.

The Corrida is highly formalised. It was banned in France under the Grammont Law which was passed in 1850 making cruelty to domestic animals a crime, and was for its time a very enlightened piece of legislation. The courts decided a bull *was* a domestic animal, but the Corrida still went on in the Midi. The penalties for a first offence were not very severe, and by changing the committee and the *toreros* for every event no one's liberty or pocket was seriously menaced.

In time, however, the Societé Protectrice des Animaux (SPA) became more active on behalf of the bulls. Certain southern politicians considered this a *nordiste* conspiracy to upset the traditional pleasures of the Midi. Numerous attempts were made by the afiçionados to get the Grammont Law amended, but it was not until 1951 under President Auriol that a bit of unscrupulous political chicanery got the amendment through, one of the principal arguments being that as the present law was unenforcable one might as well accept the status quo, otherwise the law as a whole would be held in disrepute, a form of reasoning referred to as *tartufferie*.

So the bullfight, including the *mise à mort* (the killing of the bull), became legal, but only in those towns or villages where a 'local uninterrupted tradition' could be invoked.

For the defenders of Tauromachie this was the thin end of the wedge, and having got their feet in the door they seized the bull by the horns and went to town. (A quadruple mixed metaphor: it is no use mixing metaphors if you do not do it thoroughly. Why should politicians be allowed a monopoly of the fine art?)

Before long some dubious legal decisions wrecked all pretence of restraint, for example our local seaside village, Le-Grau-du-Roi (which barely existed in 1850, and was anyway a dependency of Aigues-Mortes which had no bullfighting), got their Corrida legalised on the grounds that: 'it clearly *would* have had a tradition of the Corrida if the village had existed, so that it was unfair to prevent it from having one now.' Arguments produced for other places, charged with 'interruption', were that the arena *had* been used in the meantime (but for different purposes) or that a four year war had caused a fourteen year interruption.

Nowadays the Corrida, which is expensive to stage, takes place mainly in Nîmes, Arles, and Beaucaire. Smaller towns like Grau-du-Roi and St Gilles have them from time to time, in the same arena, but not on the same day as, the Courses. It pays to study the posters carefully. The better French arenas rank with the second division Spanish ones (there are three divisions). The Spanish, who make the rules, will not accept even the splendid arenas at Nîmes and Arles as first division, as there is no full scale operating theatre on site. A helicopter to the superb hospital at Montpellier will not do, it seems.

The Corrida flourishes in France in those places where it is a matter of fierce local pride and tradition, but it is not generally popular, and the SPA are eternally opposed to it, though their main concern at the moment seems to be vivisection. The SPA have accepted that the Courses Camarguaises, however, are neither cruel nor degrading. We would go along with that.

It is interesting to conjecture on the future of the Corrida in Europe if the politicians want a confederation to replace the separate sovereign states of the EEC. Would the people of Britain, not to mention the other northern states where a tradition of animal welfare is strong, consent to a union with countries where such medieval cruelty is common?

Bullfighting is cruel, despite the spectacle that accompanies it: the colour, the ritual, the importance of threes. There are three *picadors*, three *banderilleros*, and three *matadors*. There are three gates to an arena, which is divided into three areas, and there are three stages in the fight. In the first, after some inoffensive capework by the *matador* and his *peons*, nominally to assess the bull's temperament, but also to entertain the crowd who are paying a lot of money, the *picador* comes, riding a well-armoured horse, and provokes the bull to attack. From the saddle he drives three *piques* into the bull, just behind the shoulders. The *pique* is a lance about an inch thick with a sharp pointed end and a collar about four inches from the point, and it is driven into the bull until the collar prevents its further entry. It is this which, not surprisingly, causes all the blood, and which weakens the bull. (One would not give much chance to a boxer required to go into the ring having had a few inches of lance driven between his shoulders.)

After the bull's strength has been sapped the second stage begins. The *banderilleros* drive three pairs of barbed darts into his back. These are supposed to be carefully placed so as to correct any tendency the bull has to favour one side or the other, but they seem seldom to be placed with such accuracy. At the end of all this, in the third stage, the *matador* further plays the bull with the *faenas de muleta*, passes with the small red cape, stiffened at the top with a baton, until the moment arrives for the *mise à mort*. A measure of how exhausted the bull is by this time is found in the ability of the *matador* to walk arrogantly away with his back turned: the bull is not 'dominated', he is exhausted, and in fact it is not unknown for bulls to give up and lie down (or even to drop dead) at this time, much to the *matador*'s fury. The *matador* is supposed to dispatch the bull with one downward and forward thrust of his sword in such a way as to minimise the blood, but he often fails, at least in the less prestigious rings, and repeated thrusts are needed to finish off the poor bloody beast.

We, ourselves, no longer go to the Corrida or *mise à mort* spectacles, though we occasionally see them on film. It seems to us to be a public execution preceded by public torture. We are not sentimental about animals; we accept that beasts have to die to provide us with the meat we enjoy eating, but they should not endure a cruel death.

It is understandable but disturbing that people enjoy such a performance. It is theatrical. The men are beautifully dressed in their suits of lights, and the matadors' movements can be very graceful, almost a dance. But it would not make us enjoy a hanging just because the hangman was Rudolf Nureyev, dancing his heart out, beautifully costumed and assisted by a corps de ballet.

The Courses Camarguaises, which start in spring, are quite different. The bulls are different. The men who face them are different. The game is different. Instead of a ritual killing, whose origin possibly lies in prehistoric pagan sacrifices, and certainly dates to the Moorish occupation of Andalucia, we have a confrontation between man and bull which arises naturally from their everyday relationship.

We had started boat-building again, working on the spare cabin. A mistral was blowing, and Bill was playing a panel game on the bank, trying to move a large plywood sheet that threatened to carry him under full sail down to Grau-du-Roi. 'What's the trouble?' Laurel called up from below. 'I've got problems with the wind,' shouted Bill. 'Too much cabbage,' replied Laurel.

After a hard day's work, it was our custom to go out for a cheap workaday supper. In winter this was difficult, unless you settled for pizza, as many of the restaurants closed. Once the season started our friendly bistro L'Escale opened again, and we were sure of a welcome and a meal which cost very little, and included a fairly atrocious but tolerable carafe of Vin des Sables, red or rosé. Bill could drink a *demi* of beer here, outside the ramparts and overlooking the turning basin, for a franc less than the Express Bar in the square, but the beer at the Express was colder. When the heat of summer comes one needs to know these things. L'Escale was popular with the *gardians*, many of whom would gather at the bar and spend noisy evenings there. If the weather was good, we ate outside, where we would chat with the cook's widowed mother, the young waiter who wanted to go to England to be with his girlfriend but was meeting opposition from his family, and a strange ebullient character who rode up on a bicycle, always dressed in brightly coloured clothes and a tartan gorblimey, a gentleman locally known as La Merde. He had a loud voice, a joke for everybody, and an accent that was to us totally incomprehensible. We just laughed when everybody else did.

There were two waitresses with Spanish names and skirts about as long as a width of a hatband. A lace apron the size of a pocket handkerchief hung below the front of their skirts, and they were cheerful and friendly, and always ready to doctor the menu a bit to meet our requirements.

Here the *sapeurs-pompiers* had a celebratory dinner one evening, lining up the tables, and arriving in various garments, mostly track suits and T-shirts, but unmistakable because of their military haircuts. Three of the noisiest were high on orange juice. They were on duty, they explained, and our faith in the *sapeurs* remained unshaken. They are probably the nearest equivalent to our lifeboatmen, since many of them are volunteers, trained but unpaid. The volunteers are called in when manpower is short, if there is a bad accident, or when the forest fires begin in the heat of summer.

One of the most attractive things about eating outside at L'Escale (the cuisine was simple) was looking across the turning basin at the sunset reflected in the water. The other was the strip of public garden that stood between the tables on the terrace and the road. It was so much more pleasant to look upon grass and trees than having cars passing so close that they sprayed grit into your *moules marinières*.

Since we had had no call to look their way all winter, we were struck on our first visit that year by huge heaps of gravel and cement in this very strip of green.

'What is happening in the *jardin*, *madame*?' Laurel asked of Mme Rigal.

'It is a *catastrophe*,' said Madame simply. 'The Municipality will erect a toilet.'

'No! exactly there? in the garden?' cried Laurel in horror. It would ruin the view.

'We have done all we can. It seems they may do what they wish. It is a disaster.'

We were not only horrified but intrigued as well. For not two yards away from the proposed toilet stood the Tree of Liberty, which had been planted there by the Mayor himself last Bastille Day, July 14th, with great ceremony. The town band (well, three of them: two saxophones and a drum) had played, the schoolchildren had been present in Revolutionary costumes, there had been patriotic songs and solemn speeches about Liberty.

The Tree, a young lime, had been planted with a very special looking trowel, and wreathed in red white and blue ribbons, and we all sang 'The Marseillaise' with one of the saxophones a little behind the tempo of the singers.

The Tree of Liberty did not look too well nine months later. The ribbons were torn to faded rags by the mistral, and its roots were buried in a dribble of aggregate. Liberty to do what? we wondered.

'We must hope for the best,' sighed Mme Rigal, setting before us our workday *steack-frites*.

One of the features of an association, in France anyway, is that its importance is measured by the size of its member-ship. Our Association is dedicated to the interests of a number of boat-owners and/or dwellers, but the number of these who can be accommodated in a given amount of water is limited so it was considered necessary to have other sorts of members who could be said to support our aims, perhaps because they hoped one day to live afloat, or who owned a boat but lived elsewhere.

Mario, our President, was neither and both. His caravan was parked discreetly on the canal bank and he owned two boats; the *Nérée*, which was an old barge full of large machine tools, which he used for his many boat-building activities, and the *Isles de Stel*, which was his restaurant barge. Or part of it was his. No one could keep up with the constant litigation which affected the ownership of this barge, even though Mario pinned up the court orders for us all to read on a notice-board which also contained the pictorial history of her building.

Mario once lived in a house with his wife, and by all accounts it must have been an interesting life, for there are many differing stories, some so different that it is hard to realise they are describing the same people and events. When Mario left and, so to speak, engaged the services of Martine by dragging her away from her husband, the lawsuits started and it was advisable for Mario not to have any property as lawyers dashed about sticking writs everywhere. He therefore moved into a caravan, the actual ownership of which was completely obscure.

This rather upset the Association for one of their strongest claims was that they were ameliorating the banks of the canal and as everyone knows, a caravan is synonymous with disamelioration. Mario had made great efforts to screen the offending caravan, but one fine day in April the local authority, who do not in any event like people who live in boats, but who are positively paranoid about unauthorised caravans, arrived to inspect the canalside. They said nothing in their report, but let drop a few remarks of an ironic, cynical or satirical nature, not to say sarcastic even, and an informal meeting of the Association was held, at one of the picnic tables, to see what Mario was going to do about it. As usual the meeting was oiled along by bottles of rosé.

Mario never did things by halves, whether it was leaving wives, acquiring mistresses, building boats, or moving caravans. The next day a large bulldozer with digging attachments arrived and a lorry delivered two long, heavy, steel girders, which were off-loaded close by the old barge *Nérée*. The caravan was towed round to the *Nérée* and a gang of willing helpers assembled rather as wasps gather round a picnic. This was likely to be an event with a considerable possibility of disaster, and therefore thoroughly enjoyable.

The U-sectioned girders were placed about six feet apart like railway lines to run from the bank to the *Nérée*, and the caravan's wheels were introduced into the ends. Very carefully, with much use of wedges, chocks, crowbars, curses and cries, the big twenty-five-foot caravan was nudged by the bulldozer along the girders. As its weight gradually left the bank, it started to heel the barge over and the girders took on a threatening slope. The caravan started to tilt, and much care was needed to see that it did not run away downhill and roll off the far side of the barge and into the canal. When at last its wheels were on the reinforced hatch covers of the barge and one end was overhanging the water, it was necessary to turn it in place until the long dimension was within the sides of the barge, and so that it balanced safely on its two centrally placed wheels. At last, with the wheels wedged and the ends chocked up, Mario, with the accustomed cheroot clenched between his teeth, was able to pause.

The latter part of the exercise had been watched by two officers of the local council who had arrived with an ominous envelope for Mario. Mario saw them standing the other side of the fence. He beamed.

'*Voilà!*' he cried. 'There is no more caravan.'

He walked over to the fence and pointed out with glee that the caravan was now part of the barge. The *fonctionnaire* smiled thinly.

'I see a caravan *on* a barge, I do not see one as *part* of a barge,' he said. Mario did not reply. He walked aboard, descended to the hold of his workshop and struggled up with his welding machine. Seizing some pieces of scrap steel he welded the caravan to the barge and then removed its wheels. 'The caravan has ceased to exist; just as the wheelhouse is welded to the deck so is the accommodation that was once a caravan.' This time it was the *fonctionnaires* who said nothing. They left without delivering their letter. And what was once a caravan discreetly screened behind bushes and a few low trees until it could be easily removed when no longer needed became an eyesore in full view of the road. Probably it would never be lifted ashore again. Being a commercial barge, the *Nérée* cannot be ordered to move on. We expect the local authority will bide its time; like the bank at a casino, they usually win in the end.

Martine told us that the roof still leaked and the view was less interesting; would Laurel not like to *troquer* (swap) our barge for her caravan? It was her perenniel little joke.

She looked as if she would quite like to swap Mario for almost anything that week. The affair of the *fonctionnaires* did not please him, although he appeared to have won that round, and he was in a difficult mood. He came to us with a small key.

'My ex-wife has been rifling my mail,' he said. 'It is only thus that she could learn my business so well. I have had to padlock the *boîte postale*; your mail comes there too, so here is your key to the padlock.' We thanked him. He and Bill wandered over to the outdoor workbench to discuss whatever was in progress, and for Mario to have a long and bitter grumble at his ex, of which Bill understood about a quarter, but always remained in Mario's good books by keeping silent and nodding sympathetically.

The padlock may have eased Mario's mind, but did nothing to cure our particular problem with the *boîte postale*. This was not the standard issue, aluminium and with a flap. It was extremely simple, painted green, just a metal box standing on the regulation height pole, with 'Stop' painted on the door below the slit. It had presumably been one of Mario's efforts when he was more in a hurry than usual. The welding was not perfect. It stood at the roadside in the long grass among the fennel stalks and hedgerow plants, which the snails love. The snails got in the box. Snails also love glue. Whenever we spent a few days away, our mail would be seriously censored by snails, and our files contain letters and postcards, considerable parts of which have been read, marked, and inwardly digested by gastropods.

> Our friends send us views-of-the-coast cards,
> Bread and butter and thanks-to-my-host cards,
> But to no avail,
> The industrious snail
> Devours the most of our postcards.

Neither of us has much need of doctors as a rule. We have lived a mobile life for many years without any great trouble, but now suddenly, Bill felt he had to get some help. He had barked his shin badly on the edge of the gangplank, and though the wound had skinned over, it was, after three weeks of Laurel's best nursing, still swollen, sore, and obviously not healing inside. We went to the local GP's surgery (how can one fail to have confidence in a doctor whose surgery is in the Rue Pasteur?). The waiting room was decorated with naïve paintings of Aigues-Mortes, and we waited our turn as one does in England, only here one neither made an appointment nor gave one's name. Order was established – '*Qui est le dernier?*' – and stuck to. The *docteur* opened the door, the next in line received a hearty handshake and was swept into the surgery. Our turn came, and immediately Bill was put on the couch, the doctor was kind enough to say that Laurel had done all the right things, but . . . He opened the wound, and while Bill communicated loudly with his maker about design faults in the human body the doctor removed a substantial clot of blood that had refused to disperse. He powdered the wound with antibiotic, neatly bandaged it and we paid 80 francs. When we first arrived in Aigues-Mortes we had taken our cat to the vet with some small problem and had been charged 120 francs. Bill congratulated the doctor on undercutting the vet and assured him that he would continue to get our custom. The doctor, taken aback but amused by the comparison, told us that his charges were fixed by the Ministry of Health. Presumably the vet's were not.

5

Promenade in Pescalune

*'A la sason del cocut
Tan lèu plogut, tan lèu eissut.'*
. . . .
'When cuckoo do fly
Quick wet and quick dry.'

The affairs of the Association were at a crisis, as they often were. Boubou, our Secretary, had written to the Mayor six times in the past year and had been fobbed off or ignored. At one point the *mairie* lost the entire correspondence. We all wished to know whether the concession would be renewed, and what our position was.

Now a new Mayor had been elected, and showed signs of being a new broom. He had already turned various waste plots in the town into small parks with seats, instantly occupied by old men warming their kidneys.

This time the letter Boubou wrote was a strong one. We all got a look at it before it was sent, and our delicate English sensibilities were rocked. It condemned the Mayor for ignoring six letters. It roundly chastised the *mairie* for losing the previous correspondence. It accused the Mayor of imagining that people who live on boats are a mere band of chicken stealers who might safely be set aside, instead of a respectable and indeed international Association, consisting as it did not only of French, but Germans, Swiss, and two English journalists. ('That should give him a fright,' chortled Boubou.)

'Are you really going to send that?' queried Bill mildly. 'You don't feel it exaggerates a little?'

'For Paris it would be a little too strong,' admitted

Boubou. 'Down here, they expect the *coup de poing*, the punch on the nose.'

The seventh letter achieved spectacular results: a rendez-vous between the Association and the Mayor the following Monday, no later. A delegation was appointed, consisting of Mario, as President, Boubou as Secretary, Jean-Claude as Treasurer (the only one of us who lives on land), Serge who runs the tour boat *Pescalune* which spends the winter in the old canal and the summer moored conspicuously under the ramparts, so he is well known, and Laurel, who was asked to go with them for reasons perhaps not unconnected with the respect in which writers are held in France. They asked Bill to go too, but he said the delegation was big enough, and Laurel's French was better than his. Also his lack of patience with local government officers is legendary.

On Monday afternoon, then, our band of brothers, unwontedly dressed in suits and skirts instead of T-shirt and jeans or *bleus de travail*, climbed the echoing stone staircase at the *mairie*, Laurel feeling less like part of a delegation than one of a bunch of malefactors summoned to see the Headmaster. At first it appeared that she was not wrong.

The new Mayor was indeed a *'prof'* at the local school. His subject was history. His grey suit was impeccable, he was the epitome of respectability from his neat grey hair and reassuring glasses to his polished (but not vulgarly so) shoes. He even wore dark socks, and his tie was unimpeachably unmemorable.

After the formal introductions he weighed straight in. 'Your letter did not please me at all,' he said severely. Boubou, by common consent spokesman, gave a conciliatory ahem.

'It is the seventh letter, M. le Maire, and see! it has achieved the desired result, which was not the case when we wrote to your predecessor with the utmost *politesse*.' The Mayor disclaimed all knowledge of previous correspondence, it did seem as if the previous Mayor had well and truly lost it. Boubou apologised for his letter, but not with much conviction, the Mayor apologised for the administrative incompetence of his predecessor with a certain relish, and it was agreed to start afresh.

We explained our position as recognised squatters, which is what it amounted to, and that we were anxious to know if the concession would be renewed. Mario pointed out (we knew we could not keep him quiet for long) that money from his *own pocket* had gone into the lengths of railway lines waiting to be used for the proposed slipway as soon as he got the go-ahead. Mario, we must remember, comes from Dunkerque, where an Aberdonian would be considered a big spender.

'I, as Mayor, have little to say in the matter of waterways. The port near the ramparts is run from Port Camargue [the marina on the coast four kilometres away] and the canal where you are is still under the Navigation Authority. However, as you know, when the by-pass canal is built all this will change.'

Exactly, we said, and we did not want to find ourselves swept aside by events.

'This summer the first Salon Fluvial will be held at Aigues-Mortes,' announced the Mayor, to an inaudible flourish of trumpets. 'It is an event of global significance [the French use 'global' when they mean all of France] because all the bodies controlling the waterways will be present. I have met you, I have listened to your case, I understand your concern. I suggest we see what happens during the Salon.'

With this we had to be content. Serge got a bonus, however. As we left the Mayor neatly cut him out, like a *gardian* cutting out the bull he wishes to select from the herd, and booked *Pescalune* as hostboat for the Salon.

Pescalune was built, or rather converted, by Mario, who likes nothing more than messing about with boats, in his case made of steel and the bigger the better. Her name comes from the nearby village of Lunel, where, legend has it, the village elders were discovered using a basket to fish the moon out of a *roubine*, and are known to this day as moonfishers: *pescalunes*. This is a myth that is widespread in other parts of the world, and suggests wiliness rather than stupidity. What better cover for smuggling or poaching than to persuade those in authority that you are just moronic yokels fishing for the moon? Ho! ho!

Pescalune is run by Serge and his wife Danielle, who live on the pretty little barge *André* with their small daughter Aude. In summer the *Pescalune* does 'the triangle', as we call it: a tour round part of the Petite Camargue. We went on board one fine spring day, with sixty other people, starting off from a spectacular position in the Bassin d'Evolution (or turning basin) under the ramparts, with the Tower of Constance (La Ponchuda in local slang) at our back. The boat, which is 33 metres long, turned slowly and passed the open railway bridge, after which the waterway splits and goes left down to Grau-du-Roi and the sea, while the right branch continues the Canal du Rhône à Sète. *Pescalune* turned left, and went down the Chenal Maritime towards Grau and the sea. It is narrow, and only six feet deep in parts. It goes straight as a ruler after the bend by the saltworks, where we could see the huge rectangular pile of sea salt, higher than the ramparts of the town, but shortened now by the winter's use on the freezing roads of France.

On our left the flat salt pans extended almost from the ramparts on the south side of the town right down to the sea. On our right were the vineyards of Le Mole, patched with *étangs*, and scraps of pasture, and the strange tufts of marsh grass and everlastings, with stranger names, *saladelles*, *salicorne*, *salsepareille*, all starting with 'sal' in recognition of the salt in which they grow, some in circular blobs or hassocks, some in rangy tufts and straggling bushes, all with the brown earth flecked with salt crystals between them, too salty here for grass.

On a good day on the *Pescalune* you can see the three

things that most conjure up the Camargue, the black bulls browsing on a patch of pasture that has escaped the salt, the white horses on the track at the canal's edge, and a flock of pink flamingoes in the wetmarsh. It was a good day, and on the salt pan side for good measure were a thousand seabirds, white and grey, gannets and gulls wheeling silver in the sunlight.

The bridge at Grau-du-Roi lifted for us and we breathed a sigh of relief, for we had heard Serge complain loudly and bitterly about the Bridgekeeper here, both he and his bridge were crotchety, he sometimes would not open if he did not feel amiable, and sometimes the bridge itself was *en panne* and refused to open. When this happened, *Pescalune* was forced to reverse the four kilometres back to Aigues-Mortes, a manoeuvre not at all easy in a *péniche*, which is basically what she was, with a covered area containing tables and benches, a tiny bar for light refreshments, and a pleasant deck space with more benches outside.

After holding our breath at the lift bridge, we left the channel that leads out to sea (French *péniches* are not allowed to go to sea) and turned sharp right into the River Vidourle. This is not a big river, but it is wider than the canal, and more winding. On the banks were more vineyards and pastures, and thick woods of umbrella pines where egrets had made their nests, an astonishing contrast between the white of the egrets and the almost black green of the pines. The birds have learned not to fear man since they are a protected species, but a hundred years ago when their plumes were prized for fashionable ladies' hats, they could not have survived in so obvious a habitat.

We came then to the gates of the Vidourle. These massive floodgates, enlivened by a huge sun design painted on them, prevent the floodwaters of the Vidourle from inundating the Camargue, which is below the river level. The Vidourle can rise to ten metres above normal in an hour or two, and at such times the gates are closed. Now the river flowed peacefully, the guillotine gates were open, and we turned right, under one of the gates, and back into the canal.

A few hundred yards further on, on the opposite bank, Serge quietened the engines and slowed the boat down almost to a stop. Speaking softly over the loudspeakers, he told us all to watch for holes in the river bank, the nests of the *guépier*, or bee eater, and for the birds themselves.

They were there, bright as parrots, green, orange yellow, blue: rainbow birds flashing in the sun. A little like a large kingfisher, but with a pale bluegreen breast and a longer beak, they winter in Africa until the spring flowers of Europe attract the bees and wasps which are their food.

The last leg of the triangle took us towards our starting point, the Tower of Constance, brooding over her mirrored image in the dark calm water.

Then we were back in the Bassin having done a round trip, or rather a triangular one, of a couple of hours in wild land, where nature reigned and the presence of man was hardly noticeable, a delightful and refreshing morning.

Our attempt at payment was charmingly refused. 'You are our friends,' said Serge.

Laurel had joined the library. (How many towns in England with 4,000 inhabitants can boast their own municipal library?) It was small but pleasantly airy, up a spiral staircase in an annexe next to the *mairie*, and was open in the afternoons only. It was presided over by Dominique, with whom Laurel loved to discuss anything under the sun but particularly books. Dominique had the pure spare face and straight fine brown gold hair of an early Venetian portrait, and had lived for a while in England, consequently was one of the few we met who understood our occasional attacks of culture shock. She was born in Bordeaux, and to the Aigues-Mortaises was just as much a foreigner as we were.

She lived at the Mas Rancier with Serge-the-brother-in-law-of-Jeannot (not to be confused with Serge of *Pescalune*, or Serge the waiter at the Express Bar with the three-legged dog) and consequently she drove past *Hosanna* every day.

Spring is asparagus time, and she called by one day with a gift of about four kilos, grown on the Mas, fat and white and appetising, and an invitation to lunch. This was our first meeting with Jeannot the drummer and his family, as we were bidden to apéritifs in his part of the Mas, stone built, stone floored, and with a huge stone fireplace where a fire was burning. The day, though sunny, was cool after a day of wind and a night's rain.

Jeannot explained to us how the asparagus is grown. In January and February the soil is fertilised and heaped in mounds along the rows of plants. Long sheets of plastic are placed over the mounds, to prevent weeds and blanch the new shoots to a perfect whiteness, giving the fields round Aigues-Mortes the appearance sometimes of a rough sea, as the plastic flickers in the wind and reflects the sunlight, or sometimes, on still days, of a giant corrugated iron roof. Migrant Moroccan workers begin harvesting from mid February to the beginning of March according to the warmth of the spring, and continue till about the 1st of June. The plastic is then removed, the tops allowed to grow wild and feathery, to put nutriment back into the plant for next year.

We then returned to Serge's quarters for lunch in a cheerful kitchen sitting room, with a trestle table laid with a Provençal cloth, a bench against the wall on one side and chairs on the other. It was also our first meeting with Micot the potter and her husband Jacques, and Blaise, Dominique's 'previous son' as she put it, a lad of sixteen, while Paul, the child of herself and Serge, was nine.

We had asparagus, of course, loads of it, with butter or a *sauce hollandaise* if you preferred. We had a delicious rabbit stew, perfumed with herbs of the Garrigue, the maquis up beyond Nîmes where the best rabbits grow. We had cheese and *fougasse* with strawberries. *Fougasse* is an Aigues-Mortais speciality, a little like a crusty sponge cake. It was a convivial and excellent meal, a French Sunday lunch which left one feeling quite deliciously full until bedtime.

We asked them to supper the following Tuesday. Dominique remembered with nostalgia the curries she had eaten in England, so that was what Laurel cooked. A lamb curry, a vegetable curry, and an egg curry, which is one of her best, and all sorts of sambals and samosas to accompany them, followed by fresh pineapple.

Before dinner Dominique took Laurel to call on a friend with some kittens, knowing that we were looking for one. The mother was an 'Isabelle', what we call a tortoiseshell, and the Americans a calico cat. Laurel had hoped for a tortoiseshell but the only female kitten was a tabby (Danielle of *Pescalune* took it for little Aude a week or so later.)

Alas, little Paul found the curry too strange and exotic, and even Serge, though politely tasting everything, and coming back for more of those dishes he liked, had an odd considering look on his face. Conversation was a little stilted. Paul made a sparing meal of rice and pineapple. For him the kittens had been the high spot, the adult conversation was boring, and he fell asleep on the sofa.

Not one of our more sparkling social occasions, we felt, but perhaps there was an underlying reason. A month or so later, when Laurel was visiting the library, Dominique said: 'You must come and see my new house in the ramparts.'

'Are you no longer at the Mas?' asked Laurel.

'No,' smiled Dominique. 'For a while things have not worked between me and Serge and we agreed to part. We are still good friends.'

We do hope our curry supper was not the clincher.

That Sunday at the Express we met our friend Claude. He was wearing a smart white cable jersey with 'Yacht Man' embroidered on it (a nautical image is very fashionable in France) and was puffing on his manly pipe. He was not completely inseparable from his friend Basil, with whom he lived; in fact if Basil was having a fit of the sulks, or had become somehow tiresome, Claude liked to saunter round the Place by himself. He knew it enraged Basil.

The first time we met him we had asked if he was from Aigues-Mortes, since we were eager to meet that shy and rare bird, that lurked mostly behind the counters of its *commerces* and wouldn't come out to play. 'Mon Dieu, no,' he said, with a certain amount of horror, 'I come from Lorraine. From Nancy, to be exact.' Laurel had had to kick Bill sharply on the ankle, she knew that he was about to make an appropriate comment and it might have been beyond her French to explain it politely.

Claude was always keen to introduce us to someone important. He sometimes said he was in communications, sometimes in tourism (at a very high level) and sometimes in publicity. He seemed to know a great many people who could help us with our researches into anything at all, but when it came to the point we always managed to meet people without his assistance, except that he introduced us to Assunta, who on this warm day had discarded all but one cardigan.

Today Claude wished to tell us about a splendid wine he had discovered, not at all dear, and with a nose! Mmm! *superbe*! he kissed his fingers. A kind and expansive person, he had invited ourselves, and Jane and Clyde the Americans, to dinner only a few days after our first meeting with him. The first floor apartment where he and Basil lived was superb. The exterior, like many houses within the ramparts, was modest, but usefully faced a pizzeria across the narrow street. Once upstairs, the only word for it was magnificent. Whatever Claude did (and it did not seem to take up much of his time) Basil was a dealer in antiques. He had nothing so low class as a shop, however. He was a specialist. He found whatever you desired, and bought it for you on commission. He and Claude were always disappearing off to antique fairs. The apartment was graced with beautiful and curious things, which both of them

clearly loved; some of them priceless antiques, others little oddities which they were fond of. There was a model steam locomotive, beautifully made in polished brass, from which Bill could scarcely be distracted. There were Tiffany lamps, a splendid enamel and gilt clock, and a painted wooden angel from Russia that Laurel could gaze at eye to eye, since it stood about five feet tall.

Her passion for the Byzantine communicated itself to Basil, and when they found a mutual interest in Art Nouveau and Deco, they were away in a flood of chat, which was a good thing as Basil, unlike Claude, spoke no English; and could not therefore communicate with Clyde. Jane spoke excellent French, with a Boston accent, Laurel's was good but not accurate, and the whole party went with a swing. Claude and Basil loved the good things of life, but were not, alas, cooks, explained Claude, semi-apologising for the take-away Sauerkraut and Alsatian sausage that were warming up in the microwave oven. Any lack of finesse in the kitchen was balanced by good wine and good company and we spent a lively evening. We discovered that they lived a good deal on take-aways, which could be of excellent quality from the Sabdès brothers, or cheap and cheerful from the pizzeria opposite.

In the bathroom was a poignant reminder of a bachelor household: a pail of soaking socks stood in the bath.

We woke next morning to the unmistakable sound of a shotgun. Several shots followed by shouting. 'Damned *chasseurs* again,' Bill said.

'No,' replied Laurel, 'there was a woman's voice and women are seldom *chasseurs*.'

'Haven't you heard of man-hunters?' Bill said and went up to the wheelhouse to have a look round. He was in time to observe a lady driving fast on to the bridge while a man took aim and fired his gun again, peppering the vehicle with shot.

'Oh,' said Bill, 'it's only Bernard.'

Bill is not quite as casual about guns and a wild-west approach to human life as that sounds. But Bernard is unusual, even in this stretch of canal.

Bernard lives in the barge *Massabielle* moored some hundred metres ahead of us. We call it the Survival Barge. He would scorn to be a member of the Association, he would rather be totally independent. He has a large family (eleven children, he says), several of whom have now left home, four dogs, securely tied up but terrifying, and at least one goat. Several of his children visit him from time to time and stay in caravans alongside the berth.

Aboard *Massabielle* all is neat and tidy and smartly painted. Whatever their lifestyle these are no river gypsies. The whole family live in the *roef* (the after accommodation) except a couple of youngsters who sleep forward next to the *salle d'eau*. The entire hold is lined from floor to ceiling with shelves of preserved food in huge jars as if for a siege. There are hundreds of rabbits in hutches, all well kept and clean. There are caged birds, there are engineering parts, and trays of growing plants. The place is a factory. Bernard and family are very nearly self-supporting and could be for long periods if they had to.

With that number of relatives and Bernard's firework temperament, there is nearly always a crisis of some sort in his vicinity, though seldom actual shooting.

On one occasion loud shouts came from the bankside by *Massabielle*. This time women were crying, the dogs were barking, the goat had jumped on to the highest spot it could find, bleating; and for a while the air rang like a shipyard with a full order book as Bernard slowly and effectively demolished a fairly new Volvo car with a sledgehammer. When he is in one of his moods we avoid him.

He was badly wounded while serving in the French Navy as an artificer in the Indo-Chinese war. His head is still full of shrapnel, his wife says, no possibility of surgical intervention because in that case *pouf!* she indicates graphically with a snap of the fingers the instant death of

Bernard. Every so often a piece of shrapnel moved and caused strange mad things to happen in Bernard's brain and rendered him impossible for a time. He gets a lot of sympathy and tolerance all round, as well as plenty of living space to himself.

In fact Bernard was a good neighbour. He was generous with both his time and his undoubted expertise as a diesel engineer. He was good company. His children were obedient, though we would not have trusted them to be scrupulously honest if we were strangers. We were not sure if he had a garden somewhere (he seemed to work twenty-five hours a day), but he certainly had access to huge supplies of fruit and vegetables, wooden trays of which were often given to us in sufficient quantities to feed a platoon. The canal authorities and the local government were not on good terms with him, but plenty of respectable people were. It seemed that his outbursts of violent temper were reserved for his family and civil servants, which latter nowadays only approached him by letter. This was ideal for Bernard: he never collected his mail.

'People I like do not write to me,' he said simply.

Massabielle was not connected to water, electricity or telephone. They collected their water in large cans using one of the many vehicles that always surrounded their mooring. They made their own electricity by generator, and they guarded their plot with four aggressive alsatian dogs, each of which was tethered to a long chain so that their beats converged just enough so that one dog could touch the next. It was impossible to approach the boat while the dogs were on guard and they always were. They were never off the chain, though that is not unusual in France. It was necessary to call to those on board from outside the radius of the chains and the dog nearest the gangway, which had several bites to its credit, would be restrained while one was welcomed on board.

The French are remarkably sanguine about dog-bites in these circumstances. People we know who had been bitten by Bernard's dogs or by others in a similiar position regarded it as their own fault. Bill was careful about the dogs.

From time to time the authorities gave them notice to quit their berth. The family ignored this, and nothing ever seemed to happen. No one liked to argue with Bernard.

When we had an hydraulic pipe burst which flooded the engine room with oil, it was Bernard who came to deal with it, accompanied by a couple of sons and a stack of rags to clean up the mess. No charge, he said, you are neighbours. The same with the water pump on our main engine. He fixed it. Neighbours. Nervous neighbours.

We gave him a bottle of good wine from his native Alsace.

The next time we heard shots it was not in fact Bernard at all, but someone living opposite him in a canalside chalet. It was hot, the windows were all open, and the chalet dweller had been deeply offended by the noise not only of Bernard's generator, working late at night in 'the factory', but that of the commercial barge moored alongside him. The resident had expressed disapproval by loud shouts – '*Ça va durer longtemps?*' – directed across the canal, and firing his hunting gun into the air. Bernard set the police on to him.

'One cannot fire guns for reasons that are not serious,' said Bernard righteously.

Abrieou a trento
Se ploouvie trent'un
Farié maou en degun

Thirty days does April run
If it rains for thirty one
T'will do no ill and displease none.

April Fool's day in France is much what it is in England, except that you are an April Fish, not an April Fool. If the children can manage to pin a paper fish on to someone in authority, they do, but it is less easy on a warm day when Authority is not wearing its jacket or macintosh. Pins tend to be felt through a thin shirt, though sellotape is a boon to the disrespectful.

In the middle of the television weather broadcast on April 1st a fish swam across the bemused face of the forecaster. That, we felt, was more like it.

On Holy Thursday it was the custom in Provence to collect all the eggs in the barnyard, in order that they should not be mixed with those laid on Good Friday. The Thursday eggs would be used for the traditional omelette of Easter Sunday, but the egg laid on Good Friday had marvellous properties. It never went bad, so the market ladies said, but dried and became as hard as stone. It was carefully kept in the sideboard, where it would protect the house from all kinds of disasters, particularly thunderbolts. We could have used one in Le Bourgidou, which seemed to attract thunderstorms.

Suddenly Easter was here, and Poitavin's window cleared out the streamers and masks and tearful pierrots, and replaced them with Easter eggs, nests of chickens, and tins of chocolate sardines.

With Easter we get the traditional outcrop of marriages. There are no marriages in Lent, but in Provence, for some reason, May is not a month to marry in either, so there is a short period between Easter and Mayday which must be seized if the lovers are not to wait till June. Nowadays these weddings are noticeable to outsiders for the procession of decorated motor cars driving through the town with horns blaring continually, not so musical as the church bells of our towns. There are the wedding photographs to be taken in all the more romantic backgrounds, and in Aigues-Mortes virtually the whole town is photogenic.

Marriage was not always so easy. The Camargue had in the past a large population of Protestants who had been there certainly as far back as 1700 and the Camisard revolt, and probably further. The Catholics and Protestants were mostly tolerant of one another, which is rare indeed, but the tolerance did not extend to inter-marriage.

If a couple wished to marry across their faiths it was necessary for the girl to *enlever*, or abduct, her beau. They would go to the station, and in front of witnesses the girl would say: 'Hear me! I, Mademoiselle So-and-So, abduct Monsieur Such-and-Such.' They would then depart in the train while the witnesses rushed back to the village to spread the news. The couple would go only as far as the railway junction, and in a day or two would be back and it would clearly be necessary and honourable that they should marry. The *enlèvement* declaration avoided any possible accusations that the girl had been abducted by the man, a delicately tactful form of Gretna Green wedding.

And the family had all the fun of a marriage feast afterwards.

6

Muguet, *malpractices and marital discord*

'Oou mes d'abrieou
T'alaouges pas d'un lieou
Qou mes de Maï
Faï ce que ti plaï.'
. . . .
'Lighten your clothes by not a feather
Till the end of April weather
Come the warmer days of May
Do what you will, throw them away!'

The First of May in Provence was once celebrated by decorating the village well with pots of flowers and electing *la belle de mai*. Young men would cover the threshold of their beloved with flower petals (old maids might discover a branch of fig on their doorstep, or worse, if known to be sharp of tongue, a briar).

Nowadays it is the Fête de Travail, Labour Day, and it is the custom to offer your friends a sprig of *muguet*.

It is a bringer of good fortune, they say, good for strengthening the heart, and against spasms. For a week the *muguets* (lily of the valley) had been pushing the other flowers out of bed, today it was on sale everywhere, even outside the baker's. Since lilies of any kind toil not neither do they spin, we do not see the connection with labour, but to the French, the First of May is synonymous with lily of the valley.

To us it was an inconvenience, as Bill likes to present Laurel with a replica of her wedding bouquet on their anniversary at the beginning of April. This needs little cream rosebuds and lily of the valley. The rosebuds are easy, but when *muguets* are requested there is great sucking of teeth by the florist, if not a scornful laugh: it is too early, *voyez-vous*, do not you foreigners know that all over France the pots of *muguet* stand, disciplined in regimented rows, schooled to bud in three weeks' time and flower for the First of May?

Since we have been in France we have had to compound with Laurel's strong objection to artificial flowers, and complete the bouquet with lily of the valley made in Hong Kong.

Our neighbours charmingly presented us with the genuine article on Mayday, which is of course a holiday. Whoever would work on the Fête de Travail? This pleasant custom of giving *muguet* to one's friends on Mayday led us, the following year on April 23rd, to mark St George's Day. We put all the flags up on *Hosanna*, invited the neighbours to lunch at the picnic table, and gave them all red rosebuds. The florist, not reckoning St George's Day, had not put a premium on red roses, and they cost a lot less than the *muguets* a week later.

After the traditional *muguet* swapping we went along to the Express for refreshment and a look at *Midi Libre*. 'Look at this,' chuckled Bill, as he scanned the columns.

Everyone at this time was much entertained and deliciously shocked by the affair of the Commissaire Jobic. This Police Inspector of a Parisian suburb began an investigation into financial corruption perpetrated (he said) by a Government Minister, and he seemed to be getting too close to some dirty linen that the government did not want washed in public.

Jobic did not accuse the Minister of personal dishonesty; he acknowledged that the frauds on various local government building contracts had been committed to finance the election campaign of the ruling Socialist Party and the President, Monsieur Mitterand.

Someone unwisely tried to silence the Commissaire, not

as the real Mafia do, permanently, but by charging him
with living off immoral earnings and thus ensuring his
suspension from duty. Outraged, the Commissaire spilled
more beans than ever. He took cats out of bags and set them
among the pigeons, allowed skeletons to come out of
cupboards. *Il vendait la mèche*, as the French say. Each day
witnesses were produced with names like Fati la Grande,
Zouzou, and The Mackerel, who peopled a Parisian under-
world as colourful as it was astonishing. We had frequent
recourse to our dictionary, since the words describing the
odd professions of these people were hardly familiar to us
in English, let alone French.

These witnesses for the prosecution, whose rivetting
testimony was followed daily by a delighted media circus,
were intended to blacken Jobic's character, but the Commissaire, by deft cross-examination, demonstrated that
they were lying, that he was being framed, and to the
unceasing joy of the public went further and further into
the murky background, dragging in more and more
politicians' names every day.

We all had a good laugh for a while, the French a little
ruefully because though they do not have any faith in the
personal integrity of their politicians, they do not like to be
reminded how well-founded their feelings are.

At a certain point, public opinion decided to become
outraged. The Government, faced with ever more allega-
tions of fraud against its members, unsportingly declared
an amnesty for all politicians so accused; and worded the
amnesty with such exquisite care as to exclude most of the
rival right wing politicians. The popularity ratings of the
Government and its leaders fell dramatically, and confidence in any politician of any party with it.

It was about this time that the French President, who was
not personally under suspicion (though his colleagues and
friends were) was over in England lecturing the British on
civic duty. We are very fond of the French, finding most of
them friendly, good-humoured and with that all-important

ability to laugh at themselves. Their faults are tempered by the right degree of cynicism in their make-up. Bill's father did not agree. He observed on September 3rd, 1939 that we had ended up with the wrong ally and the wrong enemy, and though he later modified his opinion of the Germans to some extent he remained convinced to the end that on the whole one was safer with France as an enemy than as a friend.

Though Bill does not share his father's views he has always felt it odd that a country which has had seven different constitutions (two monarchies and five republics) in the past two hundred years or so without apparently finding one that is good enough to endure, should so optimistically think it can organise a viable confederation of Europe. As we go to press they are now proposing to increase the number of constitutions to eight. Enough!

We in England, who have had the same constitution (albeit with some peripheral tinkering) for a thousand years can claim a better track record. The trouble is that virtually every country in the EEC has only been in existence in its present form for two shakes of a duck's tail, and they appear to have no sense of the continuation of history.

We find it is quite hard to convince the French of this.

Mario's marital problems were having their effect on Boubou's barge *Escaut*. Mario had agreed to do the ship-wright work necessary for the conversion. Now that his struggles with his former wife had become also a struggle with the full force of French Law (in other words his 'moonlighting' had been exposed: 'I am denounced!' he cried, dramatically) he could no longer be seen doing any such work, even if he were doing it for friendship which we all knew to be the case. The court, he explained, would not believe him. Nor would anyone else.

This left Boubou in a difficult position. The roof and part of the hatch coamings of his barge had been removed and it was no longer weather-tight. The barge *Escaut* was one of the few remaining Canal du Midi barges which used to ply between Sète and Bordeaux on the Atlantic coast, via what is possibly the most beautiful and among the most imaginatively engineered canals in the world. Being something of a rarity among boats, Boubou's wish was to convert her as both his studio and living quarters while retaining the original outside appearance as closely as possible, or at the very least the silhouette, for obviously he would have some need of windows.

So a new gang of lads arrived, though they seemed to work at long-spaced intervals (the full moon only perhaps). It looked like being a long while before any real progress was made. One of the first things to be constructed (not because it was urgent, but because its foundations underpinned various other matters) was the combined swimming pool and garage.

Many barges carry a small car with them. We have once done so ourselves, though no more. It was a nuisance on deck. Boubou had the brilliant idea of converting part of the hold measuring some four and a half metres by two metres, and two metres deep, so that his car could be carried in it, and when not so occupied in hot weather it could be flooded and used as a swimming pool. We were all watching the development of the *garage-piscine* with fascinated interest, but now work had slowed down and almost ceased.

Mario was in a foul mood. He and Martine had invited us to a Sunday barbecue, and we arrived in the middle of that bitter silence that follows a row. They both spoke to us, and the dog, but not to each other. Having decided that it was less insulting and perhaps more helpful to stay, rather than be called away to an emergency phone call, we endeavoured to behave normally, so that they could recover their tempers.

Mario had soon drunk enough to enjoy himself, interspersing his stories with outrageously unkind jokes about

Martine's cooking, which we were eating at the time, though of course the main dish, the barbecue, was man's work. If it's fun, it always is. Martine was quiet, she ate and drank very little. We enjoyed her apricot tart, which Mario said was inedible, and left rather early.

As we looked back, Martine was in floods of tears.

It was not completely the most embarassing meal of our lives. That record is held for ever by an English tea-party to which we were bidden by Bill's immediate superior in a new job. Our children were two and five, his a little younger. We had a new puppy, our children could not bear to leave it at home. First mistake. Once welcomed into the brand new house, with piles of earth still round it where a garden was being constructed, our hosts kindly insisted that the puppy should be brought in from the car. We concurred. Second mistake. The inevitable happened and the puppy left an indelible memento on the new carpet in the hall until then an immaculate and delicate shade of blue.

Our hosts said it did not matter, through clenched teeth. The tea was good, Laurel remembers a delicious banana cake. Bill has blotted the entire episode from his memory. Our children behaved within the bounds of reason, and afterwards went upstairs with the other two to play in the nursery. Third mistake. As we adults talked earnestly round the tea-table of this and that, and the recipe for banana cake (our hosts were very forgiving about the carpet) there was a wail from outside the French windows, where the youngest child sat in a pile of earth having fallen out of the upstairs window. He was filthy, but unhurt. The rest of that afternoon is a blank to both of us.

Mario's barbecue ran the tea-party close, the shortage of incident being balanced by the acidity of the atmosphere.

The next morning Martine was knocking on the door to see if we had survived her cooking. Mario had gone to start a job at Port Camargue, out of reach of his ex-wife, he hoped. He had to finish decorating a new restaurant before the season in June, and would be working from six in the morning till ten at night, Mario fashion.

This arrangement did not last long. To come back to Martine and the caravan at nearly midnight and leave again at five in the morning was punishing to both of them, the rows became more frequent, and one day Mario left, and did not come back. After a couple of days he had still not returned, and Martine came to cast some of her woes in Laurel's lap.

'He's got a woman there in Port Camargue, I know it well,' sobbed Martine. 'He must be staying in her apartment.'

Laurel felt that even Mario would have a hard time satisfying a new light-of-love after a sixteen hour day's work, but did not say so. Could she with any conviction encourage a belief that Mario would, in time, return, since his beloved boats were here, let alone a chastened Martine? She could.

The day continued badly with a disquieting telephone call from England, saying that one of Laurel's ancient aunts was unwell, but that our kids were coping.

All in all it had been a depressing weekend.

7

Boat shows and boa constrictors

'*La trona sorda*
Emplena la gorga.'
....
'Thunder unheard in distant mountain
Fills the source and flows the fountain.'

Bill was making a cradle. It was a beautiful thing; the walnut pieces fitted together with pegs so that when it was no longer needed it would pack flat. He had gone extensively into the mathematics of rocking on the backs of envelopes, and had asked Laurel how long the average baby was and how much it weighed, as being in the Navy when the children were born he had no very clear recollection.

'They are a lot bigger than they used to be, I know that,' said Laurel, 'I can tell from my knitting, everything is larger.' So we went to 'Tout Pour Bébé' and measured the pram mattresses.

The Granddaughter (how odd that one knows these things in advance nowadays) was expected at the end of the month. The cradle was lovingly sanded and any hard edges rounded off; then it was given a soft beeswax polish. Its rockability was carefully tested, and its moment of inertia calculated (it is occasionally mystifying to be married to a mathematician), then it was laid aside to await The Summons.

In the meantime we enjoyed the warmth and the sunshine, and the song of the *cigales* or *cicadas*, inseparable from summer in the Midi. *Ben tems per la cigala*, they say here, as we say good weather for ducks. We had just discovered that the cicada spends four years waiting underground for one brief spell of Mediterranean sun, a bit like the tourists at Gatwick on a Bank holiday weekend. The eggs are laid in summer, on a dry branch. Those that survive the lizards emerge in autumn as a tiny gold larva. If this survives the ants, spiders and birds, it descends on a silken thread after its second moult, and buries itself in the ground. The grub lies under the soil, attacked by predators and frost and floodwater (this is why there are few of them in the lowest parts of the Camargue, the water table is too high) and waits in the long dark. Four years later, one in a hundred of them who have survived will climb up to the surface one starry night in June, and sit on a twig to crack out of her last skin into a new cicada. As the sun rises and dries her newborn wings she begins her song to Phoebus Apollo that will last a month or six weeks, she will sing, drink a little, love a lot, lay her eggs and then die. Four years in the dark for six weeks of sun.

'It takes me four years to build a boat,' said Bill. 'I know all about postponed gratification.'

'We get more than six weeks' sunshine at the end of it all,' said Laurel, continuing without much logic: 'And whatever else you do, you don't sing.' 'You make enough noise for both of us,' said her husband.

Although another proverb says it is not good to work when the *cigale* sings (too hot, perhaps?) we got plenty of external painting done, and we went to the Salon Fluvial.

Aigues-Mortes is in a commanding position from the point of view of inland water tourism, being close to the Canal du Midi. The Canal du Rhône à Sète goes past the ramparts, and as a bonus the sea and its beaches are only four kilometres away. Unfortunately, during the period when this industry was beginning to develop, the town had a dullard of a mayor, a communist, who refused to concern the town in tourist development. The limited tourism that the town attracted was thus the result of its breathtaking picturesqueness, or uncoordinated and un-encouraged private enterprise, and there was not a lot of that in those days.

One result of this lethargy is that the Aigues-Mortais declined to ameliorate the canal basin adjoining the west side of the town, and the departmental Chamber of Commerce, sensing profit, carried out the work themselves and removed control and most of the benefits from the municipal authorities.

Now the mayor had changed and the town had awoken to the commercial exploitation of its liquid assets (and by no means is everyone persuaded that they should be exploited at all) and found it was rather behind in the water-rat race.

Matters reached a crucial stage when state funds were allocated for a new canal by-pass which would leave the town on a backwater, but at the same time provide it with a second chance to do something about fluvial tourism. The town decided to have an Exhibition. They called it the First Salon Fluvial, a sort of Inland Waters Boat Show, widely billed as the most important in France, a claim that was later modified to 'the most important in the South'; well, at least it was the *first*.

It did not seem as if Aigues-Mortes had ever organised anything of this nature before. The job was given to a firm of public relations people who had been responsible for other nautical displays, mostly in connection with the sea. Grandiose plans were prepared. There was to be a quay by the ramparts full of old ships to provide a back-drop. What a photo opportunity!

In the event only one old river-boat turned up and that was for sale. The organisers hastily rounded up some seagoing craft of rather recent vintage which sat there incongruously in front of the half-dozen or so stands which were all that had been taken up. There would have been more seagoing craft but nobody had remembered that the canal was only six feet deep, and some of the craft invited ran aground and could not come to the party.

Matters were not helped by a moderate mistral with winds of a mere forty knots, and the placing of the long narrow marquee that housed the exhibitors' stands exactly along the direction of the wind with a door at each end. As soon as the exhibition opened most of the glossy folders, catalogues, and handouts were swept off the tables, wall maps were blown off their drawing pins, joined by an assortment of hats and anything not fastened down, and disappeared out of the leeward door, heading south. Fortunately parents were quick enough to seize their children otherwise the smaller ones might well have gone too.

No one was going to stay in these conditions, especially as there was little to see. Most of these stands were abandoned for the second day of the show, leaving only those sponsored by public bodies, and very soon exhibitors outnumbered the visitors, until, denuded of their papers, and discouraged, the stands closed down. The next day, when the press were expected and a lunch had been laid on for them aboard the *Pescalune*, it was still blowing, but not nearly so hard. One could stand upright. The brochures had been weighted down with stones. There was a dearth of exhibitors, public and press. Someone had linked our name with *Yachting World* and we were hastily invited to become part of the official party and have lunch. The party was smaller than expected and there was plenty to eat as a result. It was a buffet provided by a restaurant at La Grande Motte, a marina for sea-going craft not far away. It is possible that the specification and money did not provide for much of a meal. This is Aigues-Mortes we are speaking of and it was the first, experimental, Salon; but on the other hand the French are not given to skimping on the cooking and presentation of food. We have to say that the restaurants of La Grande Motte, as exemplified by this one, did not impress.

It reminded us of a similar yachting occasion in Rhode Island involving ocean-going yachts, to which we were not invited. 'You missed nothing,' said a colleague afterwards. 'We got tuna salad.' It is hard to convey the depths of disappointment and scorn he managed to put into those two words. Perhaps the American caterers did not know that tuna salad is a bad weather stand-by on many yachts, and has vibes that recall the smell of diesel, fear, and imminent nausea.

On *Pescalune* it was cold meat and salad.

Being captive on board a moving *péniche* we had to listen to the speeches. And didn't they go on? If we British think our politicians are long-winded, try the French. (The Italians go on even longer but it is more musical to listen to.) Give a French politician a microphone and he is set in for the night.

This nearly became true, because *Pescalune* broke down. Miles from anywhere, except the canal banks. Of course the Prefect and the President of the Conseil Regional had urgent meetings elsewhere, and were clearly upset, so we expected to have to suffer yet more ear-torment if only to divert their wrath. Not a bit of it. Speeches are for passing the time when nothing else worthwhile can be done. Now was the time to panic. While eminent gentlemen sat drumming their fingers on the tables and smiling wanly through clenched teeth, someone gave us a talk with maps on why the money was going to run out for the *déviation* round about autumn. It was soporific stuff coming after plenty of Vin de Sables, and snores could be heard from those not anxious to get to the next *affaire*. *Pescalune* was taken in tow after a long delay and moved slowly back to her berth, and the politicians went off to make some more speeches somewhere else which would obviously start 'I apologise for my late arrival this afternoon. . . .'

The following year the Salon was held a little earlier. Someone did some homework (they persevere, these Aigues-Mortais) and had the marquee turned the other way and sited by the Bassin d'Evolution, which excluded even those seagoing boats who got there last year, because it is through a fixed bridge. This time the weather was good, even hot. They did not dare repeat the lunchtime cruise on the *Pescalune*, so they kept her moored alongside where she was used as a base for symposiums on Water Tourism. These were delayed and frequently interrupted because the organisers (the same people as last year) had decided to lay on displays of extroversion on motor-driven water-scooters to amuse the passers-by. These aquatic horrors (the scooters, that is) were powered by the same two-stroke motors as chain saws, and made a similar noise as their devotees brayed, buzzed, and gnarred, assaulting the eardrums with a force not quite, alas, sufficient to stun them into paralysis. Only one machine was needed to deafen anyone within half a mile, two were an abomination, and there were three of them. It was a great nuisance to the people and politicians at the symposiums for whom the Salon had been organised, as even the PA system put in for speeches failed to top the noise.

It became evident early on in the symposiums, when the scooters had taken a rest and we could all be heard, that here were two different attitudes to water tourism. There were those who saw it as a harmless way of getting from one place to another and enjoying oneself without upsetting one's surroundings. And there were those who saw it as a pot of money that they hoped to lay their hands on.

We do admire the French people. They are not only able to listen to interminable speeches, but they are not afraid to bend their politicians' ears to their purpose. They do not mince words. '*Carrément fou*' ('absolutely mad') was how someone was described (we agreed). Another proposition was described as '*connerie*', which is not quite as rude as its literal translation in English, but is not far off.

There was a diverting little interlude as an eccentric gentleman went past on what appeared to be a water bicycle. It was silent as he pedalled it along, and much appreciated after the scooters. Mario joked that he had better go and check the *Isles de Stel*'s moorings after the passage of so powerful a machine, and a further burst of laughter followed as the gentleman, who had been waving to the crowd on the bank and not looking ahead, came suddenly to the railway bridge which was closed. He had to dismount and crouch down beside the saddle in order to pass beneath the low bridge.

It being a fine day, and there being a full house of both press and worthies, we did not get invited to the official lunch this time, but there was a good and simple buffet by a local restaurant, and free wine and sea-food being dispensed by a nearby tourist board.

The next Salon Fluvial, it was announced, will be held in Béziers on the Canal du Midi. Everyone was very careful to make no comment. Except Bill.

'Blown it, haven't they?' he said loudly.

> Quan ploou per san Médar
> De la Récolot empouerto un quar
> Quan ploou pa
> N'empouerto la mita

> If the day of Sant Médar is wet,
> Three quarters of the crop you'll get,
> But if that day it does not rain,
> Only half will be your gain.

One of the Camargue crops is rice. It started to become important during the food shortages of the 1939/45 war. Its introduction was so successful that a positive rice-rush developed with people from all over the republic rushing to buy land and cash in. Two crops in a year! It couldn't fail.

But the boom did not last. Too many tried to grow rice of inferior quality; they did not understand the crop or the land and its variations in water table, and soon their product got a poor reputation. Much of it was only good for feeding the animals.

Rice is a more complicated crop than is often realised. Some types such as the Arborio (which makes the Italian risottos) are very tender plants. Arborio must be harvested by sickle; a scythe would damage it too much, and this made it very hard work. We were told that the workers would start off with the sickle when the boss was looking, and as soon as he turned his back – the scythe. It is little wonder that some crops failed. (Nowadays there are special harvesters to cut the rice.)

A very important person in rice growing is the *aigadier* or Master of the Water. It was his job to regulate the flows of water to the different fields, knowing by judgement exactly how much coverage each would need. Obviously in the early days such skills here were rudimentary.

Nowadays the Camargue rice is marketed aggressively, under the tradename of the Winged Bull. It needs prewashing to remove some of the starch, and longer cooking than most kinds, and our Chinese sister-in-law, who is a connoisseur of rice, was not impressed.

It was on a very hot day, but close and threatening, when Laurel saw a poster advertising the Snake Show in the Espace Régent (the village hall of Aigues-Mortes) and was intrigued. Bill was reluctant to go. He had spent enough of his younger days in Egypt and India to be wary of such things. He had, he said, no desire to see Dravidian ladies and gentlemen shoving snakes into places nature never intended.

Laurel replied that the name of the performer, Rudi Müller, sounded trustworthily German, and since children were half price it obviously could not be that sort of show.

'What do you mean, trustworthy?' Bill called down from the wheelhouse, 'the Germans are capable of anything!'

We looked at the distant thunderheads massing over Nîmes and decided that the storm was going elsewhere, and by six-thirty in the evening Laurel had got her beloved as far as the Express Bar where, after enjoying a couple of ice-cold beers on what was a very hot night, he found himself going in the general direction of the Espace Régent, and before he could say '*Götterdämmerung*' he was inside it with a large number of local people.

It is difficult to say a good word about the Espace Régent. In a town where it is necessary to be good neighbours with medieval buildings, the city fathers have erected an eyesore. Fortunately not much was visible from the street. Inside, the form and the décor were suitable only for a cash and carry warehouse, and the acoustics when a dance was held there were atrocious. But it was not bad for snake-charming.

The performance was educational. A benign and smiling young German with a straggly ginger beard and buck teeth took examples of snakes out of reassuringly strong looking containers, and walked round the circle of chairs where three rows of spectators sat. Where appropriate he let the children (and others) stroke the scaly skins. A commentary was given in a flat monotone by a lady who had obviously learnt it by rote. At first we thought this was because Herr Müller did not speak French, but on consideration realised that what he was doing required his total concentration, and chatting to the audience as well would have distracted his attention.

He started with the smaller snakes, taking them from suitcases that were stacked at the back of the hall. He showed us the difference between a viper and a harmless grass snake, which we immediately forgot again. He surprised us with the dryness of snakeskin, which one expects to be damp and slippery. He took scorpions and poisonous spiders out of rather less reassuring boxes (tupperware with ventilation holes) and his lady's eyes swivelled from her microphone as the windows lit with a flash of lightning and the lights dimmed.

He had just got to the cobras and rattlesnakes, and there

were two or three large tin trunks on trestles that had not yet been opened.

At the moment when he and his assistant were going round with the rattlesnakes there was a terrifying flash of lightning with an almost immediate clap of thunder and all the lights went out.

In the darkness, lit occasionally by flickering lightning, Bill whispered to Laurel, 'This is where the fun starts. The exit is behind you to the right.'

He was wrong about the fun. A voice raised itself above the hubbub and in an astonishing blend of authority and controlled panic ordered us to 'remain in our seats for the safety and comfort of all . . .' and the rest of his words were drowned, almost literally, by the noise of a torrential downpour, and another crack of thunder.

When the lights came on again after not too harrowing an interval (the EDF are very efficient) the two rattlesnakes were nowhere to be seen.

'Do we assume they are back in their snakeskin cases?' asked Laurel. 'I would have been happier to see them still gripped in his hands when the lights went up.'

'I'm not sure,' Bill replied, 'you observe that our HairundBeardenSerpentHandlungShaftner is walking around with a cleft stick. Check your handbag.'

'Surely they couldn't get through the zip, could they?' asked Laurel, worried.

Herr Müller put down his cleft stick, assured the audience that the rattlers were safely back in their box, and continued the show by opening the second biggest trunk, taking out a boa constrictor that was several feet long and as big round as a small tree. We were gratified to see its diameter. It had the appearance of being extremely well fed.

'There's reports of some bulls missing in Lafont's *manade*,' said Bill, and Laurel had to tell him to shut up. He is unreliable in company.

Children were called out from the audience and had their

photos taken with Boris the Boa coiled round their necks. He was then joined by the lodger in the larger trunk, an even bigger and fatter python who clearly liked children too, and looked as if he had eaten several.

We left the hall with the children still playing with the enormous snakes, and returned to *Hosanna*, dodging our way through deep puddles. We had left the skylights and windows on the boat open, the storm had been severe, and everything beneath them was wet through. Guess whose fault *that* was, and who told her so.

Laurel tried to distract her husband's mind from the mopping up which followed by telling him of a recipe for a 'dish of land-eels' (grass snakes) which she had recently discovered.

'You make a marinade with herbs, tomatoes, garlic and oil. Then it says: Take a handsome grass snake (the collared variety is best), skin it and clean it: you must remove any excrement which is very bitter . . .'

'I don't think I want to know any more,' said her spouse firmly, as he squeezed out the sponge.

'You cut it in slices and marinade all day. Then you fry the chunks before putting them back in the marinade to cook about half an hour. You can eat it all or just strain off the broth.'

'The Chinese would love it.' Our Chinese sister-in-law had often told us that snake broth fetched high prices in China, where old men who have married young brides consider it fortifies the parts that other broths do not reach.

We had mopped up all we could. Wearily we put the sponge and bucket away.

'Dear God, look at the time,' said Laurel. 'We should be in bed.' 'That's the barometer, idiot,' said her husband fondly.

8

The Old Lady dances

'*Dins lou tramble de l'air tousc*
Lèu me leissère peresous
Empourta pèr un raive blous.'
. . . .
'In a shiver of warm air
Lazily I let go
Wafted by a dream of light.'
Marquis Folco de Baroncelli-Javon

One fine Tuesday we went out for lunch, starting early as we had a long way to go. We drove across the Camargue, leaving the Arles road at Albaron, passing Méjanes and skirting the north shore of the Etang de Vaccarès, the only part of the lake which the public can see close up. We stopped to climb the lookout towers, but saw no unusual birds. The interesting wild-life keeps further away from the road in summer.

However we could see and admire the saltmarsh, the *sansouire*, now emerald green and covered with the flowers of statice, and immortelles, and the *roubines* edged with green reeds and clumps of great mace and bullrush. Floating on the water were some waterlilies, known hereabouts as the clock flower, since they are reputed to bloom at exactly seven in the morning.

At Villeneuve we turned right. The roads were getting progressively more and more rural. We were still close to the eastern shore of the *étang*, but we left this as the road surface deteriorated. Some sharp turns followed in what was apparently the middle of a farmyard and the road became a track that passed between small *étangs*. Here was an outpost of the bird-park people and a pleasant young man explained what birds could be seen and what their habits were. As few tourists penetrated this far, there were more birds, and he told us a great many interesting things, especially about flamingoes.

Shortly after, we passed a gate and were driving over beaten sand and encroaching *étangs*. We were glad of our four-wheel-drive car for several times we had our wheels in the water. Alongside the road the plant life reflected everything that liked salt. There were no trees, and scarcely any bushes, but the flowers were wonderful. The track seemed to be leading us over water for the next ten kilometres, every time we began to fear we had lost our way, a rough handpainted sign would encourage us: Restaurant Poissons, and a wobbly arrow. We continued across shallow pools alternating occasionally with sand spits and a few dunes, riotous with stiff flowering grasses, cystus and sand lilies.

We crossed a ford, drove for about half a kilometre across the sands and reached the sea at Beauduc.

At Beauduc it would be easy to believe yourself at the world's end.

The land was flat, and there was nothing to be seen behind us under the immense blue bowl of the sky but sand and water, as far as the distant horizon. Ahead of us was a limitless sea. It was now that we called to mind that the Camargue is known as one of the five deserts of France.

The rough track we had followed exists to service a *station de pompage* which pumps surplus water from the Camargue into the sea. To the south-east of it is the beach of Beauduc.

This region is made of fine sand that has come down the Rhône and been deposited in places where the littoral current has a counter-eddy. If there had been tides such as we have in Britain, the sea at low water would have been miles out, so gentle was the slope of the beach. Here in the Mediterranean the tidal range is only nine inches, but even that makes a big difference. Huge pools are left by the tide, acres of them, none more than a foot deep, idyllic playgrounds for tiny children, and full of shell fish.

In this desert was a settlement; one cannot call a place with no trees and no water an oasis. Hippies had once moved in, then moved on or grown up. There were some twenty unauthorised and decrepit caravans, abandoned lorries, vans and an old London bus. Some of these had been turned into homes and were still lived in. There were as well wooden cabins of more or less simple construction. Every habitation had an awning for outdoor living, a little fence round a sandy garden; some with a small stable and a horse. The hippies, and others of peaceful but anarchic habits, had left their rotting debris behind them, a sort of shanty-town, a *bidonville*, which is fortunately spread wide enough among the sand dunes to be quaint rather than ugly. In fact parts of it have a surprising charm if you are tolerant of other people's habits.

Living here would not be easy. The nearest water supply is more than ten kilometres away, bread and groceries even further, and of course there is no electricity or drainage. It is a good stop-over for the genuine touring caravan who has the determination and courage to get there, and there were several parked right on the beach, or among the dunes further back. Most had been towed here by four-wheel-drive cars and we began to understand the Camarguais dislike of these vehicles.

Several times we had seen the graffiti '4 × 4 out' or '4 × 4 go home' or some similar expression and had felt a little resentful, for we have a four-wheel-drive car mainly because we wish to be mobile in bad conditions over rough roads in winter. But the Camarguais complain that too often the 4 × 4s, as they know them, are used by people who abuse an ability to penetrate into places where they are not welcome, or even where they are not allowed, and worse, who organise off-the-road rallies in the wild country where sheer numbers damage the terrain and wildlife.

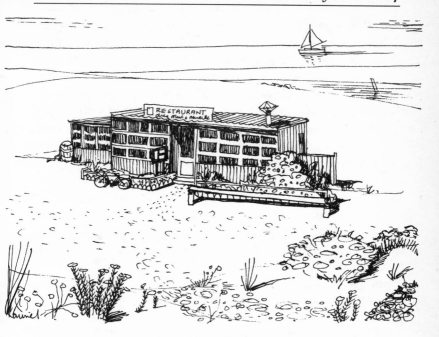

It was not hard to spot the two fish restaurants among the cluster of shacks. They were a little larger than the other buildings, the gentle rumble of a generator could be heard, and they were dignified by a wooden deck (Chez Juju) and a flowering bush fully three feet high (Marc & Mireille). These restaurants were of special interest to us as they were very primitive, of a type that is unique in sophisticated countries. They had no water laid on. They could not erect a permanent structure, but somehow they managed to attract a clientele of cognoscenti even in winter when the track is almost impassable. They each have their own fishing boat anchored off the shore and they serve only their own fresh caught fish and shell fish, cooked in the simplest way. These are served grilled, accompanied by fresh lemon on plates that do not match. Naturally there is wine and a basket of bread.

You choose your fish from the refrigerator and it is prepared and cooked while you wait. To start you can have the shellfish, though you should choose with care, for those that require much washing, such as those highly promoted *telines* that look like little finger nails, can be a bit sandy, a function of the shortage of water.

You eat inside the wooden planked structure, since the sea breeze in summer blows sand into your food, and in winter the wind sweeping the saltflats would freeze you. Even indoors in winter there was a perpetual struggle to avoid draughts, pieces of newspaper or cloth were pressed into whistling apertures with only moderate success. We wonder sometimes why we like going to Beauduc in winter. The journey is interesting, though long and some-times hazardous after heavy rain. The place is fascinating in a slightly horrific way, and the fish is excellent. The wildness of it appeals to us. We suppose that is reason enough. It is extraordinary that in one country one can find such extremes, from Juju's at Beauduc to three-star Paul Bocuse at Collonges. Juju's is a lot cheaper, but fish is never given away in France.

We chose a fine looking *loup-de-mer* (sea-bass) and when he was grilled to perfection over charcoal we ate him with crusty bread, cool white wine and enormous chunks of lemon. Perfect, because simple.

If you go to Beauduc in summer, or anywhere far into the Camargue, you might as we did once, see a marvel. Sometimes on a hot day when the air shimmers with the heat above the saltflats, mirages occur. We saw trees, invisible over the horizon, mirrored in the sky, misty blue, quivering like aspens. There are those who have seen the whole village of Les-Saintes-Maries upside down in the sky.

At such times the Camarguais say: '*La vieio danso*'. The Old Lady is the Earth, drunk with the summer and the sparkle on the sea, standing on her hands and dancing in the sky.

It was a powerful thing to have seen, just that once, the Old Lady Dancing.

On the way home we stopped for a coffee and a chat at the little café where the family are very hospitable, close by the road junction at Villeneuve. We had come twenty kilometres or more from Beauduc and were back into civilisation.

Well, nearly. There was a dog asleep in the centre of the road junction, which tells you something of the traffic conditions prevailing at Villeneuve late on a hot summer afternoon. Sitting under the shade of a huge tree in the garden, with scratching hens and a magnificent cock pecking up the leavings round our feet, listening to the doves cooing, and playing with the latest crop of kittens, we felt completely at ease, whereas going back to a city would have been a severe shock to the system. Perhaps, once you have seen the Old Lady Dancing, it is not possible to return, not, at all events, as the same person who left.

We stopped again by the wayside and came across a man gathering *sangsues* (leeches). We thought this business was superseded though Bill, who once helped manage a hospital in England believes anything to be possible with the medical profession. These were being gathered for bait, not professionally, though leech gathering was once the life-blood, so to speak, of the poorer Camarguais and Arlésiens during slumps and recessions when jobs were hard to come by.

It is still difficult to avoid accidentally picking them up in the wetlands in some parts, and the *gardians* often wear rubber thigh boots as protection.

Arles was the centre of this trade, said our leech hunter, and despatched leeches far and wide, but the method of catching was *pas agréable* in the old days: because, *croyez-moi*, the hunter waded in bare to the thighs, using his tempting legs as bait, and after stepping out of the water waited till the leeches were sozzled, when they dropped off his legs. There must be better ways of making a living. But it underlines the hardship undergone by the people of sixty years ago.

We asked one of the chemists in Aigues-Mortes, M. Delord, when the medical use of leeches ceased. As his father had been a pharmacist before him, he regaled us with reminiscences.

'Why, not till – it must have been 1955. As a schoolboy I remember my father's leech jar. One moment, I have it still upstairs.' He dashed away and returned with a round glass jar, rather like a stemmed goldfish bowl on a firm base.

'She must have very pure water, the leech, she is fussy. You will find no leeches where there is any trace of pollution. You see how she could not escape from the round bowl – she could not climb the reverse curve. They used to cost five sous each. I remember a patient would visit my father with a *coup de sang*, what we now call high blood pressure, and for five sous he would buy a leech which he would attach to his neck. When the leech was engorged with blood (it would swell excessively, you know, from a little flat ribbon to a great balloon) it would drop off and be given back. No it was not painful, there is no biting, just sucking.

'There are still leeches in the clearer ponds and marshes. Sometimes you would wonder why a horse ailed and grew thin, you would try every remedy, and do you know what it was? A leech, fastened on the inside of the lower lip, very hard to see. To get it off you cut it in half with scissors, you must never try to pull it.'

After Albaron there was a gradual return to civilisation: we were passing caravans and camping cars on the tarmac road, and coaches that venture in hordes just inside the edge of the Camargue, but do not dare to challenge the savagery and spells of its wilder interior. We encountered again the heavy trucks, lumbering too fast on roads never built to take them. There is a motorway between Italy, East France and Spain which passes some way to the north of the Camargue, past Nîmes and Montpellier, but although truck drivers are given money for the *autoroute* tolls, they prefer to take the short cut along the narrow road across the

Camargue so that they may profit personally by a few pounds at the expense of others.

The restaurants at Aigues-Mortes are *pas terrible*, as the French say, meaning that they are nothing to write home about. There are some thirty-four of them in a town of about 4,000 inhabitants, mostly concerned with peddling sustenance to the mass of tourists who greatly exceed in number the indigenous. Even in France, the land of *haute cuisine*, and also of the good local and modest restaurant, the chance of finding thirty-four good restaurateurs in 4,000 persons is remote. Taking out the children, the old and infirm, the *police municipale* (all nine of them), the Mayor and his adjoints, that would leave a statistical improbability that there could be more than one good restaurateur in Aigues-Mortes. Unfortunately, the possibility that there is not even one good restaurant remains.

We have not tried all the thirty-four reported establishments. We have not been to most of those that our French friends have described as horrible, since where we have ignored their advice we have regretted it. Fortunately to eat out of doors in St Louis' Square under the plane trees is such a pleasure to the eye that it makes up in part for imperfection in the food. If you choose your dish well and strike lucky, your meal could be memorable for the right reasons, perfection not being attainable.

Given France's reputation as the land of good cooking, every young *Français* believes he is a born chef, just as every young Englishman thinks, quite erroneously, that he is a born sailor in the mould of Drake and Nelson. *Ce n'est pas vrai. Pas du tout.* The French are quite as capable of cooking badly as the English are of being seasick. But neither will believe it.

Even the hard core of competent, trained chefs who go on year after year are not *surdoué*. Certainly there are some who are not bad, but their prices are out of proportion to their skills for any clients who have enjoyed the good cooking of Burgundy or the Perigord.

We must in fairness point out that not all see Aigues-Mortes' catering as mediocre. The Adjoint for Tourism, defining his terms with great care, claims proudly that the standard of restauration is the highest in any coastal town west of the Rhône.

Late in June we met Claude at the Express Bar. He looked like a horse with a leech on his lower lip, very down in the mouth. He had bad news.

'We must leave our apartment,' he told us. 'Our landlady has started an infamous *chantage* [blackmail]. Either we pay an exorbitant sum for the summer season, or we go. Naturally we go.'

We thought of all their lovely possessions, and the impromptu pizza lunches we had enjoyed on their terrace overlooking the rooftops, now that the warm weather was here, and commiserated.

'Where will you go?' we asked. 'Oh, we will try to stay within the ramparts. But at such a time of year, *ce n'est pas évident.*'

It was not indeed *évident*, an expression the French often use when we would say 'It won't be easy.'

At intervals during the coming weeks we were apprised of the results of their search. At last they found something in a street off the square. Our congratulations on finding anything so conveniently placed were received with the nodding of the head from left to right which means 'I hear you and I don't agree.'

Claude said: 'It is of a shabbiness inconceivable. The rooms are pokey. It is in a state altogether abominable. Basil is having a *crise de nerfs*. I fear we cannot ask you to our home for a while.'

So it was. Claude kept us informed when we met him at the Express or in the *supermarché*. They were getting their new dwelling straight, but even when clean and redecorated it was clear that Basil went into a fit of the vapours at the idea of inviting anyone to see it. 'He is still sulking,' Claude would say. 'In fact I have put him down the well.' The whole affair had upset both of them severely, but Claude managed to keep his head above water. Basil, deeply wounded in his aesthetic region, seemed to go into a fugue, and we scarcely saw him for the rest of the summer.

In any case on June 25th the Summons from England came. 'Please feel free to come any time,' said our daughter, on the phone, sounding unwontedly in need of aid. 'There's a heatwave, I'm as large as an elephant, and my brain has ceased to function. I hope this baby isn't late, I'm already having to spend all day in the bath to keep cool.'

'We'll start at once,' we said. We packed, laid the cradle, well padded, in the back of the car and set off first thing next morning. We were grandparents before we reached the ferry at Calais, and spent the next month helping with the new arrival.

9

Local amusements

'Ce que pana pas a l'estieu
Ves pas la figuro de dieou.'
· ·
'Who profits not by summer's grace
Cannot hope to see God's face.'

July and August are the months when tourism in the Camargue, indeed everywhere in France, is at its height. The French and Belgians enjoy long summer holidays, concentrated in these two months. From the start of July the radio and television are full of traffic warnings about red days and orange days, and talking about *Bisons Futés* (the Wily Bisons are those who look for the *'bis'* or secondary routes).

Those journalists not among the *juillettistes* (those who go on holiday in July) revel in telling us about 30km *bouchons* on this or that *autoroute*, together with the numbers of killed or maimed in this or that *carambolage*, which delightfully noisy word is a fine example of French onomatopeia, and means a motorway pile-up.

We missed most of our first July in the Camargue as we had been in England. We had returned from a hot English summer to baking desert heat, the boat, shut up for a month, practically incandescent. We spread awnings, washed the decks down with cold water, then opened windows, and fixed up fans, but still it took a couple of days to cool it down to a bearable temperature.

The second July was mercifully less hot, but extremely beastly, since we spent a fortnight of it being sandblasted and painted. This torture had been postponed from April, and was far worse than just having the builders in. That is a condition that we have long been used to, but since Bill is the builder the situation can usually be kept under control, and there are long spells of comfort between short spells of chaos. This was two weeks of total and uncontrollable chaos, with workmen, and their dogs.

The noise of the sand-blasting machine, the disruption, the dirt, and the impossibility of finding any peace, brought us almost to blows on several occasions. It was too hot to remain below, and too unpleasant to sit on deck, even if you could find a spot to do so. We ate out almost every evening to keep morale up, and so got to know a few more of the thirty-four restaurants in Aigues-Mortes. Perhaps the disorder on board has coloured our jaundiced view of some of them.

Laurel escaped from the noise and grit to the market twice a week, revelling in the relative peace of the shouting hucksters and amplified pop from the cassette stall. She bought local melons, peaches, and if you knew where to look and got there early, raspberries. She would almost always have a story to tell on her return.

There was a thief in the market one day, so it was clear that the summer season had begun. He looked like any tourist in psychedelic shorts, but he had tried to take the purse from the top of an old lady's wicker shopping basket. He had been seen, caught, and firmly held by a man who also looked just like any tourist, but turned out to be a policeman on holiday. The municipal police arrived, the thief pleaded, the old lady was in tears. She could not be bothered with bringing a case against her assailant, she was already too upset. It looked as if he would get away with it. The policeman on holiday began to look as if he regretted not breaking the offending arm, and apologising afterwards.

On another occasion Laurel was buying mussels and after smiling at an elderly dame next to her in the queue the dame became expansive. 'Fish is excellent for the feminine system, dear Madame. Particularly for ladies of our age, the iodide is to be recommended. There is much iodide in the *violets*, you know.' The violets were not flowers in this instance, but an expensive shellfish like a spiky whelk, much esteemed in the town, perhaps for the reasons stated by the old lady. Already out of sorts with the sandblasting, Laurel was irritated, not liking to be taken for a 'lady of our age' in desperate need of iodides by someone who looked *quite* so old and decrepit, not herself a walking advertisement for violets, which had obviously done her no good at all. Thus it was that the next woman who accosted Laurel, at the hat stall, might have got short shrift. 'I cannot decide,' muttered this lady, turning to Laurel as if she were an old friend, 'whether this [white cotton] or this [navy straw] is the more becoming. What do you think?' Laurel bit back a desire to respond that whichever one she bought, she would still look like a pekinese with a hat on, and commended the white one as cooler in the hot sun. Delighted with this advice, the smiling lady thanked her and bought the hat. The stallholder smiled at her as well. Nice to be popular with someone, thought Laurel.

Two Provençal cousins met in mid market. In America this would have produced an excited scream of '*Oh*! Good *Gard*!' but here in the Midi the ramparts echoed to '*Boouu-uu-Dioouu*!' which is the exact equivalent.

She recounted these stories later to Bill. 'Well,' he said cheerfully, 'you must have a kind face, even if you do look about a hundred.'

The tourists had arrived with a vengeance.

Here in the Camargue we found the *nordistes* (those from the north who are *carrément* uncivil, quite unlike those benign gentry from the south, the *sudistes*) pouring off the motorways like rivers overflowing in time of flood. They were reinforced by descendants of Attila from across the Rhine, most of them in camping cars, and by Caesar's cohorts transalpine, and then by our fellow *rosbifs*, those

inexplicable odd-balls from *trans-manche*. Throw in a dash of Transatlantics, a teaspoon of Scandinavians and Dutch (not to forget a soupçon of Niponnese) and you have mixed an indigestible cocktail that cannot fail to make the country-side feel poorly.

The minor roads of this delicate country that in winter carry little except horse-boxes, cattle trucks, and tractors, and not many of those, are now jammed with caravans, *Wohnwagons*, camping cars, Dormobiles, and mobile homes so huge that they would make a London bus feel insignificant. There are not that many places for them to go. In the main, *camping sauvage* (which in this context infers camping or parking of caravans outside authorised sites) is not permitted, but there are not enough police to enforce the law, and it is widely disregarded.

It is the savage caravanners and motor-homers that rouse special opposition from local people, for many of them bring their own food from home, buy nothing locally, never eat out at a restaurant, and contribute little to the community other than the obtrusiveness of their vehicles and the ubiquity of their rubbish. There are good camping and caravan sites available; some are excellent examples of what can be done, nicely disposed among trees, and well regulated, but one cannot turn the whole Camargue into caravan sites, as has almost happened to the Norfolk coast. They are already running out of names, all the nice ones have gone: Camping Soleil, Tamaris, Flamant Rose and so on. We recently saw one called The Thistles.

In Aigues-Mortes we prepared to be incommoded, to be nudged and jostled, to find no parking spaces, and to shop early or during the lunch hour, as at other times the small supermarkets were full to bursting and there were not enough trolleys outside or checkouts inside.

The summer tourism is, as we have said, essentially day-tripping. Loads of people descend daily from their coaches on tour. They did Nîmes yesterday, this morning they stopped at the old Roman aqueduct at Pont-du-Gard, and at lunchtime they were in Aigues-Mortes, and looking for the public toilets, which are hard to find and closed at lunchtime. (The new toilets blocking the view outside L'Escale reached a certain stage of building, and then all work seemed to have stopped, so the cluster of bushes by the Porte de la Gardette, known to us as Pooh Corner, because it is used by the old men and others taken short, had become more noisome than ever.)

The motorists park just outside the ramparts, paying through the nose for the privilege, for this is almost the only way the municipality can earn revenue. Only persons with property inside the walls, the aristocracy of Aigues-Mortes, may take their cars in, and as many streets become pedestrianised in summer, there is not much room for them. The visiting motorists will, according to taste, patronise the several smartish restaurants round the Place St Louis or the hot-dog and crêpe pitches just inside the beautiful old gates, a sour vista of stainless steel and garish colour more in keeping with Blackpool's golden mile than a medieval city. Why does not the *mairie* do something about it, you ask? Unfortunately, though the ramparts are scheduled as an ancient monument and therefore heavily protected, the buildings of the town itself escaped classification, so La Grande Rue leading to the Place St Louis is an appalling example of unfettered bad taste, mixed with the elegant façades of Souleiado, Cacharel, and La Taste, beautiful examples of what the street could look like with some co-operation from the *commerçants*.

Though the apex (or nadir according to one's pecuniary interest) of the summer's tourism was yet to come in August, already there were some good things laid on for the visitors. There would be a Theatre Festival of a high standard, and there were orchestras and entertainers in the Place and the Chapelle des Capucins, and by happy chance or good planning these were not a continuous round of rock and roll. There were exhibitions of craft and paintings, and various runs, marathons and swims for the *sportifs et sportives*.

Entertainment of all kinds quite often occurred in the old streets of Aigues-Mortes; the *mairie* liked to give pleasant surprises to weekend visitors to temper the prices charged in the Place St Louis for hot dogs and ice cream. Sometimes there would be a juggler, or a troupe of acrobats. On one memorable occasion there was a huge dancing bear, led by a swarthy gypsy. Both looked impossibly fake, both were very real indeed. The bear wished to return to a mayoral dustbin full of snackbar debris from which its owner had endeavoured to distract it. The bear, frustrated, growled and deliberately deposited a few huge *crottes* on the pavement.

On this particular Saturday our shopping was enlivened with the sound of pipe and tabor, and merry voices singing, and into view came a band of strolling players. Their gay accoutrements streamed with multicoloured ribbons, and they sang in Provençal, as did all good troubadours, including Richard Lionheart. They were called FAI TIRAR MARIUS, which Laurel recognised as a quotation from the Provençal *Poème du Rhône*. It means, roughly, 'Haul away, Marius', a term used by the Rhône bargees of old times. The statue of St Louis looked down on them with obvious approval.

Down by the sea at Grau-du-Roi or Sète, jousting took place on the canal, a wet and hilarious frolic in which two beautifully painted boats, one blue and one red, with high sloping stern platforms opposed each other. On each platform stood a nautical knight, wearing white trousers, a striped blouson, and a straw boater on his head. He was armed with a long lance which he had already carried round the town in procession that morning with pipes and drummers, a lance which gets heavier every minute. The tradition is that the jousters process to the station supposedly to meet the pipers, who are deemed to come from Montpellier, but who now live right there by the canal; never mind, tradition must be followed. 'We looked like a band of Asterix's demoralised *légionnaires*,' said one of them.

The boats were rowed double-banked by ten oarsmen, with hautbois and drummer in the bows, and attacked each other much as the knights of romantic chivalry did, each knight armed with lance and wooden shield standing as firmly as he could on his *tintaine* (the platform at the stern) as, dipping and wallowing, he tried to unseat his opponent and topple him into the water. The harbour at Sète is not all that clean and the water there is referred to as *glauque*, which has a fine onomatopaeic ring to it, but actually means sea-green. These jousts go back more than 300 years and as might be expected a lot of folklore has been acquired en route.

The whole town and many tourists turned out to watch, particularly on the Monday of St Louis which is local Derby Day. The play was not always cricket, you might say. The French are not noted for their love of referees, but unlike *le rugby*, this was not all that serious, and the audience was allowed to laugh. At times it would be difficult to keep a straight face, even if you did not know the language, because there was obviously a certain amount of wrangling between competitors and referee.

It was important that the jouster should be as heavy as possible, and therefore hard to displace. A redoubted former champion is said to have weighed 130 kilos, he is one of the few to have achieved over a hundred successful jousts. The cognoscenti bemoan the fact that jousters nowadays go into training for the event by eating a special diet to put on weight. This is not considered cricket. One should be a giant descended from giants.

The rules about dress are rather stricter than the rules of play. The white dress is obligatory. One participant who rolled up his trouser legs to the knee was hailed by the judges from the shore: 'Loulou! Your dress is not *de rigueur*. Lower your trouser legs.'

'What?' said Loulou. The crowd was noisy.

'Lower your trousers . . .'

The jouster obeyed to the letter, exposing what the

French describe as an *anatomie de toute beauté* to the delighted throng.

The nicknames are as joyous as the play. Where else but in France can you find men weighing over twenty stone called Loulou, or Bon-bon Noir? And Mimi in the Blue Boat, who refuses to be disqualified.

'What for, disqualified? and he, the other cheater, why is he not disqualified also? Me, I do not descend!'

'Mimi!' pleaded the judge, 'Be reasonable! You are blocking the tournament!'

'Come and get me!' said Mimi.

'Mimi! It is your President who speaks!' but to no avail.

The crews come not only from Grau-du-Roi and Sète, but also from the surrounding towns, Mèze, Montpellier, and Frontignan. It is enough to plunge Sète into mourning if an outsider wins.

All along the banks of the canal are restaurants and bars where good sea-food and drink are served all day long. Wins and losses may be celebrated or drowned. It is party time, and it makes a change from bulls.

The Sètois dialect is just as difficult as the Aigues-Mortais. We are quite unable to work out if the two towns can understand each other. Possibly they can, for we are told that after the port of Aigues-Mortes silted up hundreds of years ago, it was the Aigues-Mortais who moved over to colonise the newly created port of Sète.

We celebrated the end of an appalling two weeks of sand-blasting and painting by a visit to the town dump and a party. The events had to be in that order: the mess and debris left by the workmen necessitated clearing up both the boat and our mooring on a massive scale. Burning rubbish was out, forest fires were blazing all over the Midi, fanned by high winds, and we had no desire to add to the troubles of the *sapeurs-pompiers*. There was too much gunk to sneak it into the big bins down at the port, even if these had not been full now the tourists had arrived. There was nothing for it but to load the huge paint tins, sticky balls of used masking tape and torn hardboard, plus all the tins, bottles, packets and melon rind discarded by picnicking painters, into the car and take it off to the dump. Boubou went regularly. 'You can't miss it,' he said. 'Past the *sapeurs-pompiers* and look for the seagulls.'

We found it all right. The smell hit us before we saw the seagulls. It was not a pleasant place to be on a hot day in July, though the seagulls seemed to love it. So did a good many North Africans, who were picking over piles of objects, one person's rubbish often being someone else's treasure trove. They were winkling out cushions, a cooking stove, refrigerator shelving, and useful bits of wood. One was even musing over a TV set. We held our noses, jettisoned our contribution, and got away as fast as we could. As we turned the car to go we saw that our big paint cans were of interest to the scavengers, but not to the seagulls.

The party was much more fun. Everyone came, Mario and Martine, Francine and Boubou on the eve of departing for their summer cruise, Jean-Claude and Nise, Serge and Danielle and little Aude, the Swiss, the Germans and even Bernard and his wife for a quick swallow (mercifully without the eleven children), though he did not usually socialise with the peninsula. It was a great success. Our progress inside the boat was much praised, Martine again asked if we would not like to swap for the caravan, and we went back thankfully into our normal, fairly peaceful routine on the morrow.

In mid July the Music Festival takes place all over France. It recalls our St Cecilia's day, but is much more a matter of local people in every town and village in France making music rather than professional concerts.

Aigues-Mortes did its best, but it is not very musical. All day in the square small children with little talent thumped out piano exercises on a long-suffering instrument. There seemed to be no school choir or orchestra. (Maybe they were all on holiday.) A lady gave us a few tunes on an electronic organ with asthma.

One of the best turns was Caroline's English class. Caroline was an Aigues-Mortais who had been brought up in Australia, and returned to France as an elegant young lady. A dozen five and six year olds who evidently adored her gave a lively rendering in choral speech of 'The Kangaroo from Wallamalloo', complete with Australian accent. The other good turn was the choir of the *Troisième Age*, the Pensioners, who sang some very creditable Viennese waltzes. Laurel noticed among them a beak-nosed gentleman whom she had had to fight for a place in the crowded carpark. He claimed that his imminent per-formance in the choir trumped her orange badge.

The Mayor sat listening, enjoying a drink, as were we, at the Express Bar. We hoped he too would sing, knowing he had a strong voice when in church. He contented himself with applauding loudly, especially one of his little nieces at the piano. She was the least worst of the pianists. For some reason the *peña*, the town band, did not play at the Festival. Perhaps they considered themselves profes-sionals.

On Sunday mornings the market was now much larger. The practical stalwarts who had been there all winter, vegetable and fruit stalls, cheese, meat and fish, Annie the flower lady, the garden plants, the second-hand clothing where we bought all our work clothes (and some of our others) and the oyster stall; these were joined by African vendors of shell jewellery and sunglasses, leather hand-bags, hairy artists selling oilpaintings, pottery and crafts. Sure now of warm weather and spendthrift tourists, they happily splashed out their six francs per metre, which is the reasonable sum asked by the municipality to pitch your stall on market day.

On this particular morning one artist managed to avoid

even that modest charge by setting up an easel. He was, he told the policeman who sells the rental tickets, painting, not selling. Ho ho. He wore a Van Gogh sunhat, and a terribly clean smock, and dabbed away at a finished painting trying not to ruin it until a tourist – surprise! – bought it.

Our after-market drink was taken far under the Express's awning in the deep shade. '*Ohé, les Brittanniques!*' said Serge. His dog panted in the coolest spot she could find. He told us of a dreadful meal he had had in England, lamb with mint sauce, he said with his lips crisping, and Rosé d'Anjou, which was far too *sucré*. It would be to anyone used to the stomach-blasting rosés of the sand dunes.

In the afternoon we went to the Courses.

Every Sunday afternoon in every village the Camarguais

indulged their passion for bulls, the Fé de Biou. The Courses Camarguaises were in full summer swing.

We went quite often. The arena to the south of the town overlooked the *étang*, there was, one hoped, a sea breeze, and as usual the tiers of seats were full. The loudspeaker system (which was far from hi-fi, the French correctly pronouncing it as 'iffy') was playing the same Spanish tangos and paso dobles as last year, but the tape was a little more worn and scratchy, and the spring rains seemed to have got into the speakers and made them crackle. This was not a first division arena, though it had its moments, and the current champion *raseteur*, or tassel cutter, Luc Mézy, was an Aigues-Mortais taxidermist.

The doctor arrived, and took his seat in the infirmary, the President sat in front of his sometimes reluctant microphone, and the Course could begin.

The arenas in the villages have the same relationship to the big bull-rings at Arles or Nîmes (both situated in ancient Roman arenas) as that of a small town cricket ground to Trent Bridge. The analogy is not inapt, for at the start of each Course the team of *raseteurs*, together with their *tourneurs* walk onto the *piste* dressed head to toe in white like a cricket team taking the field. They are known as Les Tenues Blanches, the Men in White, and whether they play left or right-handed is as important to a *raseteur* as it is to a cricketer. However, they walked out onto sand, not grass, to the tune of Bizet's 'Toreador', to which it was impossible not to clap in rhythm as everyone else did.

After saluting the President they took up their positions round the boundary fence, the *barrière*, the righthanders on one side and the lefthanders on the other.

When the bull was released from the dark *toril* onto the blinding sand of the arena it was given a full minute to adjust its eyes to the light. A promising bull, he used this minute to snort, wheel about, paw the ground, and look dangerous. Then a few bars of a fanfare fought their way through those speakers that were still functioning; this signalled the start, and the Men in White vaulted over the barrier and took up their positions, *crochet* in hand. (The *crochet* is a small four-pronged hook they use to lift and cut the tassels, and they and their girlfriends wear gold and silver replica *crochets* round their necks.)

During the Course, which gave the bull fifteen minutes, the *raseteurs* must seize one or more of three tassels from the forehead of the bull. Bound securely to its horns with a regulated number of turns, regulated knots and regulated string, were a red *cocarde* and two white *glands* (three tassels in all). There was prize money on all of them, even the string left when the tassels had gone, and the prizes increased in proportion to the excitement as local traders donated more and more money to the prize fund.

'Natalie Fashion Shoes gives ten francs more,' the President was saying, as this particularly wily bull held off all comers.

'The Express Bar gives ten francs more,' (Assunta was an afiçionado) as the bull chased a *raseteur* and leapt into the *contre-piste*, to a roar of delight from the crowd.

'SuperU Supermarché raises the prize by ten francs to three hundred francs.' Then minutes had passed and only one tassel had been won, by a triumphant youth who held up his hand to show the prize.

'And the management rounds the prize up to four hundred francs.' They were fairly safe, this bull went back to the *toril* with all but one of its attributes intact.

The Camargue bull, as we have explained, is of a different race to the Spanish bulls. It is small, black, swift, and cunning. Its horns are lyre-shaped, and as long as a man's arms. The rules of the game do not allow the *raseteur* to sneak up and grab the *cocarde*; it has to be taken on the run, from within the arena, and the bull can run a lot faster than the man. Thus a technique has been evolved.

The red wooden barrier around the *piste* is about four feet high, and outside that is the *contre-piste*, a narrow run round the whole arena six feet or more wide. The spectators are perched in tribunes, with the front row of seats about six feet above the ground.

A *tourneur* attracts the bull's attention, allowing a *raseteur* to run across in front of it, from left to right if he is right-handed, the opposite way if he is not. As the bull perceives the *raseteur* moving, he turns to go for him. The *raseteur* must judge his run to pass in front of the bull's head before it achieves full speed, preferably when it is turning, make a grab at the tassels attached to the horns as he passes, and then, pursued by the bull, sprint like mad for the barrier, which he leaps and ends up clinging to the outer wall of the *contre-piste*. Sometimes his leap is so urgent that he surmounts the wall as well and lands among the spectators. (We did not normally sit in the front row, being choosy about whom we have on our laps.) The slightest misjudgement in sprint or leap and the bull is helping him on his way, with a bunt from a forehead if the *raseteur* is lucky enough to find himself between the horns, but occasionally with a sharp pointed horn in the thighs or buttock. This causes a penetrating wound that may become seriously contaminated, as the flesh is torn rather than cut by the horn and it seldom heals quickly or easily. It is almost unknown for a bull to get hurt in this very rough game, but *raseteurs* are often gored. Several are badly injured every year, and ten in all have been killed.

Sometimes the bull, who is often more experienced at the game than the men, will follow the *raseteur* over the barrier, and very occasionally will get up among the spectators, which provides great hilarity for those on the opposite side of the arena. Notices display the warning that '*La direction ne répond pas des accidents*' ('the management disclaim all responsibility') not only because bulls can join the spectators, but also because after the sixth bull the professional part of the afternoon comes to an end, the rules change (or rather disappear) and there is a *vache* or *veau* for the children or the inexperienced, or sufficiently drunken tourists, to play with. Do not suppose that these *vaches* resemble the contented dairy animals of British farmyards. They are not ruminating Daisies. These are rangy athletic lady members of Bovine Liberation. They run as fast as the bulls and have as big a pair of horns and are not noticeably any less aggressive. Nor are they always female. They are quite often all Bull and a yard wide. However, they do have the points of their horns *emboulées* (padded).

Laurel noticed the same beak-nosed old gentleman who had fought her in the car park and sung waltzes with the Pensioners, sitting in the front row. This is where the empassioned afiçionados sat, armed with old cardigans or long padded pairs of ancient jeans to lash the bull with when it got into the *contre-piste* (and it was considered a poor bull that did not jump the barrier at least once in his fifteen minutes in the smaller arenas, though we notice it happens much less often in the bigger ones). Beak-nose was sitting on a scarlet cushion, and as the bull's horns whistled past his shoes he leant forward and belaboured it with his cushion. As the bull dashed round the *contre-piste* he took with him a ripple of legs, raised out of reach of the horns, to be lowered again as he passed. A blue wave of blue jeans.

10

Méchoui *and Mas Madame*

*'Oou jue et oou vin
L'home deven couquin.'*
. . . .
'Gaming and drinking
Stops men thinking.'

One of the things an association in France may do with its funds is to hold meetings of members and to provide refreshments for those attending. Our Association decided to hold a *méchoui*, a sheep roast, on the peninsula.

Mario was the organiser. Naturally Mario had returned when he finished work on the restaurant in Port Camargue, and he and Martine were all smiles again. He it was who ordered the lamb for roasting and got the assistant chef of the *Isles de Stel* to come and make *tabourlé*. Mario it was who welded up the barbecue base from half an oil drum, and made up the spit with its two handles. Wives or consorts (the terms were much the same in this locality) arranged paper plates, cutlery and glasses, made salad, and produced enormous quantities of wine. Others of us erected tables on the uneven ground, lent chairs, provided lighting for later, and then helped Mario, who was centre stage in all respects, set the lamb on the spit in the hot afternoon sun. The charcoal was glowing, thanks to Mario's inspired use of his oxygen cylinder; never has a charcoal fire so quickly taken hold.

All the men took a share of spit turning. It was not as popular a job as it might have been for there was no shade, the fire was very hot and the spit handle was short, but we soon mounted a parasol over the spit turner and established that he had ready and immediate access to the galvanised bath containing iced water in which reposed wine, beer, and Coke for the children.

It is hard to believe that nothing went wrong. Forest fires were blazing out of control up country, but we damped down the surrounding grasses and kept our barbecue within bounds. It was a splendid evening. The lamb came to the point at dusk, when the proceedings were interrupted in order that everyone could cover themselves in anti-mosquito sprays, ointments and lotions. Of course everyone had forgotten to do this for we never learn (do we?) that mosquitoes come out and dizzy about at dusk, and those horrid little pregnant females bite. So there was a brief delay before the lamb, succulent in its bed of rosemary and mint, and herbs of Provence strong enough to overcome the waft of lemongrass and Jungle Formula, was carved, served, and enjoyed.

After the feeding the singing started. To us British, the Welsh are held out as the race that bursts into song at the slightest opportunity. In France there seems to be no social occasion when the party do not sing both in chorus and singly. They really know their songs, which range from the jingo (beside which the patriotism of 'Land of Hope and Glory' fades to a lukewarm insignificance) to the self-deprecatory ironic, which shows that however patriotic they may be, they are also realists.

After a number of choral songs each of us sang in turn. The Swiss sang, then the Germans, then it was Albion's turn, and we decided that Laurel had better sing solo because Bill has a voice that sounds like a gate being opened on rusty hinges while at the same time entrapping a cat's tail. She performed adequately, and then it was the turn of Monsieur Prolix.

That is not his real name. Bill, who has a habit of giving people nicknames, produced this one owing to the gentleman's habit of interrupting our work or worse still our repose, and telling us his life story. While Bill had been incapacitated with his shin wound, sitting with his bandaged leg raised in the shade of the cockpit, Monsieur Prolix had taken pity on the invalid and had come on board uninvited, accompanied by his enormous and unwelcome dog which was quite as big as he was and totally out of his control, and in between his desperate attempts to man-handle his outrageous animal had lightened Bill's boredom with many repetitions of old times as an engineer in the French Army of the Air. He had been incapable of realising that a man with a resourceful brain could be entirely happy planning earth-shaking schemes for the twenty-first century, or drafting witty and erudite letters to *The Times*, while apparently taking a siesta. For his part, Bill was developing Cooper's First Law of Canine Relationships: the smaller and wimpier the man, the bigger and wilder the dog.

One of M. Prolix's talents (as he had, oh so often, told us) was his expertise on the piano-accordion, which he liked to play in the traditional style known as *bal musette*, that pleasant tinkly music that goes with Pigalle and Mont-martre in English films about France.

Bill now had his revenge. He had insisted that M. Prolix should bring his harp to the party, and when everyone was agreeably drunk, M. Prolix was entreated to play. Rather to our surprise he was reluctant, but there was no getting out of it. Strong men went to his car and helped him bring over his instrument. Many times (oh, so many times), he had told us that it weighed twenty-two kilos and imposed a great strain on the kidneys. It produced, he said, hernias in strong men. The strong men helping him brought out a music stand, a heap of music, a special stool, and a spotlamp. He may have seemed reluctant, but by heaven he was well-equipped.

Whenever Frenchmen take up any hobby they do so with gusto and the right uniform. No tentative start for them.

Any Frenchman who decides to take up cricket (there must surely be one or two?) will not just turn up at a club and ask for a game, rolling up his shirt sleeves and changing into his sailing plimsolls. Oh no. His first action would be to go out and buy the proper kit. He will turn up the very first time dressed in immaculate whites with the correct boots and pads, a V-necked white cable-stitched sweater with red and yellow bands round the neck and hem, a little peaked cap, and a Botham-autographed bat. Not to mention the box, though on second thoughts if that necessity were to have been pointed out to him it is probable he would have changed his mind and taken up volley-ball instead. There are things which the English are prepared to hazard that the French might not care to trifle with.

M. Prolix, therefore, had a complete accordion player's kit. He set up the music stand and the light, posed his stool in front, changed his glasses, selected his sheet music, opened it out on the stand and peered short-sightedly at it, leaning forward so far that the twenty-two kilos hung round his neck almost overbalanced him.

At this point he nearly reneged, saying that Mario had given him too much to drink, but this feeble excuse was howled down by the audience. We had all had too much to drink. Everyone waited in silence. A child giggled and was hushed. These were the rites of passage; we could not have the mass until the host had been consecrated. He settled his glasses more firmly on his bony nose, twitched his moustache, and shuffled his music.

It was apparent that M. Prolix was having difficulty seeing the music. He was a very small man and his very large instrument was getting between him and the stand on which the music was placed. The light was not bright and the focal length of his glasses was probably designed for reading a book. There were some encouraging noises from the crowd and the first signs of genial impatience. This was not the usual setting for *bal musette*, which is more or less the French equivalent of pub music. One expects a large jolly man in a beret, smoking a *gauloise* and playing fast and continuously by ear while the folk dance or sing, drink or make love. We have known one such performer play for three hours pausing only to refill his glass, and never repeating a tune.

There came a tremendous rushing noise as M. Prolix drew apart the ends of his gigantic organ and inflated its bellows. Some notes, quavering and not very tuneful, were pushed out, they then seemed to lose courage and fall to the ground. After a couple of wobbly bars he hesitated, missed a beat or two while he peered intently at the page and went on a few more bars. At first he got the notes correct but with so little success at rhythm that the tune was unrecognisable, then he faltered and played a series of wrong notes. Bill, who had had enough to become a bit exhilarated, said in a loud *sotto voce*:

'He's playing the mosquitoes, not the notes!'

It was excruciatingly bad. With the final disharmonious chord there were suggestions that the player had now included the full-stop.

It recalled performances by the Portsmouth Symphony Orchestra, or concerts by Florence Foster Jenkins. Everyone was enjoying themselves, and begged him to continue. With a resigned sigh he consented to an encore. The audience was giggling, except for Mme Prolix who loyally maintained a serious demeanour while turning the pages for her husband. Laurel endeavoured to silence her own husband, while giggling herself, then at last, as the piece came to a halt the audience applauded, forgot him quickly, and broke into a Burgundian drinking song. A few stalwarts helped the accordionist re-pack his gear, and a few brave souls earned themselves heavenly grace by thanking him for his performance, but he never recovered. His little boat remains moored at the peninsula (he did not live aboard and used it only occasionally). He was last seen heaving his reluctant dog into the boot of his car. Perhaps he is staying at home to practise his comeback.

We ourselves turned out to be the star turn of the evening, to our surprise. Mario put on some Spanish dances, including a paso doble. We were sufficiently exhilarated to shed thirty years, grab a table napkin and do our bull dance. The audience, delighted at this unexpected entertainment, joined in the *'olés'* with huge enthusiasm, and encouraged us to go on much longer than we should. The bull had to die with her paws in the air and have her ear cut off to be presented to the *matador* before we could sit down again.

They still talk of our paso doble at Le Bourgidou.

Thanks to our Franco-Australian friend Caroline we received an invitation to a *manade* that was giving a demonstration of how to train horses for the bullring. Horses are not used in the Courses Camarguaises, only in the Spanish Corrida where the bull is put to death; so before accepting the kind invitation to the *ferrade* we ascertained that no bulls were to be slaughtered in this show and went to see what lay in the techniques.

The *manade* at Mas Madame consisted only of the Spanish type of bull which is bred specially for the Corrida, and was kept by a retired *matador* who had managed to retain the slim-hipped figure so favoured by these types, helped, we noticed, by having no pockets in his trousers, though that may be to avoid getting them caught on a horn as the bull goes by. He gave demonstrations of the different passes and types of cape work used in the ring, and then one of the local boys from the school of *raseteurs* (they perform in the Courses Camarguaises) entertained everybody by playing with one of the large Spanish bulls. Without a cape he encouraged the bull to charge him and side-stepped neatly several times. Then he had the bull charging right across the ring so that it was going at full speed; he stood absolutely still with his feet together and at the last moment leapt into the air and somersaulted over the bull's back as it passed beneath him. He did it several times to show it was no fluke, and one could clearly see the bull was baffled. One often sees this sort of thing done with the smaller and wirier Camargue bulls but to leap over the much bigger Spanish bull requires unusual skill as well as courage.

There was then a training session for the horses used in the preliminary parts of a bullfight by the *picadors* who spear the bull from horseback. These horses are very well padded for they are charged by the bulls, and we have seen a *picador*'s horse tossed onto its side (the *picador* beneath it) by a bull, so its padding is not for nothing.

The lives of the *toreros*, all those who go into a ring with a bull, are at risk. Nimeño II, the French star, was badly tossed a couple of seasons ago and paralysed, and television in the Midi showed the toss in relentless slow motion for days afterwards.

Two years later, after partial rehabilitation, he has killed himself rather than face a life without his Suit of Lights and the plaudits of the crowd.

When bullfighting restarted in France they had to use mainly Spanish bullfighters and Spanish bulls. The French had a great incentive to rear their own bulls because the Spanish suppliers used to see them off very badly. Though the *matador* or his representative has the choice of the bulls, they found when they were delivered, and too late for change, that the Spanish had not sent the goods ordered: the French were supplied with the bull with the crumpled horn, the bull which limped and so on. The Spanish regarded the French as mugs ripe for the picking, and considered the Corrida in France to be a bit of a joke. Gradually the French got things in order, and today the 'sport' is well established with good French bullfighters and French-bred (Spanish type) bulls which though reared in the Camargue, are not the same breed as the local black bulls, and the *manades* do not mix their stock.

The show in the private bullring finished with a display by an elegant young lady rider trying valiantly to stick darts in the back of a bull and not succeeding very well, after which the fires were lit. There was a barbecue, and a huge *paella* was made in a pan about two metres across, while in another pan hundreds of mussels were cooked, and a gipsy band played very loud flamenco music until it was coming out of our ears. Perhaps it is best to hear flamenco like rock and roll, from a distance of a quarter of a mile. Or over the radio, when you have at least the choice of turning the volume down.

11

The Feast of Saint Louis

'Pluio d'aous
Douno d'ooulivo eme de mous.'
. . . .
'August rain
Brings oil and wine.'

The heat now became crushing. Any work at all had to be done before ten in the morning, after that one endeavoured merely to keep cool. We spread awnings to shade the boat, drew blinds to keep the sun out, drank pints of water, and gave thanks for the slightest breeze. When we went to town or into market, we used those streets that we knew to be in shadow, or walked under the arcades, understanding perfectly the Marseille taxi driver who when charged with driving on the wrong side of the road turned round, took his hands from the wheel and used them to illustrate this deathless pronouncement:

'In the Midi you do not drive on the left or on the right. You drive in the *shade*.'

All our meals, from breakfast to supper, were taken out of doors, in the shade of an awning.

The swimmers, who had been with us since July, were now here all day. Boys of all ages, all with one voice, and that fortissimo. All intent on cooling off in the canal (which is forbidden, but tolerated), and when that palled to look for mischief, swinging on our mooring ropes, setting fire to the flower barrels, and throwing each other's bicycles into the water. Our siestas were disturbed by shrieks and splashes, and we found constant remonstration very wearing.

We were therefore secretly delighted when we realised that Martine's alsatian, Dinky, was causing these youths some problems. He was stealing their clothes. Time after time we would see him trotting off with a shoe or a T-shirt in his jaws, and ten minutes later he would be back for something else. The boys were too intent on their own misdeeds to notice those of Dinky's, and loud were the accusations and angry the falling out of friends as it came time to go home to their *soupe* and their clothes could not be found. Whatever they were saying in French was clearly the equivalent of the Suffolk expression: 'My mum'll wholly mob . . .'

We envied Boubou and Francine on *Escaut* who had gone cruising for two months up the Saône. We desperately wanted to get away ourselves, but even after all the work we had done we were not fit yet to go to sea.

We did not need much convincing, after the ghastly experience of sandblasting, that we had earned a holiday, and decided that we would go for a cruise by canal down to Sète. So the masts had to come down again.

A little bit to the west of Aigues-Mortes, set among the *étangs* and marshes of the Petite Camargue, is the abbey-cathedral of Maguelonne. This is a very old Christian foundation, one of the oldest. Dedicated to Saint Peter, it was the sister church to St Peter's at Rome, and while Rome was being sacked by the barbarians the popes of the time established themselves at Maguelonne.

That did not save it from later disaster for Charles Martel devastated the abbey in 737 AD. Charles (the Hammer, not the Brewer of Brandy) was the father of Charlemagne and seems to have been a busy and bloodthirsty ruler. He threw the Saracens out of France (they got as far north as Angers) but he also sacked Béziers, Agde, and the old Roman amphitheatre at Nîmes. Maguelonne was rebuilt, and in 1096 Pope Urban II reconsecrated it, naming it the second church in world importance after that of Rome, granted it the right to bear the papal arms, and granted perpetual indulgence to all who would be buried in its grounds, which seems to display a naïvely trusting faith in the future.

We reached Maguelonne on the second day of our cruise, which was already doing us good. Just to be on the move again in our boat felt wonderful. The church was a magnificent building set in amongst large trees, on a mound, the only bit of land above marsh level. We approached it along the canal, seeing it ahead for miles as we chugged along, pausing for the pontoon bridge nearby to open and let us pass. This is a footway across the canal to allow pedestrians to visit the abbey, or (more numerously) to give access to the nearby beach for a swim.

A floating bridge like none other we have ever seen, it was pivoted at one end, and opened by means of a ten horsepower outboard motor at the other. Whenever a boat wished to pass, the motor was started, the bridge driven round to the bank until the boat was through, and then the motor was reversed to bring it back to its position across the canal. A proceeding without any great brouhaha which took only a minute or two in total. There were no rules, no elaborate precautions, no hootings or barriers, and one felt that such a simple affair would, if permitted at all, take half an hour a time in over-regulated super-safe places. But it is like that in certain parts of France. If you are stupid enough to fall in the canal by stepping on to an open bridge it is your own fault and you cannot blame or sue anyone else.

There was a short secluded mooring close by. We moored, jumped ashore, and walked towards the church, keeping in the shade of the great pines that lined the sandy road.

We went to investigate a visit to the abbey and found that the entrance was on the other side, miles away, as far as the beach. 'But it is of no consequence,' said our informer, eyeing Laurel's walking stick. 'You take the train. No?'

We took the train, yes. Not a train on rails, it ran on a little tarmac road and had pneumatic tyred wheels. About five coaches and a little diesel engine cosmetically decorated to look like an old steamer, it took tourists to the beach close to the entry to the abbey. In the distance as we waited we could hear loud singing, but it did not sound like Gregorian chant. '*Oo la la la*! It is the little Indians,' said the booking clerk. 'It will be better to stand well aside and let them get away quickly.'

The train hove into view round the bend. It was packed to the roof with eight to ten year olds in multicoloured shorts, waving their towels, singing their hearts out cheerfully, the noise getting louder and louder as they approached, and changing into a mighty cheer as the train swirled round in a tight curve and came to a stop near the pontoon bridge. In an instant the 'little Indians' rushed for the bridge, which they crossed like the hordes of Genghiz Khan. We boarded the train in peace, there were only a few of us adults for this trip.

The cathedral, which is no longer used for services, was cool and quiet on such a hot day, its thick stone walls keeping out the heat and its unglazed windows letting a cool breeze filter through the building. We recalled that such is its exposed position that in the Middle Ages the Prior was given permission to cement up the northern windows in winter, that the people be not frozen by the mistral.

The See of Maguelonne is now amalgamated with that of Montpellier, and the Bishop chooses to reside at the latter where there are fewer mosquitoes and rather more flesh-pots. The old dormitory and refectory of the abbey is used as a retreat for severely mentally handicapped persons and are kept quite separate, but the church is used occasionally for concerts.

Naughty St Louis pillaged the stones of Maguelonne to build the ramparts of Aigues-Mortes, and there were those who blamed the failure of his Crusade and his death from the plague in Tunis on his having committed this sacrilege. Neither his pillage, nor his failed crusades prevented him from being beatified very soon after dying. Mind you, the pillage went on long after his death, for the ramparts took many years to build.

We took the train to the beach next morning before moving on. The only building on the sands was a wooden decked café, which served the sort of thing needed for a long day on the beach. We sat down there for refreshment. Ice cream needs refrigeration, coffee must be heated, and the *steack-frites* promised on the blackboard would have to be cooked, and the blue EDF van parked outside seemed to indicate that the café had a small electrical problem. There was no trouble with the coffee, which was adequately hot. Children were coming continually for ice cream, so that was not it.

We did not have to watch very long from our seat under the awning to discover what the little problem was, and spent the rest of our elevenses with tears in our eyes trying not to laugh. Every customer stepping over the aluminium threshold received a noticeable electric shock. Children, ice cream in hand, were startled but not hurt. Women were apt to go into the *ooh la la*'s. Men were surprised into short breathy words. Dogs whipped round to see who had done it. We were quite disappointed when the reliable Men in Blue from EDF found the culprit in a newly installed string of fairylights, and put it right.

Ooh la la! is a renowned French expression. What is not so well known is that the number of *la*'s is variable and extends almost indefinitely according to the degree of astonishment or surprise. Thirteen is the most we have ever recorded. Bill, being a statistician claims to be the first to notice that women tend to stick to two *la*'s, and that when they exceed this they jump straight to four: *Ooh la la, la la*! and very rarely to six. Men on the other hand are much more variable, but always give out an odd number of *la*'s. Thus we have heard once or twice (but only from men) the almost casual *Ooh la*! Many more times: *Ooh la, la la*! and its variant: *Ooh la la, la*!, and more rarely the signs of extreme agitation with five, seven, eleven or the record thirteen times. Much individuality of expression is available in the manner of subdivision of the *la*'s. Two at a time is the norm, but threes are only used in conjunction with twos. Bill is further investigating whether the subdivision into groups of three and two *la*'s at a time has any morse code significance. He claims once to have heard SOS broadcast, but Laurel thinks he is pulling her leg. It was more likely to have been CON.

We continued our cruise for another three weeks, and returned rested and refreshed to the peninsula of Le Bourgidou, at Aigues-Mortes. Boubou and Francine, already back from their cruise, took our lines, and welcomed us, gravid with news.

The concession had not been renewed. The Association was in disrepair.

Mario the President had quarrelled with Jean-Claude the Treasurer, who had resigned.

'But,' said Boubou, 'though sad, this is not of great significance, since if there is no concession, then there is no *raison d'être* for the Association. *Ça n'existe plus.*'

We were sorry. Apart from making the position of all us boat-livers a little precarious, we genuinely regretted the passing of the Association. 'What do we do now?' we asked. 'Must we leave our berth?' It seemed that everyone had been asking the Navigation Authority this question. The reply had been soothing. 'Stay where you are for the time being,' the Navigation Authority had said. 'Nothing is going to happen quickly. *Pas de panique.*' So we continued, all of us, in very much the same old way.

Mario had had a bad summer. With the loss of the concession, there went his schemes for a repair slipway. His ex-wife and his lawyers were in the process of forcing him to sell the *Isles de Stel*, which at present was his livelihood. Martine had been unable to get a decent seasonal job, despite doing all kinds of training sessions run by the Government for the unemployed, and had ended up as a *plongeur*, washing up in one of the busy restaurants.

We had much to talk about when Francine called by with the bread. She felt physically much better with the summer weather, but was deeply concerned about Nicholas, who was working in Nice, and had a *petite amie*. 'She is his first, you understand. He is not managing her very well.' It seemed that the *amie* was still a schoolgirl, spoilt, sulky, selfish and hysterical, whose doting but exasperated parents had thankfully given way to her desire to live in with Nicholas. However delighted he might have been to begin with, he rapidly realised that the situation was far from idyllic. He made the breakfast, worked hard all day, then prepared supper while she did her homework, since her *bac* (A-levels) was more important than his bread-winning. If housework and cleaning had to be done, Nicholas did it. 'And moreover,' sighed Francine, 'he does not *like* Nice. He longs to be back here on the boat with us.' One weekend he came to see them, complete with *petite amie*. The visit was a disaster. She had given Nicholas no time to talk to his parents, she had been graceless, inconsiderate, and rude, even to Boubou, whom everyone loves.

At intervals Francine would recount the story as it continued. Nicholas was in a bind, both financially and emotionally, and was too inexperienced to get out of it. Francine and Laurel shook their heads and made wise remarks to each other. 'It is so hard to watch your children make mistakes, and know that advice is unwelcome. By the way, have you seen my cat?' 'Which cat,' asked Laurel, as Francine had three. 'Megalo, the black and white one. He did not come in last night.'

We found him later shut into our forepeak. He leaped out and streaked for home. Bill had rechristened him Mogadon, as he spent much of his time asleep. He was Nicholas' cat, but Nicholas had wisely left him with his mother. He could not be expected to cope with a cat as well as a girlfriend.

The 25th August is the Fête de la St Louis, which in Aigues-Mortes is translated to the nearest weekend in order that it can be spread over several days. (We are unable to get a convincing explanation as to why St Louis, who was a king, should change sex when he has a *fête*. We try hard to master the French language, but at times like this find it difficult to take seriously. Like it or not, it is la St Louis.)

The Fête is popular with everybody. Those townspeople who went on holiday try to be back in time for it, adding to the crowds. It is the high spot of the tourist season, colourful, rowdy, a very jolly affair. It always rains, but that is good for the grapes.

All but the grumpiest inhabitants dress in medieval costume, and there are magnificent processions with St Louis and his Queen on caparisoned horses, with a mounted retinue of soldiers, followed by peasants, market-women, lepers, beggars, even the two camels from the Petite Camargue karting track join in. The blue and yellow banners of the Capets, the French Royal Family, fly everywhere. There is a medieval market, with produce and crafts from as far away as the Cévennes. There is a medieval inn nestled into a corner of the ramparts, serving very unmedieval food and drink: pizzas, spaghetti and *pastis*. If you feel like joining in the processions, costumes can be hired, and entitle you to free drinks every now and then, to say nothing of the chance of appearing in full video in Japanese drawing rooms: 'Ah so, here Fate St Rouis, in Flance.'

Laurel is entirely at home and happy in long skirts, and a wimple under her big straw hat. Nothing, however, not even free drinks, will get Bill out of his shorts and denim sailing hat. Not in that weather, anyway.

After dusk the crowd gathered on the quay to wait for the

VIN
des
SABLES

climax, which was to be the arrival of the Royal Party by torchlight from within the town, and St Louis' departure for the Crusades. To keep the crowd from getting impatient for an event which stands no chance of being on time, the committee had organised an *animateur*, for which there is no exact English equivalent, though we suppose 'entertainer' would be nearest, if misleading. This is a breed of animal without which, it seems, nothing in France can ever take place at all, not supermarket openings, or fashion shows, or even Father Christmas, but the *animateur* is there with his braying laugh, his awful jokes, and his ice cream cornet microphone. This *animateur*'s status was down among the pests, for he soon had the crowd resenting both his presence and his amplified witticisms. '*Il n'est pas doué,*' observed a French tourist dourly alongside us. It was an understatement. He was certainly not gifted.

The culmination of the Fête, the torchlight procession re-enacting St Louis' embarkation for the Crusade arrived at last. It used to be done on the last evening, but is now repeated nightly, as it is extremely popular. The procession was as before, with all the royals, soldiers, horses, camels, lepers, etc., but (*Bou Diou!*) no bulls. It wound its way under the portcullis of the massive Porte de la Gardette, *flambeaux* flickering and smoking, and round the ramparts to the yacht quay where passing boats moor. (In King Louis' day the port was on the other side of the town, now silted up.)

Awaiting our hero was the *nef*, or medieval galleon. Well, an old fishing boat bin rose on, as they say in our part of the world. It has been medievalised with a chipboard aftercastle and forecastle painted with medieval windows, and a flimsy looking mast and spars, all of which gave the *nef* a top-heavy look. We were privileged to see the first ever embarkation three years ago. We watched with some anxiety, as Bill's knowledge of the relationship between the centres of gravity and buoyancy of such a structure led him to believe that it would never fly.

'They're not going to ride all those horses on to it, are

they?' he said, horror-struck for a short moment. Then he permitted himself a slow smile, remembering that he did not like horses. At first it looked as if the royals at least really were about to board on horseback (it is very hard to part a Camarguais and his horse, we could almost swear they take them to bed with them) but someone's better sense prevailed and the royal party were persuaded to dismount and embark on foot. It was fairly clear that, as we had watched the newly painted *nef*'s arrival from Grau-du-Roi only that afternoon, there had been no time to rehearse. The royal party and followers, all horsemen but none of them knowing the first thing about boats, rushed up to the aftercastle where thrones awaited them, and the lesser minions did the same up to the forecastle.

It was inevitable that the weight, though well-spread fore-and-aft, would be unevenly dispersed athwartships, since all of them wanted to be on the side where the photos were being taken, and the boat gave a lurch and took on a perilous list that could have tipped them all in the canal had not reason fairly quickly prevailed. Since there was no longer an engine in the *nef* it had to be discreetly towed. It seemed that all was ready, but as we said these were not seamen.

The tug was going full ahead, with the tow-rope under great strain, but no one had thought to cast off the *nef*'s last mooring rope. A kindly tourist obliged, and with great suddenness the *nef* leapt forward, depositing most of its passengers on the deck in a heap of spears, shields, cheap satin and *fleurs de lys*.

While they were picking themselves up and disentangling their lances the tug broke down, and drifted to a halt ahead of the *nef*.

The *nef*, with awesome inevitability, hit the tug a sharp blow in the rear, and the royal party again took a voluntary on to the deck, and there the two ships stayed for some time, apparently awaiting a fair wind.

The dramatic effect of Louis' departure for the Crusades

was a little reduced. He could not even plead that he was awaiting the turn of the tide, as he could have done in northern waters. Stealing his ramparts from Maguelonne seemed to be affecting his luck 740 years on.

Since then, lessons have been learnt and the spectacle is all that everyone could wish, if less eventful. All passengers in the *nef* remain on what you might call the ground floor, and keep unwontedly still. They brace themselves, but do not actually wear safety belts. Their numbers have been reduced. It makes no difference. There is still an air of impending disaster hanging over the exercise.

King Louis gave his own seaport city of Aigues-Mortes a very liberal charter and it prospered. Every vessel passing within sight of its lighthouse on the Tower of Constance had to pay tribute. But the sea is merciless; over the years it receded and Aigues-Mortes found itself several kilometres inland. King Louis XIV took away their generous privileges when a new port was founded at Sète.

Nowadays Aigues-Mortes lives on salt and tourism, and in August they harvest both crops. There are two large salt-pans in the Camargue, which has been a source of salt for thousands of years. The Salin-de-Giraud in the east of the Camargue is the larger and is a very industrial complex owned by a big chemical combine (Pechiney). They produce some 800,000 tonnes from 11,000 hectares, most of which is used chemically or sprinkled on frozen roads. They have built a town for their workers, one of the ugliest towns in France and quite out of keeping with the country around. It would look at home surrounded by slag-heaps in the outskirts of Lille; here we can find no redeeming feature in it. The company have also bought up all the surrounding land, closing many of the old public accesses, particularly those to the sea. By this policy they also reduce effective opposition to any developments which might normally come from affected neighbours. Worse, they are pressurising the politicians to build a bridge over the Rhône here.

The Salin, and its friendly colleague Solvay, who also has

a factory at Salin-de-Giraud, find it difficult to get their products to Marseille by road, having to make a large detour via Arles which has the lowest bridge over the Rhône. That they should grumble about this is odd for Solvay presumably chose to establish itself close to its raw material, salt. It ought not to expect to be close to both source and customer, but, in search of ever increasing profit, it does. In conjunction with the Chamber of Commerce at Marseille, they propose a new road bridge over the lower Rhône into the Camargue. This would serve the factories but would also open the way to a great deal of through traffic. Before long the need for the trans-Camargue road to be up-graded to motorway standard would be canvassed. Wedges have thin ends. This road would thrust a dagger into the very heart of the Camargue, and that would be the last straw. The scheme is being strongly resisted by conservationists, we hope to God they win.

The Salins du Midi, which produces half as much as Giraud, is at the other end of the Camargue, just outside Aigues-Mortes and has been run in a slightly more sympathetic way. (We can find no explanation why one enterprise should be in the plural and the other in the singular. See previous note about the bafflement of the French language.) It produces table salt with a blue whale on the packet, which one can buy in England. It employs some 400 persons from Aigues-Mortes and district, and is the main occupation of the Aigues-Mortais.

Salt water is admitted (usually it is pumped) into shallow pans several acres in size and allowed to start evaporation. As its specific gravity increases it passes from one pan to another, gradually getting redder and redder in colour, until it reaches the final pans which have special floors, and it is there that the salinity becomes such that salt crystallises out on the bottom.

It continues to do so throughout spring and the hot summer, when at last the surplus water is pumped off and the layer of salt, several inches thick, is harvested and piled in huge heaps known locally as *camelles*.

This work of harvesting was once done by the men of Aigues-Mortes with wooden shovels and wheelbarrows, working all day in the full heat of high summer. It was heavy work, but one in which they took a lot of pride, for strangers found the work too arduous and seldom stayed. In 1893, the Aigues-Mortais staged a strike to which the management responded by bringing in Italian workers. At first the Aigues-Mortais sat back confident the Italians would not be up to the work, but they underrated the blacklegs. Soon the work was going well, and the Aigues-Mortais, furious, turned upon the Italians one evening and attacked them. After the fight some fifty Italians lay dead.

Later, in June 1940, when Mussolini declared war on France he referred in his speech specifically to the need for revenge against the assassins of Aigues-Mortes.

One fine but windy day in spring we had been taken on a tour of the farthest parts of the salt-pans by our friend Néné who had retired from his post as a sort of estates foreman to the company. He had seen to the maintenance of the extensive network of roads, dykes, sluices and also those parts where the bird life was protected. He had a great interest in birds, knew their habits and the places they liked to nest and frequent. It was a lovely outing into wild country that was largely untrodden by man, and when we returned we could see across one of the bright red, latter-stage salt-pans the low, long line of Aigues-Mortes' walls, catching the afternoon sun and above them the bright blue sky, a visual song in France's national colours, blue, white and red.

During the war Néné had lived in a little cottage in the middle of the marshes. He had been lucky for the Germans had not bothered him, or his parents. They had a large garden, and there was always the odd bird for the pot. Others had not been so lucky, though in the main the German occupiers had little impact on the Camargue. They concerned themselves with the Garrigue, the higher heath land above Nîmes where there was cover for the resistance fighters. As one local said: 'It wasn't much good trying to organise the Maquis in the Camargue; there was nowhere to hide.'

Any war-time unpleasantness in this area was the work of French collaborators. There was a concentration camp for gypsies not far from St Gilles. Not much is known about it and few local people had anything to do with it. We do not think France is very proud of it.

There is record of some resistance among the Aigues-Mortais, and the war memorial records the names of those who were deported and did not return.

The Aigues-Mortais have a marked 'behind the ramparts' complex. There was in the old days a lot of inter-marriage and they kept themselves apart from the rest of the locality. Even now there are three typical Aigues-Mortes noses that come from some dominant genes, and are to be found among a lot of the people.

Aigues-Mortes is the richest town in the area. Historically this comes from the salt which was an extra to the local agriculture, added to now by tourism.

Other towns have arrogated to themselves titles pertaining to the Camargue now that the area is becoming well-known. Both Arles and Saintes-Maries-de-la-Mer call themselves 'Capital of the Camargue', even though Arles is not in the Camargue. It is, however, where most of the inhabitants go to do their main shopping, except those in the west, the Petite Camargue, who go to Nîmes or Montpellier. St Gilles calls itself the Portes de la Camargue, and that is fair comment as it is on the border and on one of the roads leading in. One of the oddest is the dirty little town of Salin-de-Giraud which manages to call itself the Capital Démographique de la Camargue. It ought to be possible to give them another title based on the similarity of the two words *sale* (dirty) and *salin* but our French is not up to it.

Talking of wartime France, there is an interesting explanation of why Jean-Paul Sartre became famous. His masterwork *L'Etre et le Néant* was published during the German Occupation. At this time the Germans had seized all the brass weights for melting down to make munitions. The book in question weighed exactly a kilo, and quickly became a best-seller. He never looked back.

12

A background of bull

'E i'a qu'un crid, bram estrange que
s'ause,
Un bram que crèis coume uno fernisoun
"Li Biòu! Li Biòu!", trounadisso que
passo.'
. . . .
'One hears but one cry, a strange cry,
A cry which shudders to a crescendo,
"The Bulls! the Bulls!" as they
thunder past.'
Marquis Folco de Baroncelli-Javon

After we came back from our summer cruise we renewed
our acquaintance with the bull population by going to the
next village to see a more rural *course*. In St Laurent
d'Aigouze the arena is in the centre of the village with some
of the seating in the shade of the plane trees. One side of the
arena abuts the parish church, and the grandstand has
been built in to the side of the church. The bulls seem to be
allowed to change their clothes in the vestry, or at least use
it to wait their turn.

There were some good bulls due that day. We wanted to
see Barraie and President, two of the best. The champion
bulls' names are well known, they are stars, and it is they
who draw the crowds, though a good bull well matched to a
good *raseteur* is probably the best attraction. The champion
bull of all time was Le Sanglier, whose monument may be
seen in his home town of Le Caylar, where the local hotel-
restaurant also bears his name, a source of confusion to
visitors for a *sanglier* is a wild boar, and there are no stuffed

tuskers featured in the hotel's decoration: it is all bull. Barraie is this year's Biou d'or (Golden Bull), and the champion *raseteur*, Luc Mezy from Aigues-Mortes, says of him that he knows all the *raseteurs* and their techniques and it is impossible to fool him; he anticipates intelligently and heads off the *raseteur* as he runs, and takes up a dominant position in the arena which makes it difficult to get him on the turn by surprise.

Whether the bull actually enjoys the game is another matter. A bull in a herd is normally a peaceable animal once the 'pecking order' is well established, but on those rare occasions when he is challenged he is a fighter. His famous bad temper is probably no more than a display of aggression at being challenged, and on the farms he does not generally regard the *gardians* he knows as challengers. He probably considers them to be inferior.

Experienced *manadiers* say that the typical bull does not want to go into the ring, but point out that this is because he much prefers, like Ferdinand, to stay out there in the meadows munching grass and ruminating among his cows. The sight of the cattle truck is enough to make some wise old bulls disappear into the thickest groves of tamarisk from which they are hard to dislodge. The *gardians* also say that almost all bulls are frightened of the cattle truck; they tremble in all four limbs, and leave visible signs of their anxiety on the floor. They resent their imprisonment in the *toril* awaiting their performance, but this may not be due to a dislike of the impending games so much as the natural reaction of semi-wild animals to being shut up. At the end of their fifteen minutes in the arena, where most bulls join in with enthusiasm, they trot contentedly back into the *toril*; some, however, seem to want to stay out and have to be led back by the *simbeu*, the wise old beast with a bell round his neck.

During the game a good manoeuvre by the bull is acknowledged by a musical salute over the loudspeakers known as a *Carmen*, and after a good overall performance the same music plays the bull out. One can get a surfeit of mangled Bizet over a summer. We have seen certain bulls respond to the *Carmen* like an actor taking a curtain call. The bull is a complex, beautiful and intelligent animal, and worthy of our respect.

It has recently been announced that the Club Taurin of Beaucaire is to erect a monument to those *raseteurs* that have been killed in the ring. So far as we can tell there has been only one case of a bull being fatally injured in what is after all a rough game, but over the years there have been ten men, which seems to establish statistically the odds in favour of the bull. As five of these ten have come from Beaucaire (strictly speaking it is outside the Camargue, but is one of the great centres of bull worship) this seems to be a good place for such a memorial, though whether the predominance of Beaucairois among the victims is a measure of local enthusiasm or lack of skill is not for us to say.

The memorial will cost about 200,000 francs and will consist of a high-relief stone carving some three metres by three metres. This will make it rather more impressive than Beaucaire's war-memorial and cenotaph, which puts the local preoccupation into proper perspective. Most of the deaths have been from injuries; in one case a bull's horn drove through the unfortunate man's heart. This bull was called 'Napacun', which is the phonetic spelling for a condition that is usually referred to in England as the singularity of Samuel Hall. There was also once a famous bull called 'Napaca' who was doubly unfortunate.

After the six *courses* are over the bulls are released together into the arena where three *gardians* guide them out of the gates into the streets. Outside the arena wait a posse of mounted *gardians* who position themselves round the bulls and conduct them out of town. This is the *bandido*, a word with the same root as abandon, and as with the *abrivado* it is the occasion for all the local youth to join in. Apparently it is not an old tradition, this harrassment of the *gardians*, older folk say it has arisen largely since the war, and bemoan the lack of discipline among the young. We seem to have heard that song elsewhere, but have noticed that there seems to be less vandalism if the young have something dangerous to do. Bullgames beat motorbiking.

Because of this horseplay, for want of a better word, the *manadiers* no longer let their best bulls run in the *bandido* or the *abrivado*, where they could be injured. This duty falls on lesser bulls. We suspect that some *manades* keep *bandido* specialists who do nothing else and are trained to run home. The whole world is becoming more and more specialised; why should bulls escape the trend?

There is some pleasant wild land between the salt-pans and the sea clear of the unlovely developments at Port Camargue. There was once a little more, but some of the land was bought by a wealthy industrialist. This is not uncommon. For many years property in this region has been at a premium, a large part of the land being in the firm hands of La Banque de Henin, and the supply limited.

No attention to the purchase was paid until suddenly it was announced that a new luxury restaurant and retreat for the very rich would be opened. First class chefs had been engaged, access was by private helicopter only, and the prices would ensure that hoi polloi kept out.

Whether the local authorities (all of them are either communist or socialist) were enraged by the aura of exclusive and élitist opulence, or whether they were really concerned to protect the Camargue and avoid the undoubted disturbance by helicopter to both wild-life and humans, we cannot say. Writs were served, the place was closed almost as soon as it opened on the grounds that no planning permission had been obtained and it looks like being a feast for the lawyers. People are in fact very keen to conserve the Camargue, though it is being whittled away all the time by local authority, the worst examples being Port Camargue and La Grande Motte, two of the biggest and ugliest marinas in Europe, that are not popular even among yachtsmen. (Yes, yachtsmen go there; there is not much choice, but they would have preferred a mooring where the architects had not taken grandiose leave of their senses.) Another problem is: for what is the Camargue being preserved? We speak elsewhere of the single-mindedness of the ornithologists, but there are the hunters of several different types of game, the sailors, the bug-hunters, the bull-sports fans, the horsemen; all are fighting their own corner and they only come together to ward off the military (who, as always and in every land are up to no good in beauty-spots) and the builders of roads and railways. The fuss hereabouts over the track of the TGV, the *train à grande vitesse,* will ring familiar bells to the managers of British Rail. It does at least look as if it will avoid the Camargue: ah, but whose vineyard will it go through? Not mine, *pardi.*

House prices are high hereabouts. A small three-bedroom house of no especial merit in Aigues-Mortes is on offer at the moment for about 800,000 francs, and a reasonable sized house in the country with an acre or two will be well over two and a half million. With so many anxious for a piece of this pie, how will it remain unchanged?

August ends with massacre on the roads as the *aoûtistes* (those who take their holidays in August) head home. It is *la rentrée*. The last two weekends are full of red and orange days, motorists are advised to start for Paris at dead of night, and travel anywhere but on the motorways which were built for the purpose, and anyone with any sense leaves the car in the garage while the stampede goes on. The supermarkets are full of stationery and school books, and satchels to carry them in.

Then suddenly it was all quiet again. The weather was still, hot and sunny, but the beaches were almost empty. The old men shuffled gratefully back to their favourite benches round the Porte de la Gardette. The waiters in the square had time to lean on a tree and smoke, and ogle each other.

Serge the waiter at the Express had time to greet and chat with *les Brittaniques*. 'You will spend another winter here, then?' he said. We told him, yes, but that next year we really did want to take *Hosanna* to sea. 'What will you do now?' we asked him, knowing that his was a seasonal job. 'Me,' he said, 'I'm going down to Grau to be a fisherman. If you get away to sea, I'll see you there. *A bientôt!*' We forgot to ask him how a three legged dog would cope with a fishing boat.

'You cope all right on a barge, with one good leg,' said Bill comfortingly. 'She ought to manage with three.'

Mme Poitavin's window is decorated with bunches of grapes, and vine leaf garlands.

The *vendanges* are about to begin.

13

La vendange

'Vin de Setèmbre
Li fremo fai estèndre.'
....
'September wine
Makes the women incline.'

The hundred days it takes to build a bunch of grapes from an insignificant panicle of tiny white flowers had been fulfilled.

As early as mid August, analysis had begun in Jeannot's vineyards. The precise moment of the *vendange*, the grape harvest, is now decided by science, like the picking of a Birdseye pea. One hundred grapes were taken at random, diagonally across the field. When the acidity and sugar balance are right, that is the moment; *mais c'est le temps qui commande*, said Jeannot, it is the weather that rules. If the earth is dry, the *vendange* can begin. If there is no balance between sugar and acid content, *le vin n'est pas nerveux, il est mort* (the wine is flat instead of being lively). Jeannot gets perhaps a week's notice of the *vendange*. But we are far from the jolly picturesque *vendangeurs* of old times, happy peasants toiling day long, picking the grapes into photogenic wicker baskets, and laughing in the September sun when the crop is good. A *bon ramasseur*, a good picker, is hard to find these days. 'They are needed immediately but will not come,' says Jeannot. 'They grumble at the pay and conditions, they want days off. Then if you start one vineyard and finish, and another is not ready for picking, or the weather turns bad, you must lay them off for a few days, which they *supportent très mal*. All this trouble for three weeks' work. *Ça va vite et fort, le vendange*, fast and hard.'

A machine is fast, can be worked or wait a day, and is hired for the time it is needed. It harvests four hectares a day, into great plastic bins, which drive straight to the *Cave Cooperative*. He hires as many machines as he needs to get the harvest in from his two hundred hectares, preferably in two weeks. Why bother with people? But is it coincidence that all the great vineyards pick by hand?

The Fêtes Votives, the local festivals, used to be held in August, after the cereal harvest but before the *vendange*, while waiting for the grapes to ripen. Legend relates a marvel at St Laurent d'Aigouze, the year the grapes were late ripening, and the Fête prolonged itself for three riotously drunken weeks before the *vendange* finally ended it.

There are many vineyards hereabouts, and much wine is made, not of the highest reputation.

In 1863 the phylloxera insect was first noted in British vineyards having been brought over from the USA. It soon spread to France and virtually ruined the French wine industry within a few years. However, it spared many vineyards in the Midi region of France. Down here on the edge of the Camargue the vines are planted in sand and the water table in winter is barely under the surface. In 1865 when flood control was rudimentary it was higher still, and the lower vineyards were often flooded. The vines in the Camargue, it was said, stood with their feet in the water, and it was these vineyards that escaped the plague. When the French were everywhere else deprived of their *coup de rouge*, the Languedociens were able to sell their inferior wine at a high price. Fortunes were made, but instead of reinvesting the money in improving the stock, the local folk went in for quantity to produce as much as possible as cheaply as possible for a thirsty market.

When the traditionally excellent vineyards of the North and West at last re-established production with new phylloxera-resistant vine stock, the people turned back to the good wines eagerly, and left the Midi with a reputation for brewing rubbish.

That reputation persists and is not entirely unjustified, especially among the co-operatives, though there are many vineyards making good wines if you look for them. Other winemakers visiting the region are shocked at the generally low standards of husbandry, viticulture, and oenification in some of the vineyards. An Australian who bought a local *domaine* and in no time was winning prizes at blind tastings (he won another this year) was reportedly asked to what he attributed his success. He replied with Australian tact: 'Well, we scrubbed the floor for a start.'

This is not to say that all local winemakers are bad. There have been valiant attempts to upgrade the local produce, and change the image. It started further west with the

Faugères and Minervois wines, and such producers as Chateau Gourgazaud, and Chateau Canet from the latter region stand up well, in our opinion, against wines of a much higher snob value and price. Nearer to home the white Picpoul de Pinet from round the Etang de Thau is a perfect companion for the shellfish that grow in the *étang*; it is similar to a slightly less dry and rather sunnier Muscadet. Locally, we have found very few thoroughly enjoyable cheap wines in the Costière de Nîmes, or Vins des Sables, or in any of the local co-operatives. Of course we have not yet tried all the *domaines*. People tell us that this or that *domaine* is good, but some are disappointing or over-priced for their quality. We go on trying.

Mostly the good wines of this region are made above the Camargue in the upper parts of the Costière, and they are outside our scope. Within the loose geographical boundaries we have set ourselves we have come across a pleasant red wine from Pierrefeu, near Vauvert, and a very good rosé from Ste Colombe les Rameaux, near St Gilles. The cheapest wines from the co-operatives in this region sell for about five or six francs a litre, but to get a worthy wine it is necessary to pay twenty to twenty-five francs a bottle. This is not unreasonable, for good oenification takes trouble as well as skill. It is probably true that the best wine from hereabouts selling at say twenty-five francs, is more enjoyable than a similarly priced generic Bordeaux.

That is our opinion. We are not Masters in Wine, nor experts in any form, we are simply people who enjoy drinking wine. We are the customers at the end of the chain, and it is for people like us, not the experts, that wine is made to be sold.

We discovered the reason for having found so few drinkable local wines when we visited the Maison du Vin near the Espiguette lighthouse and talked to the resident *oenicologue*, Maurice Issert. We found that the cheaper wines of the Camargue region, the Vins des Sables as they are called, shall not grow old. Age will definitely wither them and the years condemn. Some of them, he said, are past their prime after six months, and most are gone by fifteen. But they are sold long after this by the *supermarchés* and restaurants, who have not even bothered to keep the wine in an even temperature. It is cheap, this wine, but fragile. Just because it costs little does not mean that you can abuse it. So it is almost never drunk at its best, young and well cared for, like a baby. By the end of the year, he said using his hands expressively, there is merely a shadow of what the wine had been in spring.

But, he claimed, some growers are improving their methods. They do not like the image so often presented to the public on TV of an industry dominated by musculaı hooligans who overturn Italian tanker lorries to protect their trade, instead of improving their product. He gestured violently, miming the single-handed up-ending of a forty-tonner and going on to open all its *vannes* (cocks).

The growers are not helped by the local restaurateurs, for it is in the restaurants that visitors come to meet local wines at close quarters. This rather confirms our view that local restaurants are not all that good, though he was criticising their owners as *sommeliers*, not as cooks. Deep cellars are unknown, and the wine finds itself next to the ovens or a radiator, and if the restaurant closes for the winter the wine is all too often left until next spring, even if it is well over the top and already overdue for drinking. He added that the English tend to let even the great Bordeaux wines get overaged, commenting that the limiting factor in wine preserving is the cork. For great long-living wines he recommends changing the cork at every ten years or so.

Many of the restaurants hereabouts overcharge: it puts people off, he said. We have a long way to go to educate the restaurateurs, he went on, sketching with his hands a fight worthy of Cassius Clay.

Too many people believe that all red wine should be served at room temperature, he told us. Some of these Mediterranean reds, as M. Issert would like people to call them, profit from being served a bit cool, about fifteen to seventeen degrees celsius, he recommends, adding that only the robust, great old wines really cope with temperatures of twenty degrees.

What he likes to commend from hereabouts are some of the better white wines, which is surprising, given the region's image as a producer of red and rosé. But these *domaine*-bottled whites do not come cheap.

M. Issert likes to look at wine growing in the French Mediterranean as a whole. You can see that the idea gives him pleasure, the hands dance with the idea of entity. 'It is historic, it is *traditionel*.' Then you can take it all together, the everyday Vins des Sables (Vins de Charettier: Waggoner's Wine he called it) and the really good products of some of the vineyards, which for quality and price are now doing well in a field where the market in well-known vintages is increasingly perturbed by massive Japanese buying.

One of the pleasures of living in a boat is that one is spared the capriciousness of living on land, subject to strikes and bureaucracy. Nevertheless there are occasions when one is grateful for shoreside comforts and incommoded when they cease.

Bill put down his powerless electric drill with a few choice words. In the middle of a delicate piece of woodwork the current had failed again. Our fuses were *sauté*, but not as deliciously as potatoes. Jean-Claude had resigned from the Association, which anyway was in desuetude, so a small group of worried barge-dwellers gathered on the bankside. Laurel was using our word-processor at the time of the disconnection. Boubou was using his. It is *grave*, is it not? Work had been disrupted. We ourselves had lost five pages of deathless prose. Beards were pulled, even twisted in anguish; a new cable became more desirable with every breakdown, but it was Saturday; nothing could be done. What would everyone do over the weekend?

We on *Hosanna* might have said 'Blow you Jacques' for we

had a generator capable of giving us all the power we
needed, but it was not the quietest of machines, it needed
starting and stopping, as well as servicing every hundred
hours and, diesel oil being expensive, we preferred vintage
EDF if we could get it; it is cheaper, cleaner, and quieter.
Mario offered to try to fix up something later in the day, for
it was evident that another of the underwater wires had
failed, leaving only two usable. One should be able to
manage with those if everybody would be economical.
Mario had first to make the *soupe de poissons* as the *Isles de
Stel* had a party scheduled for Sunday. Mario was neither a
professional chef nor a professional electrician, but was a
man of superb self-confidence. Bill determined to watch his
electrical wizardry later on, just as Laurel planned to
watch the making of the soup. Bill was not completely
electro-illiterate, having wired *Hosanna*, but he had no
confidence in continental installations, holding that they
seemed to be wired contrarily to all he had learnt in
England. Judging by the way everybody on the peninsula
did their own adjustments and repairs on a trial-and-error
basis, this seemed to be a fair assessment, so to avoid
trouble he had fitted fast circuit breakers on all the wires
coming into the ship, and had fixed up our own private
earth. Nevertheless he sometimes came out of the *cabane* on
the bank with a sense of doom, singing 'nearer my God to
thee' in an off-key tenor voice, with that wondrous
expression on his face of a man who has had a vision of the
Almighty.

Laurel had met Martine in the *supermarché*. The obligatory
three kisses were exchanged, Laurel as usual forgetting
which side to begin. 'C'est pas grave,' said Martine.
    How were things, asked Laurel cautiously. With Mario
and Martine it was not always a good idea to ask, and if the
reply was introduced by '*Boff* . . .' ('An expression indicating little enthusiasm' as the dictionary calls it) it was as well
to remember a pressing engagement rather than undergo

half an hour of vivid sociology at the butchery counter. But this time Martine was cheerful, being allowed not only to work on, but even to drive the *Isles de Stel* mainly because the summer crew had gone, one to Australia, and one to care for his mother, a *marinière* whose foot had been taken off in a bight of mooring wire in Rotterdam.

'And you, how does it go?' asked Martine.

'Very well,' said Laurel, adding a few items of news before cunningly saying:

'Unhappily the electricity cable is again *en panne*, so we cannot use the *traiteur de texte*. Is Mario very busy, or can he spare time to assist with the mending?'

'He has to make *soupe de poissons* for sixty people this afternoon, but I will remind him,' Martine assured her.

Tired of housekeeping, and with no power for the word processor without starting the generator, Laurel went round to the caravan after lunch, kicking her shoes off on entering as the rain had been heavy, to ask if she could watch Mario make *soupe*.

'A little coffee? Tea, perhaps? No? Then let's go to it,' said Mario. 'The kitchen on the *Isles de Stel* is small, but *professionel*, so that is where we cook.'

Laurel replaced her shoes, Mario did not, and they scrambled through the big saloon window of the *bateau restaurant* which lay alongside Mario's decrepit barge-cum-caravan. It made an amazing contrast. The barge Mario lived on was ill kempt, short of paint, and rusty. The caravan perched on deck was none too weather proof, and in heavy rain the roof leaked. The *Isles de Stel*, however, was immaculate, with cheerful tile-topped tables along each side of the saloon, a bar at one end and two superior loos outside at the stern, each with the carpeted walls which are such an unexpected feature of the modern French 'WC'.

The galley, entered from behind the bar, was indeed small; little bigger than that on *Hosanna*, but as food was mostly kept in lockers outside, it did very well. Mario padded out on deck, barefooted, unearthed an enormous *marmite* from a deck locker, and began to scrub it vigorously in one of the two huge sinks.

'These aluminium things,' he said disgustedly, 'they never look clean. I would prefer *inox*, but imagine what it would cost! This aluminium one is already *mille balles!*' (which is near enough a hundred pounds).

The two sinks and a big fridge took all one wall, and opposite were a large gas oven, four giant burners, and another by itself for the *friture*; all of these stood at table height over the engine so there was no storage space under them.

The *marmite* being cleaned to Mario's satisfaction, he hefted it on to the back burner, lit the gas, and began.

'I can give you no recipe,' he had warned Laurel already. 'No, it is not a secret, but *je ne dose pas.*' He slopped in the remains of a bottle of olive oil, and quite a 'dose' out of a second bottle, probably a third of a litre all told.

Seven kilos of soup fish then came out of the fridge. Mario picked them over with care, lobbing them one by one as he approved them into the *marmite*, whose top rim was well above his head. There were breamlike *sar*, gurnards of various kinds, *pageot*, stargazer, grey mullet, and a long thin fish like a pink ribbon, the only one more than three inches long. All the fish went in whole, with a few pieces of stale bread 'for liaison'.

On the front burner Mario had put a smaller pan of water, adding salt and thyme branches. When it was boiling he threw in two kilos of little green shore crabs. As they turned scarlet, he occasionally stirred the unseen contents of the other *marmite* at the back with a huge wooden paddle a good three feet long. He tipped the pan so that I could peer in: the fish had already melted into a grey paste. It became pinker as he added three large (750 gram) tins of tomatoes. 'Fresh tomatoes are better, but too dear just now.' A head of garlic went in, then five or six leeks, a large onion, two carrots, a head of fennel and six potatoes. All these were roughly cut up in the hand, without benefit of a chopping board.

Martine entered through the window, and began to lay the tables for the morrow; Laurel gave her a hand, glancing in at the galley occasionally to see what transpired. Mario had added the crabs and their cooking water, and a good many jugs more to liquefy the soup. Then he lugged out an object the size and shape of a pneumatic drill, which he plugged in before standing it in the *marmite* where it lurched against the side as it churned. It was the mixer.

'*Solide*,' he said contentedly. '*Professionel*.' Mixer was a rather tame name for such a redoubtable engine: at the base of the thick steel spindle was a castellated grinder, which made short work of fish bones and crab shells.

'If the restaurants buy six kilos of fish for their soup, after they have sieved it they throw away three kilos of "*restes*"; they have not time or patience,' he snorted derisively, adding proudly: 'You will see, when I finish, there will be only three spoonfuls of "*restes*".' He added a 400 gram tin of tomato purée and gave the whole brew another stir with the paddle.

Laurel mused on the paucity of his '*restes*' and concluded that it was due more to the *professionel* crab crusher than his reserves of patience (a quality he was not known for on the peninsula). Also there were his origins in Dunkerque. After helping Martine to fold napkins and place them in the polished glasses, she took her leave. As she clambered through the window Mario was cutting hundreds of slices of bread and drying them off in the oven. 'The saffron goes in at the end of the cooking,' he called after her. 'Come with us tomorrow, and you can taste it.'

Then he went with Bill and Boubou to commit an act of temporary magic on the electricity cable.

It was not only the soup we tasted on that brilliant September Sunday. The *Isles de Stel* drove along the canal, slowing down sometimes so as not to disturb wild-life on the bank; a flight of egrets among the parasol pines, or a heron fishing. Mario was driving, happy as a lark, micro in hand, broadcasting a commentary on the passing scene. He also tried to get us to read all the legal notices on his corkboard, which indicated stages in his quarrel with his ex-wife.

'You know I must sell the *Isles de Stel* because of her?' he said. '*Ah, la p* . . . that she is! Look here, what she has done!' We pleaded non comprehension of legal words and distracted him by looking into the galley. 'But she will see! I have a much bigger boat now, three times as big! But it's a secret. Tell nobody.'

The galley was in the charge of a young trainee chef, who had almost missed the boat, driving up on his motor bike at the last minute, with many excuses, one of them being exhaustion from overwork. 'Overworked! You mean over-slept!' scoffed Mario. 'Everyone knows what kind of work on a Saturday night causes you to oversleep on a Sunday morning.' He dug the young man in the ribs, grinning. 'Of course, I have cooked nothing, so you have two hours to make *déjeuner* for fifty-four people.' (Heads had been counted as the coach arrived.) The boy was used to Mario's fooling, and laughed as he donned his apron and entered the galley to check what still remained to be done.

Martine, acting as hostess, was wearing a black crushed velvet dress whose *décolleté* almost met its extremely short hemline. From there to the floor a pair of long bare legs ended in high-heeled sandals. Bill enjoyed the scenery. Eventually we both went up to the top deck to savour the outdoor variety.

Our fellow guests were a charitable organisation, the Society of St Vincent de Paul, having their annual outing. They all lived close to Clermont l'Herault, in the foothills of the Cévennes. We were introduced to the President, M. Gallego, over an *apéritif* made of peach juice, which looked innocuous but astonished the gullet, and were told something about the charity. Among other ways of raising money for lepers and the children of the Third World they made *oreillettes*, a speciality of the Montpellier region. Little pillows, we wondered, or little ears? We had met pasta in the shape of little ears in Calabria, we told M. Gallego: *orecchiette al rape*, served with garlic and broccoli. Our mentor sucked his teeth.

'No, this is a delicious *patisserie*. There is much art in making the layers; you must ask the ladies how it is done.'

We found ourselves a table already containing three women, were introduced to the eldest, Mme S., who was eighty-six, and sat down. The other two, Mmes Panafieu and Fabre, were mere chicks of seventy or so.

The *soupe de poissons* was excellent. For Mesdames it appeared to lack salt, which they all added with a heavy hand, and while we walloped into the beautifully persimmon coloured *rouille* (the peppery garlic and mayonnaise sauce that accompanies fish soup in the Midi) they opted more for the grated gruyère on their croutons. Too much garlic, they warned, upset the stomach. Mmes S. and F. drank water, leaving the local *gris de gris* for us and Mme P., who would only accept a third of a glass at a time, but drank them so fast that she kept pace with us pretty well.

After the *soupe* there was a pause during which we asked about the making of *oreillettes*. Each lady had a different answer. They began to interrupt each other and argue among themselves, inserting the 'Madame' that is supposed to soften the rudeness of strongly expressed opinion.

'No, Madame, not margarine, it *must* be butter.' 'But, Madame, I find that margarine makes the layers rise better.' 'No, it must be butter, Madame; and of course a little orange flower water.' 'No, no, no, *rosewater*, Madame, nothing else will do.'

That was as far as we got with the recipe, as our main course (rice and *seiches sètoise*) arrived, and the cuttlefish proved a little chewy for Mme F.'s new teeth. This led to an in-depth discussion on dentures which we felt could roll along nicely without our aid, as we had no personal experience to offer.

Salad and cheese was followed by Mario's apple tart, done French style with the apples in delicate overlapping slices, and described by Martine, to the ladies' great amusement, as *tarte bateau*, instead of *tarte maison*.

As if we had not already eaten and drunk extremely well, little glasses were brought round for those who would like a *digestif* with their coffee. The ladies at our table declined at first, but when the tray came round with a choice of cognac or *crème de cassis*, Mme P. weakened, and took a glass of *cassis*. One does not go out to lunch every day, *pardi*.

Before they boarded their waiting coach back at Aigues-Mortes they urged us to come and watch the *oreillettes* being made. 'The first Tuesday of the month, behind the church just opposite the *mercerie*,' they said. We promised to remember the co-ordinates of the Foyer of the Society of St Vincent de Paul at Clermont l'Herault.

Two weeks had passed since then without an electricity cut and everybody had been very careful. When anything was switched on the Catholics had been crossing themselves and we heathen British crossed our fingers. (The Church of England is not dignified by being called a religion in France; it is a *culte*.) Which kind of crossing had proved unreliable cannot be determined, but the Weather-God got at the cable during the night once more. It is no use trying to get these continental Christians to propitiate the Weather-God; they will persist in thinking that one god controls everything, whereas every sailor knows that praying for good weather is ineffective. Or if not ineffective, then it produces perversely the opposite conditions to those requested. Why else do the Greek sailors, in bad weather, put the ikon of St Nicolas in the bows to get wet and cold until he sees sense and abates the storm? Of course sailors accept the One True God, and even grant his Omnipotence, but it is evident to them that He delegates the weather to a junior saint, an apprentice perhaps, who is not yet very good at godding. The young saint gives the impression of having lost control most of the time, but he is not malicious; he always apologises for his worst errors with a spell of fine weather, and this lulls us into the feeling that all is being well managed. It is not. Never.

This time insurrection threatened on the peninsula. Despite the demise of the Association, Mario, as ex-President, and now tacitly appointed as payer of the water and electricity bills, was still the one we went to for practical help. As his caravan was now on the other side of the creek he was in no rush to embark on rewiring the peninsula. A deputation called on him. He was at last convinced of our earnestness, but alas he had no licence for his *fourgon* (the big, old white van) and, as everyone knows, the policemen at Nîmes, where he would have to buy the cable, are serious. No matter, it was agreed that they do not interfere with the English, or they do so at their peril. It was therefore a *fourgon* conclusion that Mario and Bill left in our old car and penetrated deep into an industrial estate to the south of Nîmes, so deep that there is no doubt Bill could not have found it on his own. To start with it is known as the Industrial Centre of the Station, but is a good couple of kilometres from the railway, the station referred to being the lorry station. And to continue, the company concerned with electric cable had no sign outside, on the well-known East Anglian principle that if you do not know what it sells and where it is you have no business going there.

The establishment only sold to contractors working for, or with the approval of, Electricité de France. Did that apply to us? Of course not. But Mario was not going to say so. He is a Dunkerquois. It took him some time as he had no documentary evidence, but he managed to convince the manager that we were not only persona grata with EDF, but that Bill was negotiating to purchase the entire company or something like that. Bill, who was wearing a pair of workstained overalls, did not look the part of a ruthless specialist in take-over bids, but after a half-hour of concentrated diplomacy (otherwise known as a pack of lies), they left with 120 metres of heavy cable in the back of the car. Bill was inclined to think that Mario would have done well in a career on the Stock Exchange.

On their return they decided, despite the strong wind, to get straight to work, slinging the cable from poles over the water this time, rather than run it under the canal. The only poles available to take this lengthy span belonged to the telephone company, but Mario was in no mood to let a minor detail like that stand in his way. Bill had a moment's concern that the live electricity cable might induce currents into the telephone wires close beside it thus exposing us all to the risk of amps in the ear-hole. His companions either did not know what he was talking about, or decided that the risks were acceptable. Too cautious, these English. No sense of sport. They should wear rubber boots. Or rubber ear-muffs. Or both.

Mario was pushed up the ladder which rested against the first pole. The pole wavered, but he succeeded in fixing the wire to the top. He did the same with the second pole. The third pole cannot have gone very far into the ground, for under the weight of the ladder it started to cant over towards the canal. Mario descended the ladder with some speed. No matter, here were nautical folk; the pole was given a forestay and shrouds (the latter an appropriate rigging for a high voltage line) and Mario went up the ladder once more.

At last all was connected. *Hosanna*'s meter went backwards again to everyone's fascination. It seemed as if the whole neighbourhood were summoned to watch this phenomenon. Mario tightened a few connections, gave the meter a sharp blow with his enormous fist and it reversed its travel. We had electricity again. We were all too tired to take the old cable down, and anyway it was lunchtime and everything stops for the French lunch. The old cable is still there several months afterwards; who knows, pieces of it might come in useful one day.

Laurel meanwhile had watched the proceedings from

Hosanna where she was hanging out her sheets, taking advantage of a strong drying wind. As she hung up the last one, pegging it securely, the basin in which she had brought them up on deck was carried away across the canal by a strong gust. It was a good basin, floating well. She ran to the car and drove down to the bridge, across the canal and back the other side. With the help of her walking stick she managed to retrieve the basin from the canal without falling in, assisted by holding on to a large dog that happened to be handy. She recognised him as Martine's Dinky, over there on business of his own, but pleased to help. Wiping the duckweed from her basin and walking stick Laurel could see on the other side of the canal a vignette: a vivid little picture. At the top of a pole, swaying dangerously on his ladder, was Mario. Bill and Boubou were on the ground, feeding cable from the reel. Across the creek Serge of *Pescalune* was making large 'Let it come!' gestures. She decided that they could all be left to get on with it, and returned to her washing.

14

La chasse

We have said elsewhere that the Camarguais religion is the bull, but that is strictly a local religion, though none the less intense for all that. One might draw comparison with parts of northern Scotland where the principal church is that known as the Wee Frees (most of its adherents that we have met have been far from wee, and with their plethora of restrictive interdictions they can hardly be called free either). But if the Wee Frees is the dominant local religion, there is still plenty of place for the Church of Scotland.

So in the Camargue the bull is *the* local religion, but there are still plenty of worshippers at the shrine of St Hubert, patron saint of hunters, and as near as a whisker to being the patron saint of all Frenchmen.

Hunting, or *la chasse*, has nothing to do with well-heeled gentlemen dressed in pink and riding over each other's land after a particularly cunning piece of vermin. In France *la chasse* extends across the class structure. (Do not let anyone tell you that class does not exist in France. It does, but they refer to it differently.) Everybody who can afford a gun to shoot game with, a dog to get in the way and occasionally to get lost in the excitement, the appropriate outfit of bandoliers and imitation commando clothing without which a man would not look the part and therefore lose face, and finally the necessary permits, will be keen to go out and kill something. He must wait until the right season, for the rites of this religion are very strict and extremely complicated. Every hunter has to know his killing catechism (he is helped by a little green booklet that he is given with his licence, rather like a child is given a prayer book), and heavy penalties attend infractions if the sinner is spotted by the *gardes champêtres*. Different birds and animals come in and out of season at different times in different departments, so presumably the wise hunter must know his departmental boundaries too. To add to the confusion the season is further cut up because shooting round here is forbidden in vineyards until at least a week after the *vendange* is over, or rather is expected to be over, the object not being to avoid lead in the grapes but to minimise the chance of winging some poor unfortunate who is picking them. Where workers are still used they are very often North Africans, so this is a most humane and liberal concession by the authorities, there being quite a few local hunters who would not mind at all shooting the odd African.

Most of the real wild game has been shot long ago, but there remain a few targets: rabbits and hares, protected species (sometimes), and a few migrating birds who have not yet learnt to fly above four hundred feet when crossing France and Italy. (Why does Darwin's natural selection take so long?) But so big is the industry, and so profitable, that game birds are bred specially to be sold to various hunting clubs in order to be released so that they may be shot.

Of course in England too, birds are bred in captivity for the sporting gentry to massacre. In the Suffolk village where we once lived there was a small piece of land that belonged to a charitable trust. It lay next to the Lord of the Manor's large estate on which pheasants were bred for game. Each year the use of this little patch of land was auctioned to a resident of the village, the proceeds going to assist the local poor. Each year Sam, the postman, outbid all comers, and each year he planted corn which he did not harvest. As soon as Lordie's gamekeepers released their birds for a shoot they flew over to Sam's to feed on his fallen corn and get themselves caught in his traps. His Lordship was powerless. Why did he not outbid Sam? we asked. Couldn't do that, awfully bad form: he had to grin and bear it, regarding the outlay as his contribution to the postman's pension fund. Sam must be long gone, and there is a new Lordie: who harvests his pheasants now, we wonder.

Quite close to our mooring near Aigues-Mortes there was a game farm where various birds were raised under secure netting about eight feet high. The birds were bought from a hatchery as chicks, and are reared most carefully to be ready for the appropriate season. There are wild duck, pheasants, partridge and quail, and all have different seasons.

Contrary to the usual English view of *la chasse* there are many species that are never in season, as they are protected. One is the famous pink flamingo which can be seen in vast numbers in the shallow *étangs* hoovering up krill. There are the white egrets, and other birds such as kingfishers.

The Camargue is also the home of the wild boar, though this animal is fast disappearing, not because of the hunters, but because of the tourists with whom it finds it difficult to share a habitat. We are waiting until an open season is declared for hunting tourists once the wild boar have finally disappeared, for the French must have something they can shoot. The odd Belgian's head mounted on the wall would be quite acceptable to some Frenchmen.

The wild boar is such an important game animal that, like the salmon in Scotland, it has different names for different sexes and different ages or sizes. It usually appears on menus as *sanglier* or *marcassin*, and is in season from 1st September to 29th December, the season being limited to enable the species to survive, which it does with difficulty. We arrive at the paradox where an animal in danger of becoming extinct because of hunters is artificially preserved and encouraged in its fecundity by the very hunters who wish to destroy it. Bill thanks God he is not a hunter because he would not be able to sleep at night trying to resolve this paradox.

The wild boar is not so common in the Camargue as in the Aude to the west. There it takes the place of the bull, except that the Camarguais do not hunt their God, while the Audois think of nothing but killing and eating theirs. Asterix the Gaul is their hero. *Par Toutatis!*

The sad thing is that the boar is bred at all in captivity to be released and hunted. (He is also bred to provide 'wild boar' for sale in supermarkets and restaurants.) This breeding for hunting provokes a dilemma to the French. While they see nothing untoward in breeding birds to be shot at great expense, they are querying the wisdom of doing the same for boars. Hunting a boar is not a simple matter of looking up at a flock of birds and scattering birdshot in their general direction and seeing how many fall on your dog. The boar has to be tracked, identified and then shot at fairly close range with a rifle. He is a dangerous beast which can kill a man and why should he not if he is being hunted? It sometimes takes a whole day from dawn to dusk to stalk a boar, and even then the hunter may not bag it. Boar hunting is an obsession and takes a lot of a person's time.

When the boar is shot it is eaten. Of course. It is a strong taste but good. As it is sometimes a bit tough to roast, the popular method of cooking is to make a civet (or a rich thick stew) and serve with plenty of white beans cooked in boar-fat. It is a dish distantly related to a *cassoulet*, but only distantly. It is eaten with loads of strong red wine of the grenache/sirah grape. It should not be marinaded. There is much mysticism about the cooking of boar and there are restaurants whose chef's reputation is built on it. And it is because of the gourmands that the 'raised' boar is not being well received. Its taste is too much like that of ordinary pork. *C'est le cochon, quoi*?

Not only the taste, but the hunters themselves are beginning to feel the same way. The wild boar is sensitive to sound and smell, steers clear of humans and is difficult to track down. The boar which has been elevated by man sees man as a giver of food, is not the least bit afraid of him, and runs up to the hunter expecting to be offered a tit-bit. Where is the sport in that?

A few miles from here two hunters, a father and son, appeared before the court this week having been caught shooting chaffinches last February by *les garde-chasse* (a singular sort of plural calculated to drive mad all foreigners who are trying to learn the language), and offered for excuse that there was nothing much else to shoot at that time, as if that was justification for some indiscriminate massacre. (Tourists watch out!) Neither the state nor the local hunters' association would have that; it was pointed out that not only was it the birds' nesting season, but also that this species was absolutely protected.

They were fined 2,000 francs, plus a further 1,000 francs damages on behalf of the poor birds and had their licences suspended for two years. The damages on behalf of the birds seem to us to be a commendable form of justice, though as the chaffinches presumably died intestate we cannot imagine who actually gets the 1,000 francs. And given the hunters' apparent disrespect for the law, the suspension does not seem to be all that effective a deterrent, but what else can the state do?

It is thought that there would be four times the population of wild duck here in the Camargue if they were not hunted. There is one wild animal alone that could be shot but is not, and that is a species reputed to be found only in the Basse Camargue: the black rabbit. Whether this is due to superstition we cannot discover. In our native Suffolk the Devil is reputed to take the form of a black dog. But a rabbit?

Once the *vendánge* is over the hunting starts in earnest. Since our mooring is surrounded by vineyards, our early morning sleep is quite frequently disturbed, especially at weekends, by a barrage of shot and shell that might seem to presage another D-Day landing. Sometimes we hear spent shot raining down on our deck, a clear indication of disrespect for the law, for the vineyards are on the opposite side of a road, and no one is supposed to shoot over a road, or in the vicinity of a canal. But infractions of the general law by hunters are overlooked by police; to do otherwise would provoke popular reaction. It is only offences against the interests of the hunters themselves that are rigorously pursued.

We were sitting at the Express Bar, when Claude came up to us with a much more cheerful expression, and an address in the district of Gers for superb *foie-gras*. He brought good news. 'We have found a house in Marsillargues,' he said.

It was old, and charming, had some land, and best of all good outbuildings. They would renovate the old house, which had small rooms, and let it in summer, because as everyone knows, in summer small rooms are not an inconvenience since one lives outside on the terrace, no? The outbuildings they would transform into their own dwelling, with large rooms. It sounded like an excellent idea. Basil's morale had much improved, and he was sometimes to be seen talking to the waiters in the square, though we noticed he kept away from Bill. 'You will visit our new house of course,' insisted Claude. 'It is only a few kilometres away, but it needs so much work before we can move in.' We said we would look forward to seeing it.

15

La Fête Votive: all bull and a yard wide

'*Oou mes d'octobre
Qu'a ges de raoubo que n'en trobe.'*
. . . .
'Who has not a shawl to wind one
In October better find one.'

On the day of St Francis of Assissi we went to the Refuge des Sources (Assistance aux Animaux) which lies next to a vineyard on the road from Arles to Nîmes. It was a grey day in early October, and we were looking for a cat. We were in the Garrigue; an area of heath and scrub that stretches between Nîmes and the mountains, noted for succulent rabbits and army manoeuvres. Our every foot-step crushed summer-dried thyme and *sarriette* as we approached the Refuge, till the air was full of a perfume heady enough even to overcome that of dog. Said dogs had signalled our arrival with a cacophony of barking, no one at the Refuge could fail to know that they had visitors. Among the few trusties who were allowed to range freely outside the enclosures were a huge black dog (very loving, they said; we soon discovered that it knocked you to the ground before covering you with kisses), and an ancient bitch, something like a corgi, with a square ground plan and trailing dugs.

We found not one but two cats to our liking among the sixty or so of every kind and colour that slept, sat, leapt or spat in the airy rooms giving on to the trees and scrub of the enclosures. One, a small thin sandy tiger, was winding affectionately among the beds and armchairs which had been thoughtfully spread with old clothes to provide a nice human smell, and the other, a velvety blue, was resting watchfully in the arms of an English girl called Sheila, who seemed to think that this was the one for us. We took both cats (*'Carrément deux?'* said the lady in charge, delighted), filling in forms about the probity of our antecedents and the impeccability of our intentions, and brought them back to the Refuge the following day for Benediction. We had discovered that as it was the nearest Sunday to St Francis of Assissi Day, there was to be a Blessing of the Animals and in the Provençal language too; it was hoped that the Master of the Félibrige (a prestigious society for the promotion of the Provençal language) would attend also. Presumably our newly adopted cats would be used to Provençal.

The day was still grey, the dogs as noisily welcoming, but this time there were many cars, and the dogs would quieten down at intervals if you kept a distance from their enclosures. The more boisterous trusties had been sequestered for the time being, as visiting dogs and cats were everywhere, the cats on leads or in baskets. There was a herd of charming goats (if you stayed upwind and trod on plenty of thyme) and a Shetland pony that had been rescued from a pitch dark shed, quite blind; now gradually recovering its sight in God's good daylight.

Emerging from a vehicle was a tall man with white curls, the calm thoughtful face of an academic, and a briefcase. That will be either the Abbé or the Master of the Félibrige, we decided, and engaged him in conversation.

'We have brought our cats to the Benediction,' we explained.

'Ah,' he smiled, 'it is with this I have come to occupy myself,' thus confirming that he was the Abbé Petit even if we had not seen a coy fragment of lace peeping from the clamped jaws of his briefcase. Such a sight in Aigues-Mortes might have given a very different impression.

No longer are the Fathers of France unmistakable in black

beret and the *soutane* with buttons all the way up the front, like Mr Noah, and eggstains all the way down. The Abbé wore a smart fawn suit and pointed Italian shoes, which disguise must entail his overhearing items of real interest from a voluble populace not recognising a man of the cloth, and one who speaks Provençal to boot. He spoke of his passion for the language, his familiarity with its poets, and his visits to lofty colleges in London and Cambridge in the pursuit of, and for the dissemination of knowledge; then he was borne away by a volunteer to meet the Master, who in tweed jacket and hat on a bald brown head looked more rancher than intellectual. He turned out to be both.

A congregation of a hundred or so people, accompanied by their dogs, cats and grandmothers, often more than one of each per family, surrounded the Abbé when he belatedly mounted a stack of breeze blocks topped by a wooden pallet, to take the service. We had watched entranced as he removed his surplice from its case and put it on, struggling against the wind. The linen was endearingly creased, and the lace hem was a little grubby, and suddenly the elegant scholar with his urbane feet on the ground gave place to the otherworldly priest with his head in the clouds.

He began in French, telling us of the creation of animals, called 'animals', he said, because they were beings with anima, or souls (to us a radical doctrine). He told us of St Francis of Assissi, whose feast we were celebrating. He then launched into praise of the Provençal language, why we should all learn it, what a shame it was not obligatory in school, as Breton is in Britanny, and the Basque language in the Pyrenees; no doubt because here in Provence we were too peaceable to use the *mitrailleuse* to get our own way like the Bretons, or bombs like the Basques. With a nod to us, the English, he reminded us that Richard Coeur de Lion was imprisoned in Vienne, and asked in what language he had written his songs? Why, Provençal of course. He fixed the French with as stern a look as his benevolent face could compose: what language did the Popes of Avignon speak in their heyday? Provençal. It was a language older than Latin, and by rights every one should be speaking it today instead of this upstart French tongue. Carried away on his favourite theme we listened spellbound as he chanted in ringing and resonant tones something whose words were meaningless to us, but undoubtedly poetry. We almost understood him as he returned to Sant Francès, as it was recognisably the story of the wolf of Gubbio. He touched on Santo Marthe (very likely her taming of the Drac at Tarascon, but we were guessing). He then exhorted us in Provençal to lift up our hearts, and about six people responded that they were so doing. The Lord, he said, be with you, and about seven people hoped He would also be with the Abbé, the rest of us mumbling agreement as convincingly as possible. Those who knew the words in Provençal then sang the Lord's Prayer, while we French speakers limped along, humming off key.

There was a sudden pause as the Abbé discovered that he had forgotten the holy water; 'Marie-Pierre! (where is the girl?) The *eau bénite, s'il vous plaît*, it is still in the car!' A moment later Marie-Pierre, an intense dark girl in a tiered Provençal skirt, arrived out of breath, clutching a cat to her sparse bosom with one hand, and a brass urn and sprinkler in the other.

After the Abbé had sprinkled as far as he could reach from the podium he gave the urn back to Marie-Pierre and went off into another song accompanied by the Majourau dóu Félibrige and a few others. Marie-Pierre placed the urn at her feet in order to take a better hold of her restless cat. As she did so a long-legged black and white spotted puppy with a festive blue frill round its neck lolloped up and took a few grateful gulps of holy water, before being hauled off by its giggling owner. There was a cheerful sound of song and gentle laughter as the rain held off.

Marie-Pierre took sprinkling seriously, gave her cat into someone else's charge, and made sure every creature present was well *asperged*, adding a sign of the cross to make quite sure, and paying special attention to the more unfortunate: a three-legged hairy dog, an old sick cat, a spherical pomeranian belonging to an ancient and adoring couple. When we left shortly afterwards the black and white puppy, quenched with holy water, was behaving with the utmost saintliness.

The restaurant at L'Escale closed for the winter before the Fête Votive began. The municipal toilet outside had just been finished, a monstrosity painted pale battleship grey and planted with barberry bushes to camouflage it.

'How could you do such a thing?' we asked the Mayor's Adjunct for Tourism when we had him cornered one day. He looked embarrassed. 'It was never intended to be so high off the ground,' he muttered.

We had a flash of intuition. Excavation work must have stopped when they had discovered the water table. Nowhere in the Camargue are there any cellars, even the wine caves are all above ground, the minute you dig more than a foot down the water comes welling up. Some architect or builder had forgotten this little detail and designed a subterranean loo. The long wait that followed must have been due to wrangling between experts about whose fault was it, who was going to pay, and what do we do now. We wish we had heard it.

In the end Aigues-Mortes got the only above ground subterranean toilet in existence.

'They've closed off the carpark,' said Laurel. 'The *forains* are arriving.' They come every year for the Fête Votive in October, and take up the entire ramparts carpark: dodgems, shooting galleries, roundabouts, tunnels of love, ghost trains, and games of chance where everyone, mesdames and messieurs, but everyone, wins a furry rabbit. In addition to yet more pizza purveyors, and hot dog stalls, there are machines to make *barbe-à-papa* – grandfather's beard, known to us as candy floss.

We resigned ourselves to three weeks of renewed parking difficulties, even though the tourists had dwindled to a trickle. The local Fête is strong meat, and meant for strong local stomachs. It is not for the tourists, though some uninformed visitors do get caught up in it. If they can find where to go.

For example the usual programme for a day in the life of the Fête starts with the *déjeuner au prés*, breakfast in the fields. Here the spectators barbecue their breakfast, washing it down with the first of the day's bottles of *pastis* while they watch the *gardians* select and single out the bulls for the day's games. So we are told. Two years we have been looking whenever it was not pouring with rain, for the *déjeuner au prés*. 'Past the HLM's, the council houses,' they said. But our foray in that direction merely brought us to the town dump, mercifully smelling less in the cool weather than it did in July.

We tried other promising-looking fields without success. If we'd joined the Golden Age Outing we would have been taken there in a bus with the other old crocks, but neither of us wish to have anything to do with Golden Ages, Senior Citizens, or any other wrinkly party, however euphemistically described. We'd have preferred to go on Children's Day.

In town there is the eleven o'clock cow (*la vache de onze heures*) which is let loose *emboulée* (with pads on the points of its horns), for the population, and particularly the young, to play with between the *déjeuner au prés* and the hour of the *apéritif*. The elders sit and watch from the cafés enjoying their second bottle of *pastis*, and occasionally beating a hasty retreat, or climbing a tree if the *vache* becomes a little adventurous. *Vache* (cow) is an approximate description. Whereas anyone who cannot tell a cow from a bull would be treated with a scorn verging on contempt, we notice that quite often when a programme promises a *petite vache pour les enfants*, it can be a calf of either sex, the main criterion being that it should be small. This smallness is a variable element. Bill is big but he has no desire to mix it with some of these small cows or bulls.

The bulls let loose in most towns and villages are free to try to go where they want subject always to the crowd who try to get them to go where *they* want. None the less occasions are frequent where the bulls end up in the bars, the shops, in someone's kitchen, and even in their bedrooms.

The bulls, when selected in the fields, are brought in by *abrivado*, a dozen horsemen to perhaps four bulls. We know several places to go if we want to watch that.

After lunch there are the bull games; but for the Fête they are Courses Libres, that is: no rules, any one may join in, and the *direction* does not respond to accidents.

The *peña* plays 'Valencia', and looks smart in red blazers and straw boaters.

Prizes are awarded with more *pastis*, the *bandido* takes the bulls home again, after the fun and games in the arena. We certainly know where the *bandido* goes, because if the bulls escape the horsemen they all come over the bridge alongside our boat and either turn left into the vineyards or right into the *jardins potager*, the allotments. At *apéritif* time there is a band in the square to listen to while downing the third bottle, and then there is a *bal* at the Espace Régent. After that, you being young and it being now about midnight, you go to the fairground, or the *bodegons* which have sprung up in garages everywhere to make sure that you do not have to forego the next round of *pastis*. The filled glasses are set out in rows, and you buy a metre at a time. You can end up having burgled your way into the ramparts (Ministry of Culture, normally nine francs per visit) and continue the party all night in one of the towers. Next day you start again with the *déjeuner au prés* at nine-o-clock, and you keep this up for a fortnight. Added to which you may receive, from a bull feeling generous, a badge of honour in the shape of a broken leg, arm, crush injury, or loss of a few teeth, and continue the party flaunting your crutches, bandages, prosthesis, or plaster. Since you won your injury in no pain at all, anaesthetics were not presumably necessary during your treatment. It would be a rare tourist who could cope with two weeks of all this.

On the Thursday of the Fête there was a special *bandido*, a competitive one. Three *gardians* from each of ten *manades*, alert on their sturdy Camargue horses, waited as one bull was released at a time from the *toril*, then the encircling horses would herd it at the gallop out of the arena onto the open land south of the town, round a sharp left turn and through the massive town walls via the narrow Porte de la Marine, along the Boulevard Gambetta, and out of the opposite gate, galloping through the streets on their way home, impeded (as is *traditionel*) by the young of the town, and away to the *manade* out in the *prés*. It is a fine spectacle, and a big crowd comes out to watch.

About three thousand had gathered at the arena. Many,

we among them, watched from the grandstand, others from their private wooden *théâtres*, but there were crowds more at the arena gate, outside the Porte de la Marine where the open land was dotted with tethered horses and cars parked, not orderly but Midi fashion, higgledy-piggledy; the usual method of parking hereabouts being Italian style: you stop the car and get out.

Some trios of *gardians* had little difficulty getting their single bull under control and herding it out of the arena, the three of them effectively surrounding the bull, one on each side and slightly forward of the bull and the other close behind. But not all trios had it completely their own way.

Laurel

One rider dropped too far back, leaving his two colleagues an impossible task. It reminded us of that epic story of the policeman giving evidence: 'Me and PC Smith surrounded the gang.' That bull got away. As the third and fourth bulls were released youths fired with booze and festivity spread the ground with straw, and fired that as well. *'Bou Diou!'* cried a great many people in the crowd. Neither bulls nor horses paid much heed, leaping the flames at full speed, Laurel observing that the bull would be cooked more by this method than was usual for a French steak.

For the fifth bull the youths threw fireworks in front of the horses to distract or frighten them, to another burst of *'Bou Diou's'*. Horses and their riders, however, were not easily put off. The standard of horsemanship was very high, to our inexpert eyes, and the horses gave every impression of joining in the fun whole-heartedly, and neither fireworks nor noisy exhausts and backfires gave them more than the *frisson* it gave to all of us.

On one occasion the leading horse stumbled as they crossed the rough ground outside and the bull swerved to avoid the horse, injuring several spectators in the front of the crowd which was undoubtedly too close, but prevented by the crush from falling back. This time the cries from the crowd were *'O! Peuchère!'* ('Oh, alas!'). There was of course an ambulance of the brave *sapeurs-pompiers* standing by at the arena gate, but a second ambulance was needed and it could not get through the parked vehicles; one major culprit (though not the only one) was a large Belgian tourist coach which had just innocently discharged a load of elderly passengers, intent on a peaceful tour of the ramparts, into this mêlée. After half an hour the injured were taken to hospital and the *bandidos* resumed.

One bull, clearly a champion sprinter, out-accelerated the horses and beat them hands down to the gate, cheered on by the crowd, and we expected him to be off into the agriculture, but no; he knew his way home and headed off through the gateway eager for his supper, undoubtedly getting home ahead of his *gardians*. Two other bulls evaded their *gardians* and put up a good show in the ring, leaping barriers like show-jumpers before finding their own way out.

While one team of *gardians* appeared and waited in the ring our neighbour in the crowd made caustic comments about the *tenue* of one of the riders, an elderly man, very smart in fawn cord trousers with a black ribbon down each side seam, velvet jacket, stock, and broad-brimmed black hat. There was good natured banter about amateur riders, then the bull appeared, and in spite of some clever dodging he was soon brought under control, the elderly rider showing superb mastery of his mount. 'He does very well, I forgive him of his hat,' said our neighbour generously.

In Arles and Nîmes, where the *bandidos* are a spectacle for the tourist, all the *gardians* are attired thus, in traditional dress of recent origin, the Marquis Folco de Baroncelli having been instrumental in realising the publicity value of such a dress to promote his beloved Fé de Biou, to the point where you could call it *folcolorique*.

But Aigues-Mortes *en fête* is concerned with amusing itself, not the outsiders. Tourists are welcome to come, but should keep out of the way. This is the local working man's sport, and it is the working man in his own environment who is playing, and wearing what he feels comfortable in.

The waiters from the Crèperie des Gardians were mixing business with pleasure, advertising their workplace on their black T-shirts, but wearing mohawk and punk wigs, and lots of sparkly eye make-up. During the half-hour injury time the youths had rebuilt the burning straw barrier. Two bulls leapt it well, but one of the trio of horses hesitated, missed a stride, and the bull was away in the gap so formed. The crowd was tight outside the gate but it parted, cheering wildly, to form a path in the direction the bull wished to go and within seconds it was dodging and weaving among the parked cars. The three riders had no chance of getting it back under control, especially as the local youths were compounding their problems. Each of these two bulls finally broke cover, dashed over the road and were once more into the agriculture among the darkling dust.

No matter. If the riders could not find them they could always follow the advice of that old Bayle *gardian* André Bouix: 'Let him run. You'll find him at the *manade* gate next morning waiting to be let in.'

On Friday, it was the *jour à l'ancienne*, lovely old carts and carriages were paraded round the arena with riders and passengers wearing appropriate turn of the century costumes, and ladies with uproarious bloomers rode ancient bicycles. On this day we had a band led by a hero of Aigues-Mortes.

Long ago before the war, back in the thirties, a few local lads got a band together and played for the pleasure of it at the Fête. Their fame spread to the next village, who requested their services. The band, formed only for the duration of the Fête, was faced with a challenge, and actually practised for a few days before doing that one, adding a sketch with comic *toreros*. They got better and more numerous, and were asked to perform at all the neighbouring arenas. A year later, their band-leader had to leave. There was an obvious successor, the cymbalist, a boy called André, but he was so young, only fifteen. They gave him the chance. His abilities as a natural performer, a comic, a musician, and a dancer, conquered all audiences. They acquired splendid uniforms, and added to their numbers a group of acrobats and clowns who specialised in bull work. Under the name of El Gallito, The Little Cock, they became famous throughout the Midi. The war interrupted the progress of the troupe, but after the Armistice they took up again with yet more verve and did a tour of Tunisia which clinched their success. Now as the troupe 'El Gallo', The Cock, they played everywhere.

Here they were at their hometown, in gorgeous uniforms, and at their head, smiling, whirling, dancing, top-hatted and silver-cloaked, encouraging his players with pirouettes and great gestures, was André Laboutière, a little portlier than he had been at fifteen years old, in 1935, but not a whit less lively. For once we went along with the

French passion for old performers. Besides, he was a son of Aigues-Mortes, one of the few whose fame has spread further than the Tour Carbonnière.

In times past, when the bulls were driven on the hoof to various *fêtes*, it was often necessary to swim them over rivers and canals. Now that they are generally taken to the edge of the village in a truck before being run through the streets for the *abrivado*, the practice of swimming the bulls has died out.

Except in Aigues-Mortes. Even here it takes place only a couple of times a year and when it does they make an event of it. The bulls are taken in a *char* to a spot on the country road to the north-east of the town on the other side of the old Canal du Bourgidou. Most of the population gather on the banks where barred metal crowd-control barriers have been erected across the road to help divert the bulls into the canal. The town band, or *peña*, is there, gaily dressed, often with straw boaters on their heads, playing lively hispanified tunes (Valencia again) with more enthusiasm than harmony. The *sapeurs-pompiers* are present in smart navy-blue overalls and big black army boots, with their first aid and resuscitation equipment in two red vans. The municipal police are *not* here, because it will take all nine of the Aigues-Mortais police force to stop the traffic on the road outside the ramparts as the bulls and horses sweep through.

Waiting on the south bank are the twenty or thirty mounted *gardians* who will try to herd the bulls after they have swum the canal. With them, and gathered for the express purpose of preventing them from doing so, are a larger number of youths and their more lively girlfriends, most of whom are in their 'gang chariots'. These are made from substantial old motor cars; the boot lids are removed and flat tops are welded on to the roofs of the vehicles, and also numerous strong handholds. Silencers are removed, so is most of the glass. The chariots are painted bright colours and carry the name of the *bande*, or gang, with the advertising slogans of the local shopkeepers who sponsor them, and who provide T-shirts for the gang. Each chariot is loaded with some fifteen or twenty young folk, who roar about the *fête* as if riding hideous dragons, rejoicing in a high profile and licence to commit minor misdemeanours, for at this time the mischief of youth is overlooked. One would think that these battered and noisy vehicles, which often have to be given a push start, contravene every known traffic law, but we were assured that they must all gather in front of the *mairie* for *contrôle* at the start of festivities. When we asked what the check was for, the authorities became a little vague.

Many of the youths and even more of their girlfriends were looking puffy-eyed and delicate. Some had arms and legs in casts. Some were finding the sun much too bright, and showed signs of imminent sleep; if they were at the *bal* till four in the morning, and up for breakfast in the meadows at nine o'clock, little wonder. There was an almost visible collective headache from last night's *pastis*.

From the canal bridge the waiting crowd could see the cattle truck and the knot of mounted *gardians* in the distance, about a kilometre away across the vineyards. Suddenly there was a shout and the crowd moved from gossip mode to positions in selected spots; some to watch the *gaze* where they would be protected from the bulls, others to a place where they could hinder the horses and tangle with the free-running bulls. Small children and dogs were called into safety while the four or five black bulls, surrounded by about twenty *gardians* galloped in a tight knot down towards the bridge of Le Bourgidou.

Last year the *gardians* launched the bulls into the canal without problems, only to have the bulls split into two groups part way across, one of which formed the *abrivado* and was herded by some of the waiting *gardians* towards the town, while the other group swam up the canal, selected their own landing and escaped into the nearby allotments where the remaining mounted *gardians* were severely

impeded in their attempts to catch them, not only by the
terrain, but also by the shouting youngsters, who left their
motos and gang-chariots and pursued through the cabbages on foot. The loose bulls ran round the suburb of Le
Bourgidou for about a half hour in all, to the delight of all
except the cursing *gardians*, the allotment holders, and one
or two worried boat owners.

This year the bulls and their escort approached the *gaze*
rather faster than last year, and the bulls, instead of making
a sharp left turn and finding themselves swimming, elected
to go straight ahead. Two leapt over the crowd control
barriers, scattering the spectators, while the foremost
escorting horses were caught wrong-footed and ended up
unable to jump, falling over the collapsing barriers with
their legs dangerously tangled in the bars. The remaining
bulls that had not jumped the barriers wheeled sharply
about and within seconds were pounding back the way
they had come at high speed. Followers of the party
jumped about in the road to impede the bulls which
promptly turned left into the vineyards. The bulls that had
leapt the barrier had had a choice of charging the crowd or
else taking to the adjoining asparagus field, and had opted
for vegetation rather than mayhem. The bulls were in two
groups about two hundred metres apart, and very sensibly
they immediately began to separate further into five
diverging escapees. The *gardians* were after them in a trice,
but these Camargue bulls are very fast bulls indeed, and it
was evident that, though they would not outrun a horse on
a level chase, the bulls had quicker reactions at close
quarters, and were benefiting by the impeding vines. The
bulls had sufficient start for the chase to be a long one.
Three were caught after about a kilometre, the others went
far away out of sight beyond the distant pine copse. After
some time they got the three back to the *char* and started all
over again with a smaller party of escorting riders (the rest
of them were still chasing the other two bulls).

This time they approached the *gaze* more slowly but at

the last minute lost control of the bulls altogether, help-lessly seeing them scatter once more in the vineyards. Helpful advice was offered by the crowd:

'Wrap the bulls in a parcel and put them in the post,' yelled one elderly enthusiast, and another added:

'Call out the CRS with their tear gas.' All round people were commenting:

'*Ça ne gaze pas.*' But the Aigues-Mortes accent is strong. It sounded like '*ça ne gazza pas.*' No, they would not swim.

There was a long wait. The *peña* struck up a paso doble. One of the waiting stallions developed amorous inclina-tions for a nearby mare, and all the photographers gathered round to take broadside pictures of the animal among considerable ribaldry, while the rider, a dignified respect-able gentleman in a hacking jacket tried hard to look as if nothing was happening.

Someone arrived to cut down a few reeds on the supposition that they had impeded or frightened the bulls. Unlikely. These bulls did not have the air of being easily worried by such flimsy things; it was clear to the waiting crowd that we had bulls here that did not relish swimming in October, and who could blame them, *pardi*? They no longer had the *habitude*. Someone offered the comment that to get bulls to *gazer* one had to drive them at the water at right angles. His overalls bore the name Listel, a local wine company; he looked as if he enjoyed drinking his work, and there was much agreement with him.

Then they had a third try. The television crew filming for the local tourist board settled into the ready position once more. The local youths put down their girlfriends. A full team of horsemen cantered at a fair speed, and this time they wheeled the bulls down the bank, the first bull entered the water and . . . turned round and leapt out again on the other side of the barrier where there were no *gardians*. He was instantly away into the vineyards. The other two bulls saw the first one up to his knees in the beastly water and put the brakes on hard, all forelegs out straight and carving deep grooves in the earth. The horses following behind cannoned into them on the steeply sloping bank. Horses started to fall, there was equine disorder and some near panic as the bulls ran back up the bank. One *gardian* got his horse between the bulls and the vineyards and the two bulls just pushed the horse bodily out of the way with their foreheads. A bull is more sure-footed on awkward terrain than a horse. All the same one had to admire the horsemanship and courage of some of the riders; it was a difficult and dangerous pastime.

Over the flat, sandy vineyards with their long lines of vines just turning now to reds and purples since the grapes had all been picked, one could see horsemen galloping up and down the straight rows. There were occasional glimpses of a black head raised as a bull had a look round, but in the main the bulls were below the tops of the vines. Though the rows are less than two metres apart the bulls could turn easily while the horses could not. It took ages to get them back to the cattle truck. One could imagine the cursing, the humiliation.

The *gaze* was abandoned. The bulls were herded together and taken along the road and over the bridge into the town. They seemed to be quite content to go that way; it is the normal thing after all. Most of the crowd had already gone. They could see an *abrivado* almost any time. It is *pas grande chose*. But to miss their *gaze*? that was *une autre chose*. We had expected most people to have enjoyed the humour and anarchy of a disintegrated organised event, but not the Aigues-Mortais. Bulls and the doing with them is on the edge of being a religion and the *gaze* is one of the sacraments. It should be properly done. One should not make a salad of it. They were still shaking their heads as we walked back to our boat.

Two or three days later a second *gaze* was scheduled, but the weather had turned and this time we had heavy rolling clouds coming up from the south-east. It had rained hard

during the night and the tracks were muddy and rutted.
The breakfast in the meadow was a special for the old folk of
the town (The Golden Age). They had been taken there in
two coaches which had had difficulty getting through the
mud, but now they were having a marvellous time with
music by the *Peña*, the whole excursion provided by the
town.

French towns are generous to both young and old: the
previous day's breakfast had been specially for the
children, with entertainment, and rides on horseback.

Across the intervening marsh the sound of the *peña*
wafted 'Valencia' on the south-east breeze while the crowd
collected. It was soon evident that the advice of the wine-
making gentleman had been taken. A track had been made
across the asparagus field, the roadway had been covered
with several inches of the sandy soil (presumably in the
hope of fooling the bulls), and the cattle truck had to fight
its way through the gathering crowd to get to an un-
accustomed road.

Two large coaches full of the old folk arrived from the *prés* and could not get through the crowd. They inched forward till they were near the front to the anger of those who had their view spoiled by the bulk of the buses. Having discharged their passengers the coaches tried to back out, failed, and then there was more backing and filling as the post office van tried to get through. He also failed. Delivery of letters in France is bad enough without the mail being further delayed by bulls. Willing hands helped the *facteur* on his way, his van detouring the jam by driving on the sloping bankside while strong men held it from slipping down the muddy bank into the canal.

At last, about twenty minutes late, not a lot for the Midi but enough to cause comment among a waiting crowd, the excitement increased and the riders came into view, more slowly than last time. But the changing of the angle did not have the desired effect. Whether these were the same bulls as last time (and it seems that some *manades* keep a few bulls who specialise in *abrivados* and *bandidos* and do little else) who had remembered, or whether they were particularly quick-witted animals we do not know, but as they approached the water they suspected something undesirable close ahead and slowed down in plenty of time. The riders had obviously rehearsed; behind the bulls there was a solid phalanx of horses, and the barriers had been braced. The bulls turned about. Two leading bulls charged the flanking horse with their heads low, long curved horns pointing forward, aiming for the unprotected underbelly of the horse; very dangerous. The horse reared in fright, and the two bulls ran under its raised fore-hooves. Not stopping to tangle with the horse, they single-mindedly kept their aim firmly in sight, and in seconds they were off into the vineyards.

The remaining bulls easily evaded and passed through the disorganised horses. We could see the four of them as they ran through the vines. Outriders had been posted on all sides of the vineyard this time, and as the bulls scattered we could see the riders manoeuvring for position, but they had little chance. The Camargue *gardians* do not rope their bulls. They claim to be able to control them by horsemanship aided by the use of the trident (a long staff with a crescent-shaped head), and they feel superior to the cowboys of the wild west who after all are comparatively new to the game, and suffer from not being French.

But they were slow to catch these bulls. Perhaps they are getting soft these days. After about a quarter of an hour they had re-captured two, and a dozen or so riders brought them to the canal and had another try with an equal lack of success. These bulls from Aubanel, the *manade* of the renowned and late Marquis de Baroncelli, down there by the mouth of the Petit Rhône, were determined not to swim.

That was the last try for this year. The gang chariots raced noisily round to the alternative route and the disappointed crowd dispersed. The television men put their gear away for the second time. At least they should have had some good footage on how not to run a *gaze*.

On the morning after the last day of the Fête, it was not surprising that the whole town smelt of *pastis*. Four thousand bottles had been delivered in preparation for the festivities, one for every man, woman and child in the town. They had run out at the end of the third day, and further supplies had had to be ordered. One of the fashions is for the rival gangs to thread their *pastis* bottle caps on a thong and make bandoliers of them. The biggest bandolier wins. Usually a gang is starting on its second bandolier by the third day. Aigues-Mortes' Fête Votive is to *pastis* what the Oktoberfests are to wine and beer in Bavaria.

There was a lot for M. Nicollin's men to sweep up, gathering together the drink tins and bottles, the greasy food wrappings, the empty cigarette packets, all the debris of Bacchanalia.

One of the men was going to have to climb up to the top

of St Louis' statue and fetch down the empty *pastis* bottle that stood within the circlet of his crown.

One might insert a few words about how to drink *pastis* if you are serious about it. Apart from the big companies like Ricard, who sponsor most of the bull-worship, there are many small private distillers who are to the trade what the great marks of Cognac are to brandy. Their product is artisanal. You do not *jouer avec*. It is serious. It is usually drunk with water which turns it into the milky fluid that everyone knows. What we were astonished to learn from a distiller who is also an analytical chemist by profession is that the oils in the roots that provide the aniseed flavour change their chemical composition when reduced to freezing point and that this affects their taste. One should never put ice in the *pastis*; but it is not dangerous to use cold water. Above freezing point, that is.

Except when the bulls came by, the peninsula at Le Bourgidou stood largely aloof from the Fête and got on with its business preparing for winter. Mario continued to lay his finger along his nose and boast of his huge new boat. We unearthed our *petite laines*, our little woollies, and by the third week in October we began to light the wood stove in the evening. The two cats had settled in well, we called the velvet one Blue, and the little tiger Tansy. The flicker of firelight caused them great fascination, and they investigated with caution. It was apparent that Blue led in everything. She had already fallen in the canal at least three times, and returned dripping to the Master's chair. Tansy fell in only once. A much more cautious cat, she never did it again.

Francine was knocking on the door with urgency. She was in great distress. 'It is Nicholas. He is in the hospital at Nice. I must go to him. I am sorry I cannot get your bread today.' We sat her down and listened with sympathy to the story. Nicholas, ever accident prone, had been frying chips, and somehow the pan of hot oil had overset. He had serious burns to his feet.

Francine spent a week at Nice, returned, and then spent another week away. On her second return she looked tired, but a little less distraught. Nicholas was in less pain, she told us. The doctors were considering skin grafting. The *petite amie* was useless, and probably to blame for the whole thing. We continued to make sympathetic noises for the next few weeks, Francine brought an almost daily bulletin with our bread, and liked to talk to our cats.

As the month ended, the leaves on the plane trees turned bronze-gold, and the chrysanthemums arrived for Toussaint (All Saints). We mused on the fact that Toussaint is a holiday in France, but nothing happens on All Souls, what we and the Americans call Hallowe'en. There were no witches' hats or pumpkin lanterns in Mme Poitavin's window; at the moment it was full of marzipan mushrooms, stuffed squirrels, and chestnuts and autumn foliage.

Yet there is so much magic in the Camargue. Not so long ago the wilder parts were a refuge for a few recluses and eccentrics of both sexes, some of whom knew herbal medicine, and got the name of Brèishe (sorcerer) or Brèisha (witch). They were also known as Masc, or Masca. There are still places called the Field of the Masc, notably at nearby Montpellier, not far from the ancient herb garden still in existence, which was probably the domain of magic and healing long before the medical school (one of the earliest in Western Europe) was founded there in the twelfth century. Spells and bewitchery were knitted into the fabric of a hard life, when some events seemed otherwise inexplicable, or blame needed to be transferred, or magic invoked. From healing to love potions is but a small step.

Here is an infallible mixture seven hundred years old.

> Eight kinds of corn I put in it
> And grease from a broody sparrow,

A pigeon's right kidney
And liver of hedgehog;
From the coq du mars the hind quarter,
Some dough from the bread shovel,
A herb named Satorna,
Reeds picked in Maytime,
And the heart of a beetle.
Strictly fasting I mix it all and pound it,
Conjuring as Na Bril taught me,
Na Bril who gave me this counsel.
Who eats of this cake is deeply wounded
By a bolt of love, more surely
Than if he had been
Pierced by a lance.

So cunning they were, the Mascs. Young girls were taught
to cross their thighs and hold down their skirts against the
vent follet, a little whirlwind swirling up spirals of dust and
leaves near the ground; what were they but the lascivious
Masc in disguise, trying to get under their aprons and up to
no good? In Marsillargues just up the road the little girls
were encouraged to throw pebbles to make it go away. To
no avail, uncountable women were impregnated by these
salacious little whirlwinds.

Nevertheless the counsel of such as Na Bril was invalu-
able. At least it kept alive a spark of hope, or gave you,
otherwise impotent, a sweet taste of vengeance.

They told you how to relieve a fever; you sat with your
back against a peach tree. You recovered, the tree took your
illness and withered and died.

For a fee they would bewitch your enemies, by means of
a *coquèl*. This was a tight ball of feathers, regularly placed,
all of the same colour. If you tried to open it by pulling both
ends, it snapped back when released. Inside it was a scrap
of rough cloth, like jute, and the feathers that folded over it,
fitted one another like the plumage of a bird. This was
always found in the pillow or eiderdown of the bewitched.

'There were lumps in our bed,' said the father of a bewitched girl not that long ago, 'but in our daughter's you could have called them clumps – there was even a magnificent rat, with a tail and all made with feathers, and hard!' They also came in the shape of birds, or coffins, according to the effect required by the Brèishe. His work was hard to destroy.

'They made a big heap there were so many. It took my father-in-law all morning to burn them, and fifty litres of diesel, they wouldn't burn, just cracked and shrivelled but stayed intact. They looked like a ball of charcoal. In the end they began to disappear.'

It was to avoid such objects being smuggled into their houses that the people hereabouts fixed a *corne de sorcière*, a witch-horn, to the corner roof tiles, just as the Chinese do to discourage evil spirits. In both the Orient and Occitan it seems, demons and mascs had the same recreation, toboganning down rooftops. The witch-horn propelled them (such was the hope) at full speed away from habitation.

The wreath of fresh flowers we had often seen on the door of newly built houses is a relic of the '*charmes*' that were once placed there to avoid sorcery.

We discovered a Provençal roof prowler far more delightful than witches or Mascs, called the Dahu. This was half bird and half cat, clad with both fur and feathers, and its legs on one side were shorter than the other, the better to cope with sloping roofs. In order to capture it you had only to make it turn round and go the wrong way. It then fell over and was easily caught in a gunny sack. The Dahu, with its built-in limp, appealed to Laurel far more than all the other odd creatures we had met coming down the Rhône and into the region. Not the river dwellers – the dragon-like Tarasque and Drac – nor the lizard Lerts, not those haunters of tombstones in Arles – the Oulourgues – nor even the Black Rabbit of the Camargue, took her fancy half so much as the Dahu.

As for the fairies – *encantadas, sarrasins, fadas,* give them what name you would – every fountain, river or grotto from the Alps to the Pyrenees seemed to have its Lavandières, or fairy washerwomen, busy beating their linen on the stones with golden beaters. Webbed feet they had, and they left prints like geese, and hung their sheets to dry in the grass or the hedgerows till dawn. Like the brownies of old England they would do a spot of housework for you now and then, coming through the keyhole. To discourage them, since they were capricious and mischievous, contributing greatly to the servant problem, you poured lentils on the kitchen floor and then left the broom outside. The frustrated fairy, unable to lug the broom through the keyhole, would suffer a fit of the vapours, and disappear with cries of rage.

So on the last day of October we saw sheets of delicate spiderwebs spread over the reeds and grasses on the canal bank. Those golden beaters had not done the fairy linen any good. The webs were full of holes.

16

A time to remember

'Per Toussant
Nèu pels champs
E ravas suls bancs.'
. . . .
'All Saints day
Snow on the lea
Roots put to dry.'

Toussaint, November 1st, All Saints. What a pity the Protestant Church has created no saints since the Reformation. Thus the image of a saint for us is pre-Tudor, we think of early Tuscan paintings, or the Flemish School, or the Book of Kells. Decorative, beautiful, majestic, but unreal. Since the inventions of Daguerre and Fox-Talbot the Catholic Church have photographs of their saints.

It must be wonderfully comforting to have a saint in the family, a great-uncle perhaps, with a sepia photograph of him on the mantelpiece in a stiff collar, standing on a Turkey carpet.

In our family we have to make do with an undoubtedly sainted aunt, who will never be canonised.

We have a cluster of family birthdays around now, so it is a festive season, coinciding in England with Bonfire Night and half-term, and in France with Toussaint and Remembrance Day. Who could possibly struggle all the way from *la rentrée* at the end of August to Noël, December 25th, without a break?

For two weeks the alleys in the supermarkets had been narrowed by pots of chrysanthemums, smelling of wet dog and causing trolley jams as two impatient shoppers clashed knuckles trying to pass each other. The market was full of chrysanthemums. All these pots were bound for the cemetery, since it is the custom to deck the graves at Toussaint. The chrysanthemum was in season, indeed it had been nurtured for this festival, just as the *muguets* are for the first of May. The form of the flower varied from a small tight button to a huge mophead, from loosely petalled and daisy-like to a tightly curled fierce looking thing that looked as if it could double as a cricket ball. The best colours were the whites and yellows, since it seems that when a chrysanthemum opts for the red shift it loses all sense of taste and dignity, and blossoms forth in unpleasant shades of rust and blood, drunkard's nose, heart attack puce, and gut pink. Laurel has no love at all for chrysanthemums, even before she knew of their inseparable link with the tombs of Toussaint. 'I wish there was a corner in the cemetery where you could put flowers for the absent dead, those who are not buried here,' she said.

'Who needs a cemetery?' said Bill. 'If you bury me at sea, all you'll have to do is chuck a few dandelions in the village pond, anywhere.' Universal remembrance is the thing. So we bought red roses, and put them on the table in the saloon and enjoyed them for the birthdays, and remembered our dead as they would have wished.

Since we passed the cemetery almost daily on our way into town, we observed the relentless march of flowers to the tombs, a trickle became a stream, a stream became a flood. In the last few days of October the cemetery car park was taken over by flower sellers, and all pots ended up in the boneyard. Old ladies staggered across the road with two large pots clasped to their chests, the flower heads nodding like old sheep dogs. Tartan shopping trolleys with ragged leaves peeping over the top gave a better chance of seeing where you were going. Bicycles arrived loaded with four pots. If it was a six pot family, it had to be the boot of the car, but *tiens*! the park was taken up by stallholders and flower pots, *peuchère*, so you parked in the road. We drove past the cemetery with extreme caution at slow speed, avoiding wobbly bicycles, children unable to see through the foliage of the plant they were carrying, and grown-ups stepping back from their car boot without looking, arms full of pots.

Just one florist in Aigues-Mortes sells 3,000 pots of chrysanthemums between 29th October and 1st November at between fifty and seventy francs a pot. Many more are sold in the supermarkets, open air market stalls, and the garden centre. The radio and newspapers will tell us, afterwards, how many millions were sold in the whole of France. It is big business. Then suddenly it was over, all pots of chrysanthemums had reached their destination, and the road past the cemetery was again as quiet as the grave.

A spell of really determined building work got the starboard side of the saloon finished and the cupboards painted out and usable by the end of the first week in November. We were keen to have a civilised birthday party, so a good deal of stowing away, cleaning and curtain hanging went on, with the cats exploring new and interesting places, and getting shut under the floorboards or in the new cupboards in moments of inattention. We went round the boat community at Grau-du-Roi and Port Camargue, issuing invitations, and lending the car where necessary as it would be a long bike ride after a celebration. When the day came lunch went on till after tea time, so it must have been a good party.

When we had made our voyage southward through the French canals we were still some distance from the warm south when the cold weather set in, and it can be very cold in central France, even in October. We had purchased our firewood and coal briquettes way up north in Picardy, where they are well-geared to the winter fuel trade. Every house up there has its own enormous pile of drying logs,

and it was simple to buy a ton or two and stack them on our deck to bring south with us. We even had some left over after our arrival in the Midi.

There is some conspiracy down here among the Provençals to persuade themselves that it does not get cold in winter. Or perhaps they have been trying to convince tourists for so long that they have come to believe it themselves. They are perpetually astonished when it happens, and discuss it in the market in tones ranging from pique to mortal insult. It is necessary to state quite clearly that there are cold days in winter. It is as simple as that. The Canal du Rhône a Sète occasionally freezes over to give people something to talk about for the next few years. One can wake to find that metal surfaces, such as car roofs and steel decks are covered with frost, and there are delicate patterns of icy lace among the reeds. Just like Norfolk. Except that in Norfolk it happens often, while in the Midi it happens occasionally, usually when there is a big anti-cyclone over Scotland which sucks polar air down all the way to the Mediterranean. The sun shines. The sky is brilliantly blue. But it is cold, and if the mistral is there to blow the cold right through your spine it can be worse than the raw, sodden cold of Norfolk.

The Camargue Calendar says that in December the Camarguais starts to think about wood for the stove. Rubbish. This year we had to start earlier than that. So we set out to buy our logs. Last winter we shared a load of holly logs with Boubou who had located a source inland. But this year he had sensibly loaded his barge with bargain logs further north during his summer cruise, and did not need any more. He graciously tried his former source but without success. None were available. There are no log merchants in the vicinity. There is no coal in the South of France. It is not cold down there, there is no need of coal. The centre and north of France are covered in forests, the like of which scarcely exist any more in England (France, remember, has nearly three times the area of Britain for the

same number of people) and it is possible to heat the
northern population without noticeably depleting the
acreage.

Not so in the Camargue. In this flat waterscape a large
tree of any kind is a comparative rarity. There are a few
umbrella pines along the canal, and a local farm nestles in a
small group of pine trees, calling itself the Mas de la Pinède
(Pinecopse Farm). Apart from these few remnants of
former widespread pine woods and a few clumps of
spindly alders and willow by the banks of the two Rhônes
there is only scrub and tamarisks, except for the majestic
plane trees that grace the ramparts of Aigues-Mortes and
shade the marketplace, the Piste de Boules, and the Place St
Louis. The Mayor would be unhappy if these were
chopped down for fuel.

So one must go further afield for wood; there are no log
merchants until you are north of Nîmes, and they have
only scrub oak and myrtle from the Garrigue. What do the
local folk burn? There are always old vines that are being
uprooted, and one sees tractors towing cartloads of these to
various houses in the neighbourhood, where their twisted
shapes make stacking difficult. None were available when
we wanted them. Even Serge of the Mas Rancier had none
left. We faced the fact that there is not enough to go round
the local residents. We would have to look further afield.

It was the first Tuesday in the month. It was cold and
sunny, and we were on our way to Clermont l'Herault to
see the making of the *oreillettes*. Bill had been lukewarm,
but as it was a beautiful day for a drive he had not found
sufficient arguments against the trip, and contented himself with explosive grumbling as we skirted Montpellier
and lost our way, as we always did.

'WHY is it,' he demanded of deaf gods, 'that wherever
we want to go, Montpellier is always in the WAY?'
Montpellier is a sprawling city, easy to get lost in. The
signposts seemed only to direct us to where we did not

want to go, geometrical spaces dedicated to commerce such as Le Polygon, or L'Antigon, or places that we had just passed; and the street Laurel thought would retrieve her mistake (it is always her mistake) was one way, against us. It is one of those cities. It is a city without a ring road, like many French cities, due to an avaricious council years ago who thought the city would prosper if everyone had to pass through the centre (cf. Lyon). They now pay the price, in coinage of outrageous disruption.

When we finally spun away from the city into the country, on the correct westbound road, our tempers cooled, and we began to enjoy our day out. Wispy clouds flew in tatters in the piercingly blue sky, presaging bad weather to come, but not, we thought, till tomorrow. We left the barren rock and scrub oak of the Garrigues behind, and moved into gentler country. The plane trees that shade the roads in summer were still full of leaf, blazing gold in the sunshine, and cast the long shadows of autumn across the road and into the patchwork of vineyards; squares of red and gold and purple, a few desiccated black grapes hung at the field corners where the *vendangeurs* had missed them.

As the road climbed towards the foothills (Clermont is at the very western edge of the Cévennes Mountains) we drove through forests, and villages became scarce. We had hoped we might find a man to sell us some badly needed logs later in the day, as we knew Clermont l'Herault to be in the foothills, and therefore on the edge of the real forests. We had an estate car, why should we not buy some logs to take back?

After Gignac our road peeled off into a ring of hills, and there in a hollow was Clermont. Hoardings by the roadside told us that there were at least three supermarkets, an Industrial Estate, a *gendarmerie*, and the gothic church of St Paul. Laurel was dismayed. She had pictured a tiny village where everyone would know everyone else's business. Now she had only vague directions. ('Opposite the *mercerie*!' scoffed the navigator. 'How will we ever find *that*?')

He had reason, as it was already noon, in a town of some six thousand people as we found later; but Laurel tends to be lucky, determined, or both.

We headed for the church square, which turned out also to be the marketplace. A power cable snaked out of the church door, keeping the fish stall cool. The *lycéens*, the high school kids, were on strike, parading with banners. It all seemed very normal.

We went into the nearest baker's and asked for the *foyer* of the ladies who make the *oreillettes*. We were taken gently by the hand and shown the building that backed on to the church, fifty metres away. '*Voilà*! It is there, madame and monsieur, opposite the *mercerie*.' Just as we had been told. In confirmation, at that moment Laurel recognised Mme F., whom we had met on the *Isles de Stel*, walking in the street, and leaped upon her. She peered at us short-sightedly for a moment, then broke into a beaming smile, and walked us down the steep narrow street to the ancient door of the *foyer*, begging us to mind the traffic; and pointing out that nothing happened now till half past two. A hand-written notice hanging from a nail on a blue ribbon confirmed that *oreillettes* would be sold that afternoon in aid of lepers.

We climbed back to the square with Mme F., again concerned that we should not be '*voituré*' by the cars who left little room for pedestrians in the ancient lanes, and as the fishmonger packed away his ice boxes and hosed down his stall we went off to look for some lunch.

We found a small restaurant which served potiron soup, memorable for its lovely rose-gold colour. We ate grilled trout and apple tart, and with a carafe of wine included we paid fifty francs each. British restaurants please copy.

On our return to the *foyer* at two-thirty we found the door ajar and peered into an infernal atmosphere thick with the fumes of hot arachide oil. Little Mme P. greeted us and all but dragged us inside, delighted that we had taken up the invitation. We were in what seemed to be a crypt, under the presbytery probably, as the building backed onto, and was below the level of the church. It was a room with a low vaulted ceiling and an arched window at the far end. Silhouetted against this ancient light and wreathed in hellish fumes, a minute amount of which was whistling out through the open window, fifteen crones were hard at work.

Trestle tables stood along the side walls, covered with clean cloths. Across the end wall, which was tiled to head height, was a work top on which burned four enormous gas rings. Each of these had its guardian, watching over her pan of boiling oil, and one of these was Mme Gineste, the organiser of the whole affair, so we fought our way through the miasma to the dim demonic figures at the back to pay her our respects. Vision improved as we got nearer, and the crouching crones became perfectly nice Frenchwomen with aprons over their cardigans, and Charentaise slippers on their feet.

Our credentials established, a lady with grey curls and a sunny smile showed us a laundry basket full of dough wrapped in a clean cloth, which reposed on a table at the beginning of the assembly line. The whole basket was wrapped in a huge woollen blanket of colourfully striped squares, the sort of thing that worthy ladies knit from oddments to keep refugees in Africa warm, but which had found a useful and no less worthy purpose rather nearer to home.

The *pâte* was the work of this morning. 'Three of us go to the baker who lends us his mixing machine. We put in twelve kilos of flour, ninety-six eggs, one and a half kilos of butter, and mix the *pâte*. Of course you add a little *citron*, and some orangeflower water to perfume the whole. Then it must repose for at least five hours.' All the mixing had to be finished by ten-o-clock in the morning so that the work of rolling out and frying could start at two-thirty.

Bill left at this point, desperate for some fresh air, and

sought the nearest café. Laurel stayed, fascinated by the purposeful logic of it all. Next to the dough in line came the apportioner. She rolled the dough into a cylinder, cut it into sections, and flattened the sections into rounds, saying that it was important to do this with the cylinder on end. A small girl then helped her lay the rounds in orderly fashion on the clean cloth. She dropped one on the tiled floor and put it back on the table, unreprimanded. Any germs adhering would doubtless succumb to the Power of the Lord and boiling oil.

Eight ladies with rollers manned the remaining trestles, the four on the right-hand side aurioled with the Society's device, painted on the wall behind them: '*Aimer – Partager – Servir*' ('Love – Share – Serve'). Armed with rolling pins of magnificent antiquity, patinaed tobacco brown with years of buttery service, they rolled out the rounds as far as possible, and then continued to stretch the paste between their fingers until it was paper-thin and the size of a plate, and fell in folds as it was placed over the front edge of the table, always on the white cloth.

The demon fryers then fried them in hot oil, one at a time, where they puffed and crinkled delightfully in an instant into delicate lacy wafers. When golden, they were removed and baptised with powdered sugar, stacked in fives on cardboard circles, enveloped in pretty paper and a ribbon to finish, and sold for thirty francs a packet. People were arriving to buy them.

'It is *aide directe*.' M. Gallego, the President of the Society had arrived to cheer the ladies on. He was kneeling beside Laurel's chair to look at her drawing, probably knowing that the atmosphere was more breathable at that level. 'We know to whom the money goes – the Sisters of Cluny, in Madagascar, for instance, or the Benedictines in Benin. We send them medicines, food, clothing, and money. And we know how the money is spent; on a clinic, for example, or a weaving shed.'

The founder of the Society of St Vincent de Paul, Frédéric Ozanam, wrote:

'The question which divides men nowadays is no longer a political one, it is social; we must know who is driven by a spirit of egoism and who by self sacrifice. We must know if society is to be more than a grand exploitation of profit by the strongest, or the consecration of each for the good of all and the protection of the weak. There are many men who have much and want more; there are far more of them who have not enough: who have nothing and will take what is not given to them. Between these two classes a war is in preparation which will be terrible; on one side the power of money, on the other the power of despair. Between these hostile armies we must intervene, if not to prevent, at least to cushion the shock.'

He was twenty years old. The year was 1833.

We noticed as we left the *foyer* with smarting eyes and our packet of *oreillettes* that the notice hanging by a blue ribbon on the door ended: 'Bundles can be taken in Mondays and Wednesdays between 10 and 12. Please do not leave anything for the poor on the doorstep.' A little too much *aide directe* on the part of the poor, we supposed.

Now in the late afternoon we had time to search out the elusive firewood. Logs are measured in France by the *stère*. Whatever its original medieval size this is now taken to be a cubic metre, and as an aid to assessment all logs are first cut to a metre's length. We folded the rear seat and prepared a space, then made enquiries around the village cafés for a *marchand de bois de chauffage*. It became apparent that our enterprise would not be rewarded.

'Yes, there is François, but he is up in the forest, or out *en livraison*, delivering.' We were ignorant of the organisation of this trade. Quite why we vaguely expected to find a yardful of a variety of logs: oak, fruitwood, birch, pine, and a bargain basement of brashings with a *responsable* at the cash desk where we could load the car as one does with plants at a garden centre, we are not clear. Now we know that logging is a low cost operation; you need only muscles, a chain saw, an old lorry for deliveries, and grandma or an ansaphone. The loggers spend their summers in the forests cutting up the trees and stacking the logs to dry. They do not bring them back to some depôt, which would cost them painful money and time. When a client wants logs the logger goes off to the forest, loads up with the required amount recut to the required size (if a metre is too big) and effects his delivery. He is never at home in working hours, and he has no convenient stock of logs ready to hand to sell retail. We went home empty-booted.

We would, alas, have to try and telephone our order. Why, you might ask, do we have a telephone if we are reluctant to use it? Because we like to call our folks back home, which is convenient and nowadays not much more expensive than a letter, and you have the satisfaction of knowing immediately that any message has been received, which is certainly not the case with the post. We both speak tolerable French and get on quite well socially, but we live in fear of the French telephone.

This is no longer dominated by the dragon operator, barking '*Ne quittez pas!*' every few seconds in a voice like a sergeant-major, and one is left to one's own devices to get through on the automatic system. Of course the French have ringing, engaged and unavailable tones different to the rest of the world and unfamiliar to us, but then they would, would they not? They also have a disconcerting warbling noise which takes a bit of getting used to, telling you your call is going through the electronic mincer on its way to its destination. But the present-day French telephone system is very efficient, except for the call-boxes; and these are an international problem.

The difficulty is ours. Trying to talk to a Frenchman on the phone, one finds that he no longer speaks the same sort of French as he does when you are face to face. He too has more difficulty understanding us. Neither speaks clearly; we all mumble and drop the endings of words, slur words together, and interject meaningless connecting hesitation noises. Like 'Well, I mean', or '*Bon ben alors*', which is unspellable and untranslatable. When face to face speech is assisted by facial expression and body language.

The Italians are considered to be corporeally eloquent, but compared to the French they are primitive in their movements and gestures. A French peasant can put more meaning into the twitch of a shoulder muscle than Winston Churchill could get into a half hour oration. If the said peasant also has a half-consumed *gauloise* between his lips to amplify his every muscular action then he is any poet's equal. We watched a Frenchman making a call in the glass-sided call-box in the Place St Louis; he was not only making most eloquent gestures with shoulders, head and his disengaged arm and fingers, but he was also waving the telephone instrument itself about as he spoke. It is an old joke that a Frenchman with his hands tied behind his back would have an impediment in his speech. It is true.

And we, for our part, notwithstanding a fiercely Anglo-Saxon demeanour, wave our hands about when we speak French. Apart from knocking over wine glasses at the table, we can be seen semaphoring our choice of produce at the market stall with even more energy than the natives, for our vocabulary occasionally falls short of our requirements, something that never seems to happen to the French. So our telephone listener cannot be relied on to understand us. Especially if he is a stranger and is apparently faced with a call from a Swiss parrot that cannot pronounce the letter R.

No remedy, we had to brave the telephone. Laurel's French is better than Bill's. Also he is the more convincing coward, and can usually find some urgent physical task. 'Look,' he wheedles, 'either of us can phone, but only I can lift the boom, or tweak the frazzentossle, or bring in the wood (what wood?) so it makes sense if you do the telephoning while I do the labouring.' Laurel falls for it, every time.

There are no nearby log merchants in the yellow pages. Boubou (who is not a native Camarguais) says this is because they cannot read, logging not being an occupation noted for its intellectual requirements. So we have to look for a free local newspaper of which there are two. One, called by the self-congratulatory name of *Top Hebdo*, gives a weekly service to the Gard department, while the neighbouring Hérault department boasts the *Hérault Tribune* (who said the French have no sense of humour?)

Laurel ran down only two merchants within fifty kilometres and was greeted by an ansaphone both times, but one of them did have a sensible message: there is nobody about during the day; try again in the evening. It seemed we had run into the same problem as before; they are all out logging or delivering.

In the evening we managed to place our order. Because

we are a long way from the trees there would be an extra delivery charge (not unreasonable) and a minimum quantity for delivery. We ordered five *stères*, rather more than we had intended, but never mind, this was the only supplier. It was Hobson's choice.

The logs arrived promptly, good oak and beech, and about a year since cutting. Admiring local residents gathered round the merchant before he could drive away and besieged him with orders for themselves and we felt a little resentful. If we could have shared a delivery it would have been cheaper. And it was we who had found him, and on the telephone too; quite a complicated bit of negotiation what with size, type, dryness, and delivery charges, so we felt a bit superior. We will have to watch that, it comes too easily to East Anglians.

It remained only to stack this large load of logs in a long low line, some four feet high, arranged so the dry mistral wind would blow through it. The cats revelled in the whole procedure, digging where the lorry wheels had turned up the soft earth, and sharpening their claws on the logs, skittering off when the unbalanced piles tumbled. Stacking was hard work, and not made any easier by the fact that our order of 30cm logs had turned out to be of all sizes from 20 to 50. Boubou, passing in his car paused to observe Bill with his small logs. 'Ah! the *coupe anglaise*: it is good but always more expensive.' Bill did not know what he meant. Laurel, annoyingly, did. She gets a bit insupportable sometimes. Boubou was referring to the fact that English tailoring (the 'English Cut') is much admired in France and costs a lot. Bill does not concern himself with French tailors; he calls them makers of loose covers.

Remembrance Day came. Aigues-Mortes has an unusual war memorial, in fact the only one of its type we have seen, and Laurel makes a study of them. Generally the French war memorial is either a simple and dignified obelisk or else an ornate and complicated affair, figuring exhausted soldiers under assault by belligerent angels. Others have soldiers in various poses indicating anguish with or without flags in stone or bronze. The memorial at Aigues-Mortes is an obelisk, surmounted by a very young soldier apparently waiting nonchalantly for a bus; it is near the Courriers du Midi bus-stop, but there are not many buses.

On November 11th at eleven a.m., the ceremony took place, since the French did not sell out the remembrance of their war heroes, as we did in 1946, to some convenient weekend imposed on us by a government of pacifist politicians who fought only amongst themselves. The area round the cenotaph was hung with tricolours and the crowd had started to gather early, some with wreaths which they placed at the foot of the monument. The new Mayor had turned what had been a dusty parade ground into a pleasant little park, with lawns and trees, flower beds and benches. The leaves had been swept up and a guard of honour had arrived from a nearby naval base under the command of a Warrant Officer and fell in facing south across the square by the end of the *boules* pitch. A very old man shuffled up and talked both to us and to the Warrant Officer who was a model of courtesy; the old man was one of the two surviving inhabitants who fought in the First World War. Now very deaf and arthritic, he was fitter than his centenarian comrade who was confined to bed. But he was proud. The first war means so much more to the French in terms of casualties, for the slaughter then was atrocious whereas, in the second, France was mainly out of the fighting after a few months, especially in the South, and this is reflected by the awesome number of names of those Aigues-Mortais who were killed in the First World War, over 130 out of a population, then, of less than 3,000, compared with the handful for the Second. For the latter many of the names are of those who were deported for forced labour and never seen again.

A small procession emerged from the Porte de la Gardette and marched across, the Mayor in his tricolour

sash and flanked by two Old Comrades' silken banners held high. All were smartly dressed in dark suits. They marched slowly and with dignity to the Cenotaph. Bouquets of flowers were placed and the banners lowered as the last post was sounded, a different call to the one we are used to, but hauntingly reminiscent all the same. We gathered round and heard three homilies, all very much longer than a British crowd would tolerate, but the French are accustomed to and accept longer speeches on these occasions. Perhaps because the weather is better and there is bright sunshine to stand under, not the rainswept umbrellas that recall Remembrance Day in England. The main homily on the virtues of comradeship, patriotism and courage was not a banal, maudlin affair; far from it, it was dignified and seemed to us to be beautiful prose, and the veteran who gave it was clear and firmly voiced. The guard of honour then saluted and rested on their arms reversed, carrying out their rifle drill in that slightly embarrassed way that sailors always seem to have, as if saying that this is what soldiers are supposed to do – we are supposed to be at sea. Then the band played the 'Marseillaise'. How fortunate the French are to have such a good and singable national anthem that everyone can really join in. It was the same band we have in the bullring, though a bit depleted and wearing scruffy clothes not reflecting the smartness of the rest of the company. We wonder if it is part of a plot to get the Municipality to pay for uniforms. The Mayor invited all relatives present to partake of a *verre d'amitié* in the *mairie*, and after a moment's hesitation we decided to accept. With one father wounded on the Somme, and the other with three ships sunk under him, at Crete, Tobruk and D-Day, we felt we had the right. We all followed the band who were playing a military march and went to have an *apéritif* in the town hall. There was whisky, gin and *pastis*, and orange juice and mineral water. Not a sign of Listel wines, or the Vin des Sables. The veterans liked their liquor strong, or not at all. One that we spoke to had been a prisoner in Germany all the war. He had wisely opted for agriculture and been well treated. On farms there was usually something to eat, he said, but he was unused to the cold, so they had given him a pair of fur-lined boots.

The feature we most missed in the ceremony, compared with Britain, was a religious service, or at least a chaplain to say a few prayers. The French constitution forbids any religious element in state occasions. The British have them all there, not excluding ministers of the umpteenth church of holy mushroom eaters – the French will have none of them. Nor do they have the poppy as a symbol. We missed that too, but were much cheered to see one in the lapel of a French newsreader on television.

17

Wild mushrooms and
wilder grammar

'A San Martin
Uyo tei bouto e tapo toun vin.'
. . . .
'On the feast of Saint Martin
Cask your wine and cork it in.'

The market was coming up mushrooms. Every time we went there were tempting boxes of wild mushrooms, some of them were varieties new to us, and a few were very expensive. We decided we ought to be more adventurous, and eat as many kinds as we could. Armed with two mushroom books, one English and one French, we started with *cèpes*. We bought two of the many varieties of *cèpes*, *tête de negre* and *cèpe de Bordeaux*; we found they took some cleaning, but were delicious with chicken and in omelettes.

We tried *pleurotes*, a beautiful dove grey, and clean, as they are beginning to be cultivated, but found them dull, with a rubbery texture.

The terrifyingly named *trompettes des morts* – the 'trumpets of the dead' – which in England have the nicer name of 'horns of plenty', are delicious on toast. They looked like black foxgloves and have a seaweedy texture.

We then tried *pieds de moutons*, the 'wood hedgehog' in our English book, which accused it of having a bitter flavour. They were a pretty gold colour, hard to clean but we found them delicious. There are many *lactaires*, the one we tried was the 'saffron milk cap', and had probably the mildest flavour of all. The egg yellow *chanterelle* we had tried before, and found tough, but very good. It needs long slow cooking.

The prize mushroom, the *amanite des caesars*, or *oronge*, was too expensive. We ate it once on the Côte d'Azur; it was excellent. *Morels* do not appear in our market, but we usually have a supply of dried ones. Including the usual *champignons de Paris*, that added up to ten varieties and we felt that we had sufficiently advanced the frontiers of our knowledge for this year.

Truffles do not appear in our market either, they grow much further up country. Tinned ones have recently suffered a crisis of confidence, as in an atmosphere of shock horror that would only be equalled by the discovery that the Crown Jewels are paste, a merchant truffler has been convicted of tinning inferior truffles dyed black. The comparison is apt, as the truffle is known as the black diamond and costs Tiffany-money.

Everyone in France knows where to pick wild mushrooms, except us. Obviously no one is going to tell us their secret mushroom corner, or only vaguely. 'In the *pinède*,' they say (there are hundreds). 'After rain, on a west facing slope. Or try up in the mountains. You will certainly find the "twisted elf's foot", and the mushroom of form unmentionable.' The mountains are a long way away and it does not help matters that the local names for these mushrooms change from village to village. We were never lucky. Laurel had been looking forward to taking a basket of assorted wild mushrooms to M. Delord the pharmacist, as is the custom, and having him weed out the poisonous ones and tell her about the others. Empty-handed, an unsuccessful mushroom hunter, she talked to him nevertheless.

'Round Aigues-Mortes,' said M. Delord, 'you should find the *rosé des prés*, or field mushroom, the *grisette*, the *helvelle*, the *pivé* as they call it here: that is the *pholiote des peupliers*. The *pied bleu*, and several kinds of *cèpes*, one of which, ' he said comfortingly, 'you must peel very carefully, as the skin is *très laxatif*. Then there are the *morilles*, but only in spring.'

Our English mushroom book is lukewarm about some of these, and does not list others. The helvella is marked not edible, but the text goes on confusingly to say that it must never be eaten without thorough cooking. M. Delord again: 'Comestible does not mean it is good. Only that it will not make you ill!' The English book does not list the *pied bleu* (rhodopaxillus nudus), is dismissive about *pholiotes*, and thinks little of *trompettes des morts* because of the texture, and suggests that they are best dried and used for flavouring. In France naughty *charcutiers* use them to mimic truffles in their *pâtés*.

It was not lack of mushrooms that caused anguish to our American friends at Port Camargue, celebrating Thanksgiving among themselves: half a dozen Cousins a long way from Mother, God, and Apple Pie. Pumpkins were plentiful, so were chestnuts for the stuffing, but they had been unable to track down a whole turkey, as it was too early for the Christmas birds. With commendable ingenuity they had bought the pieces which were available, a couple of matched but opposing turkey legs and thighs, two wings, and a breast, and they had patiently sewn the limbs all together round a good sticky stuffing, and made themselves a patchwork turkey, worthy of their pioneer ancestors.

Thunderstorms and squalls late in November had blown away most of the leaves on the plane trees. Many trees, such as aspen and poplars, had been bare and wintry for a week or two, but until now the planes were full of leaves. A thick carpet of these now lay on the ground; in the market one trod in either deep puddles or a cushion of leaves, the puddles reflecting a sharp blue where the sky squinted fast through exploding strips and shreds of smoking white, backed by distant thunderclouds preparing more mayhem before the day ended.

No one who has been in a Camargue thunderstorm can wonder at the number of charms and spells against them. Bells used to be rung to chase them away. Fossil shark's teeth were effective, said some, others swore by the bay or olive twig blessed on Palm Sunday, or *carrelets de St Gilles*, which were fragments of Roman mosaic, and perhaps accounts for the scarcity of Roman remains at St Gilles. Thunder or no, everyone is cold. The snow is coming, grumbled one old man. The winter sneezing has begun. The market is short, only as far as the Salt Tower; the dames dwindled down to a precious few. The *charcutier* is warming himself on a few oysters, swallowed down between customers. He is fond of customers, but not in the raw.

There is no one except us mad enough to sit outside the Express Bar. Mad dogs and Englishmen may show a risible fancy for the midday sun in the tropics, but we insist on enjoying it with temperatures not much above zero. Tough, we East Anglians. The French are all inside. Assunta has two cardigans on, and will not emerge. Two of Nicollin's men are working, filling a truck with dead leaves swept from the square.

Winter is a-cumin in, Lude singe tishoo.

We needed a little something welded, not important, but a light touch of the rod without which clearly the child would be spoiled. So Bill took it to Mario. The caravan was all shut up; the unlicensed *fourgon* had gone.

Never mind, Bernard got the job done for us. But what had happened to Mario?

For some time Mario had been getting gloomier and gloomier. The legal break-up of a marriage is a minefield for the parties concerned. Mario had appealed against the verdict of the court which had very roughly split the family assets, which included the restaurant barge *Isles de Stel*, down the middle, a verdict which had upset him because his wife's lawyers had imposed conditions that made the boat inoperable. Bill had to listen often to these tales of woe.

Though by temperament manifestly unsuitable to be a
Samaritan (Bill's reaction to potential suicides is quite likely
to be 'What's stopping you?'), he maintained the appropriate air of silent concern, murmuring sympathetic noises
at suitable intervals. Mario, strong man and willing helper,
now needed support.

His lawyer had counselled against an appeal, clearly
believing that the judgement was reasonable, and that any
further slight gain would cost too much. When lawyers
advise against action one should listen. The same applies to
surgeons advising private patients not to have an operation. When the professional man gives advice against his
own pocket, do not ignore it.

Mario ignored it.

The first judgement was set aside. The wife's advocate
had engaged detectives to prove that Mario was moonlighting and not declaring his income, and the judge had
threatened gaol and found generously in favour of the wife
in virtually all the judgement.

We have no comment on the rights and wrongs of it. But
Mario was devastated. He descended into a state of
depression. The *Isles de Stel* would have to be sold, but such
was the bad feeling that agreement on the sale was
improbable, and since everyone knew the score, a low price
was inevitable.

Mario announced that he was going to blow up the *Isles
de Stel* right in front of the town gates and give the town the
best firework display it had ever had. He would go into
hiding and the first we would hear of it would be the bang,
1,000 metres down the canal.

We have said before that Mario does not do things by
halves. He is also the sort of person for whom little is
impossible except tact and diplomacy. Those of us who
knew him had no doubt that he was serious, and quite
capable of carrying out his threat. We thought that this
book could well end in high drama, and hoped nobody
would get killed.

And Mario had gone, vamoosed.

We waited anxiously. Then several days later a huge vessel hove into sight upstream.

It was so wide it spanned the canal.

It was so high that its upperworks had had to be dismantled to get under the bridges.

It had two enormous diesel engines rumbling and grumbling in its interior.

It was rusty and decrepit, and was being kept afloat by a diesel pump on deck.

It was Mario's Dreamboat.

And on the bridge was Mario, cheroot clenched between his teeth, with Martine handling the controls, both of them grinning like monkeys.

Over the next three hours they backed and filled the monster, called *Massilia* (she had been a tug on the Rhine) into the mouth of the old canal du Bourgidou, shuffling *Cedrat* and several smaller fry to make room. Slightly stunned, we all helped. Martine showed us proudly round. We all had a drink. We needed it, the boat was enormous. Staircases led to cavernous spaces where water sloshed hollowly. It was rusty. There were ominous trickling noises. It had unwieldy machinery on deck, tangled with miles of heavily rusted wire. It smelt of old mattresses and diesel oil, and one cupboard had a spectacular wasps' nest hanging in it. It was not beautiful. It was Mario's pride and joy.

Mario's threats had precipitated a solution. The *Isles de Stel* had been sold (for half its real value, declared Mario, because everybody knew it was a forced sale), and with his share of the proceeds he had bought *Massilia*. He had had his eye on her for some time, as she lay almost a wreck in a backwater up the Rhône. She would become, said Mario, a high class, super restaurant barge, with terrace, night club, and swimming pool (Boubou's *garage-piscine* had given him ideas), and there would be luxurious accommodation for Mario and Martine themselves. We never doubted that he could do it. They were still having wrangles with Authority about their caravan.

We were woken at daybreak with the banging of hammer on metal, with the showers of sparks that follow the oxy-propane torch (known to English boatyards as the hot spanner, but to the French as a *chalumeau*, a word as poetically sounding as cellar-door), followed by the crash of falling steel. Mario's depression was over. He was working like the devil and as happy as a *porc* in the *merde*. We were pleased for Mario, but the machines he had to use to shift masses of steel the size of railway carriages began to fuse our electrics at regular intervals. Life on the peninsula was very much back to normal.

We are always eager to improve our French, for though our French friends are flattering about our progress, we know, especially Bill, that in the heat of battle, so to speak, it leaves something to be desired. We prepared to try the Great Dictation Tele Game.

We get the impression that dictation is no longer a feature of the English education system, if system is the right word for such an apparent state of disorder. Not so in France. There dictation is not only a feature of school life and a major obstacle in the passing-out test of *gendarmes*, but adults actually enjoy it as if it were a sort of bingo. We suppose that given the rules and trickeries of French grammar and spelling it probably is.

The Annual *Dictée* Championship starts in October with the local heats. It takes place throughout *les pays francophones*, all French-speaking countries, but also in additional countries where a fair gathering of French speakers are to be found. Australia is one (it had over 900 entrants) and so are the Eastern bloc countries where the French cultural missions have been far more successful in spreading French influence than the British Council has at encouraging English.

After some strict and heavy elimination the semi-finals

are held in Paris and the sponsors (the bank Credit Lyonnais, and the Club Mediterranée) pay for the semi-finalists to attend from all over the world. After the semi-finals, the finalists, some 300 of them, assemble in the august surroundings of the French senate.

The event this year was televised at peak time and was relayed to over forty countries, where people stayed up all night (if necessary) to watch. All the eminent literary luminaries and waney-edged writers were there. In the front row were assorted senators, ministers with obscure portfolios, presidents of learned societies dedicated to the encouragement of the French tongue throughout the world. There were actors and *vedettes*, enough senile old singers to perform the Hallelujah Chorus, *cinéastes*, a famous chef or two (cooking is culture in France), and the whole was presided over by a learned, amiable and avuncular gentleman called Bernard Pivot, who was, one might say, the hinge on whom all turned. There was a glamorous lady in a rather over-tight low-cut and short-skirted dress who interrupted the proceedings waving from person to person an ice-cream cone mike of the type that most other countries have long since abandoned. She might just as well not have bothered because Monsieur Murphy's law dictates that the person under whose nose she shoved her instrument was neither the person who spoke, nor the person whom the engineer connected to the transmitter. However, there was much good-will and *bonhomie* with interviews with finalists who had either travelled unusually long distances, or who were younger than might be expected, or who happened to have good agents.

Finally it was eyes down for the house and off they went, the *dictée* began, and everyone did it. We joined most of the French population, glued to the telly with our pads and pens. Laurel got twelve faults and Bill got fifteen and we felt very ashamed, but then later came the results.

Only two persons in the whole world got no faults at all: a

computer programmer from Paris and a teacher from Caen. As the list reached the runners-up and the prize winners in special categories (best result from a schoolchild in a French colony for example) we began to realise that for foreigners we had not done at all badly. Among the national prize-winners five or more faults were common (a misplaced accent is half a fault).

Next morning in the market place we met Dominique the Librarian (fourteen faults). In the Express Bar we came across other friends who had tried their hand at the final. When they heard our results our stock went up quite noticeably. 'Well, many of the words were to do with food and cookery, and I know those,' said Laurel.

It is not unreasonable that a foreigner should do well for we take trouble with various grammatical niceties, while the native speaker takes short cuts and easy constructions for choice. It is not just an exercise in pure spelling because French is bedevilled with two genders which generate complex agreements between nouns, adjectives and participles, to name but three of the worst. There were also some catch words which, though in the French lexicon, are of foreign (usually English) origin, and not well known to the French. Also French people make a lot of mistakes with their own very complex grammar; the former Prime Minister, Michel Rocard, a literary graduate, was severely taken to task by the French press because he said '*vous disez*' instead of the correct '*vous dites*', rather as if Douglas Hurd were to indulge in double negatives. One hears on TV or radio many errors over the masculine/feminine division of inanimate nouns, and many public signs have accents either missing or misplaced. A teacher observed to us that if we were to use the subjunctive correctly we would baffle a goodly number of local inhabitants. The problem in Aigues-Mortes is that the local argot is so strong that one has frequently to guess the word, let alone the tense.

After the intellectual exercises we went into the country for a bit. This was the start of the reed-cutting season. Just past our berth as one passes along the canal one can see the occasional man, accompanied always by a happy dog, cutting and gathering reeds into even bundles, with the bottoms of the cut reeds neatly aligned. These are stacked by the canal side for assembling into loads.

They form the best possible material for thatching; a good reed thatch will last a lifetime, and these reeds are equalled only by those of Norfolk and Friesland. Good reeds need to stand with their feet in water of exactly the right salinity to grow long, strong and durable. We were astonished to find that much of the crop in the Camargue is exported to England, even to Norfolk; astonished especially because we know a Norfolk reed-cutter who says that it is no longer economical to cut reeds in Norfolk.

Why not? If they can cut them in the Camargue, transport them by road and car ferry for 900 miles and still make it worth while there is something wrong in Norfolk. It is not as if the French have a lower cost of living, far from it, nor are the folk of the Midi known for industriousness; in that case what do we make of the Nor' folk? Perhaps we have stumbled upon the underlying cause of Britain's perennial deficit in the balance of trade; people no longer bother.

Once winter is on the way and the autumn gales are with us the barges go faster and put more strain on our mooring ropes. The earth on the banks being soft, we are pulling out the bollards which are supposed to hold us fast.

Bill went along to Boubou, the Professor, to ask advice on how to proceed. It is no easy job to dig new holes for bollards which probably weigh five hundredweight.

Boubou pulled his grey beard. Bill knew the signs. The politenesses first, then some pearl of French wisdom or wit, then the business. Boubou asked what the Anglo-Saxons thought of the case of the US Supreme Court judge who, during his candidature, was accused of sexual harrass-ment.

'Is this sort of thing peculiar to the Americans?' he demanded.

Bill said, 'You must remember that the Pilgrim Fathers were puritans.'

'Ah!' said Boubou, 'We always think that the English are puritans.'

'You are right. We are. But the American puritans had to flee England because the English puritans found them too puritan to be supportable.'

'Now I understand. Of course here in France sexual harrassment is not a crime. How could that be possible when it is one of our national sports? Imagine, some Frenchmen have not yet accustomed themselves to the idea that rape is a crime. Most policemen do not think so.'

Bill did not believe him of course, and was eventually counselled about getting his bollards replaced.

18

The Provençal Christmas

'Lou blad de Santo Barbo
Que pèr aquèu jour si gardo
A taulo fau lou bouta
Mai aco's un pla per arregarda.'
. . . .
'The corn of St Barbara
Today we sow,
For the Christmas table
We watch it grow.'

It is the custom in the Midi to sow lentils or some seeds of corn in several tiny earthenware pots on St Barbara's day, December 4th, and put them somewhere warm indoors. By Christmas the corn should be several inches high, betokening good harvests, and bringing luck for the coming year. The pots of growing corn (*lou blad de Santo Barbo*) are surrounded with red ribbon and placed on the Christmas table. If you forget to sow your own, you can buy the designer version at great expense, red ribbon and all, in the fashionable home décor boutiques in Nîmes or Arles.

Mme Poitavin has a nice potful growing in her window. Last year the seeds were for sale in the bakery, in aid of the Third World. This year Laurel had to go to the herbalist and buy half a kilo.

She planted a dozen or so grains in a small pot, and waited with eagerness mixed with doubt, as she is a terrible gardener. After ten days nothing had happened. She moved the pot further into light and warmth. One, then two, then four tiny sprouts appeared. They then grew quite fast, and by December 18th one was fully six inches tall. But there were still only four thin shoots, looking very unlike the strong healthy growth in the florists' shops.

On December 22nd the cats ate the shoots. So much for next year's luck.

The eel fishermen who roar by before dawn (at this time of year the sun does not come over our bridge till nearly nine, though it rises officially at about eight-thirty) are wrapped to the eyeballs in thick oilskins and gloves.

The eels go deep into the mud in cold weather, but it seems that there are still some being caught. Bruno appears daily in his white boat, and grumbles and chats to himself as he hauls up the tail of his eel-sett. It is a lonely job one supposes, and he needs company. He is not as surly as he seems in spite of the incessant grumbling noises. He tells us that the eels are sold to a combine at Palavas and depart immediately for far away, Holland or Italy as far as he knows; what does he care as long as they pay well. Why are none on sale here? Surely it is one of the traditional foods of the region. Because it was peasant food, says Bruno. Most people are glad to see the end of it, and the Parisians will not pay as much for eels as the Hollandais.

It was already late to be sending Christmas cards to our many friends world wide. Laurel had been searching for them for two weeks, but despite Mme Poitavin's window accurately reflecting the season with polar bears and boxes of chocolates in ice blue silk, none were to be had. The French send cards for the New Year, and a card for Christmas is a novelty. In the one shop in Montpellier that she counted on, the cards had arrived, but were not yet unpacked, and she returned from the big city empty-handed. Ingenuity would have to suffice this year. She did a typographical Christmas card on the computer.

One seasonal thing you could be sure of here in the Midi was the *santons*, the little local people, made of clay or wood or cloth, who stand around the manger in a Nativity scene that is to Provence what the Christmas tree is to northern lands. It is added to every year, and the simple stable is gradually surrounded by an entire Provençal village, windmill and all, and those biblically present at the Nativity are joined by recognisable people in local dress.

There are Foires des Santons everywhere at the beginning of December, so that everyone may purchase another figure for the Christmas crib, which may already cover a large trestle table and contain dozens of figures.

This charming custom, now spreading in England and America, is thought to have its origins in the crib devised by St Francis of Assissi to portray the night at Bethlehem. This however was made up of real people and animals. Avignon has had a crêche since the fourteenth century, and sculptures in walnut of the Holy Family were sold there in the sixteenth century. Aristocrats and wealthy families in the seventeeth and eighteenth centuries had luxurious crêches made of precious materials, blown glass, and marble; or figures made of humbler stuff but richly dressed in silks and brocades. In Naples the church at Christmas was decorated with angels, their silk and satin garments draped in exquisitely baroque folds. Nevertheless, the origin of the true *santon*, made in terracotta and cheap enough for every family, is obscure. It is decidedly Mediterranean, and was developed in its present form in Marseille at the beginning of the eighteen hundreds by Jean Louis Lagnel. He made, in the midst of bloody revolution and the reign of the Terror, little figures in the shape of the characters of his *quartier*, and deemed them worthy to be present at Bethlehem. Other craftsmen followed his example.

Nowadays throughout the Midi the biblical personages are joined by beloved figures, all with a story attached to them: the miller, the man crushing garlic, and the man with the hurdy gurdy. Visiting the Holy Family in company with kings, angels and shepherds, are fishermen, lacemakers, basketweavers, sellers of lavender, the *curé*, the doctor, grandma spinning wool on her distaff, and by ancient custom, a *tzigane* or two. The *santons* are lovingly made by artisans. Some, small and simple figures, painted or left plain so that you may paint them yourself, cost pocket money. Others, larger and more elaborate, are necessarily dearer. All of them are beautiful, and any household can get out the crêche in December, and add a new figure every year.

Marcel Carbonel, one of the great *santonniers*, has his *atelier* in Marseille. He makes his little figures in terracotta, sculpting them with infinite care. A mould is made of his *santon*, and from the mould come rows of *santons* to satisfy a world-wide demand. This is the only part of the process that could be called mass production, and the mould is discarded after a certain number of uses. He employs more than forty workers, some of whom load the kiln with infinite care, a thousand *santons* at a time, some to hand paint each *santon* when it has been fired. Gouache paints are used, which are made in the *atelier* to get the exact colour they need, but this means that these are not toys for children, since no varnish veils the intense colour, which can be damaged by careless handling or damp. His museum is a delight, a collection of cribs and Nativity figures from all over the world.

Marcel Carbonel sits at his workbench between the shop and the *atelier*, his fingers sure and gifted, working on some tiny new character, squinting at it from different angles with bright eyes. A contented man, of eighty summers.

There are a fair number of artists living near the Camargue, mostly in the area just inland. One who actually lives on the edge of the Camargue is Ponce de Leon, a descendant of the original coloniser of Florida and founder of the oldest town in the USA, St Augustine.

Sr Ponce de Leon is Spanish, originally from Seville, and could naturally be expected to have an interest in bulls, though until he moved to his present house in Le Caylar, they did not figure in his paintings. Adjoining his new home was the meadow of a bull of character whom the artist found he could no longer overlook.

This bull was discovered abandoned in the bullrushes of the Camargue marshes as a calf, and was inevitably christened Moyse (Moses). He became the family pet of the *manadier*, and having no cause to resent the human race was inclined to be friendly, which brought its problems, for Moses stepped onto the scale at 600 kilos, stripped and ready for action, and that was a lot of friendly bull. One could not afford to be leant against by such a pet, and even a loving lick was acutely uncomfortable. Sr Ponce de Leon had painted this bull in a variety of colourful postures, many of the pictures also contained the little white egret called either a *pic-bec* or a *garde-bœuf*, which sits on the bull and eats the parasites and other bugs which would otherwise upset a large animal.

We found ourselves invited to the *vernissage*, or private view, of the artist's one man show at the local gallery, perhaps because we had once purchased a modest work of art there and the proprietors hoped we could be encouraged to trade up.

Aigues-Mortes tries quite hard to be a cultural town since culture in France is not a dirty word. Most French towns can boast that they were the birthplace or residence of this artist or that writer, but Aigues-Mortes has been almost overlooked by the great and famous. Perhaps Van Gogh would have come here instead of Saintes-Maries to paint his famous multi-coloured boats if the railway from Arles had run directly and he would not have had to change at Nîmes, which is an experience to be avoided. One artist who has been here, and only because he arrived in Arles too late to see his friend Van Gogh, is the impressionist Saturnin Pissoir, but apparently he did not paint while he was here.

He erred, for a surprising number of local people are interested enough to spend money on original works. We were confident that enough local glitterati would be at the *vernissage* so decided to dress up to the occasion. Laurel does this rather more often than Bill, and it was comparatively simple for her to exercise her choice within her existing wardrobe. In Bill's case it involved the exhuming of suits which had barely seen the light of day for years, the discovery of some mildew spots, that the waistbands of trousers had shrunk, and that his smart shoes had disappeared completely.

Bill's resolve weakened, but he was on thin ice (the outside temperature was only a fraction above zero at the time) for Laurel reminded him that he had barely been out of his scruffy paint-stained trousers and half-sleeved sweater for months and he was beginning to be indistinguishable from a *clochard* (tramp), or at best a *marginal*. Muttering that to most people he *was* a *marginal*, he found a tie originating from a far distant yacht club which was not too badly creased, and a clean shirt. He paraded for inspection and approval in his navy-blue double-breasted suit, and then rounded off the ensemble with his old naval boat-cloak, a voluminous affair reaching down to his knees. 'You did say fancy-dress?' he asked.

There was no doubt that his tall black-cloaked figure added tone to the proceedings. Few people recognised him as they normally never saw him in anything decent. Claude, who considers himself something in the fine art world, came over to say he was pleased to see the English represented, and congratulated Bill on his taste in clothes, observing that the ensemble was *légèrement surréaliste* and suited the paintings. Bill has been wondering ever since whether or not that was a compliment.

After the view we decided to dine out. We have spoken about the thirty-four restaurants in Aigues-Mortes, and have said that most are not all that good since they cater for the day-trippers who do not give repeat business. The menus are written in French, and there are undeniably French touches here and there, but one might just as well be in an English sea-side resort but for the lack of ketchup bottles on the tables. All too often the 'fresh fish' is frozen, and items such as crêpes are pre-cooked in a factory (we have watched them being delivered). There are restaurants cooking good food quite well but at prices which do not compare with other parts of France. A meal which in Bourgogne would cost 100 francs will cost 180 in Aigues-Mortes, and is unlikely to be as well cooked.

There is one restaurant of a different kind to those we have encountered in the rest of France. It has no sign outside and presents the unremarkable façade of a private house in a side street, but inside the rooms are discreetly furnished and in the rear give on to a secluded walled garden. It is open in the evenings only, when all the day-trippers have gone. One must reserve, and inside it is crowded when all the other establishments are almost empty.

There is no menu, which provides a chance to talk to the *patron* about food. Price is not mentioned (but is reasonable, all *entrées* being 30 francs and all main dishes 60); there is a small, but well-chosen and unpretentious cellar, and the cooking and service are very good, in a *familiale* rather than an *haute cuisine* manner. The problem for us was that we were the only customers speaking French. All round us we heard the Camargue dialect, which we are only just able to interpret at all, and which is continually surprising us.

Two interesting points about the dishes (a choice of three for each course). One is that there were no potatoes available and the accompaniment was fresh pasta, and two, a rare thing, it would have been possible to have had a good vegetarian meal, the fresh *tagliatelli au cèpes* complementing a salad of warm goat cheese. We heard the proprietor advising the next table on their choice, saying, 'The duckling? well my son plucked them and my wife has cooked them. God knows what they are like.' The whole thing is a most relaxed and unsolemn event, and deserves to succeed.

By mid December, it was very cold, everyone said so. The Sunday market was icy, and we did not stop for a drink afterwards. Last year over December and January there had been few Sundays when a gleam of sunshine had not attracted us to the Express Bar, where often our fellow yotties gathered. This year there were few yotties about, it seemed.

Mme Poitavin's window had finally recognised Christmas with a nod in the shape of little wood sledges and green and red ribbons, and Laurel was finding out about *foie gras*. As we were not going home to England till February, we were going to have a French Christmas, this meant oysters and *foie gras*. Fresh *foie gras* came into the *supermarché* about two weeks before *Noël*, either whole, or in a roll wrapped in foil, chilled and easy to slice. *Foie gras d'oie*, that is pure goose liver, is the most expensive. *Pâté de foie gras* is cheaper, because it is a nut of liver encased in a mince of broken pieces, and *crèmes de foie* are cheaper still, since they are nearly all mince, made into a spreading *pâté*. *Foie gras de canard*, duck liver, is cheaper than goose. There is a whole range here to suit every pocket. What we found was that the fresh product tasted much nicer than tinned, and that a couple of slices off the roll of *foie gras d'oie* was not too exorbitant for a once in a while feast like Christmas Day.

Oysters from the Etang de Thau just west of the Petite Camargue are very cheap by comparison with *foie gras*, and no Frenchman could dream of Christmas without them. The Etang de Thau is larger, deeper, and more saline than the other *étangs* of the region. The French do not sit on their haunches and wait for oysters to grow on their own and then dredge them up the hard way. Oh no! They farm them, growing the little beasts from tiny little seedlings and then planting out on strings hanging from permanent frames in the shallow waters of the lagoon. It represents a considerable capital investment but at least they always know where the oysters are and can get them up without a lot of bother. The oyster industry is centred in the waterside villages of Bouzigues, which gives its name to the culture, or Mèze a few kilometres away. About half the *étang* is taken up by piled structures from which hang the strings of growing oysters. They grow mussels as well. Growing shellfish has the awesome name of Conchyliculture.

It is at Christmas and the New Year that about a third to a half of the total annual production of oysters is sold, the oyster being to the French what the smoked salmon and mince pies are to the English.

A few days before Christmas the dreadful news broke: the oysters in the Etang de Thau were contaminated. The official laboratory run by the French Min. of Ag. and Fish. had found traces of salmonella in a significant sample of the take. Every day's production is always officially tested and the safety of the Bouzigues oyster certified on each box. Now such a certificate could not be issued.

Catastrophe! The French farmer or fisherman faced with disaster of this nature has two reactions. The first is to go out and kill someone, and the second, which is a long way second but absolutely inevitable, is to cry '*sinistré!*' (there is no good English equivalent for this word, which means 'suffered a disaster') and appeal to the government for financial help, which is almost always forthcoming. Indeed we feel that it is in this way that the French Government gets round the limitations on subsidies that are ordered by the Brussels bureaucrats. Every year in turn some sections of French productive life are *sinistré* and the ritual doling out of compensating cash commences. It is the farmers' turn one year, the fishermen's another, then the vine-grower's and so on.

Those compatriots of ours who have followed the lamb wars will have some idea of the initial reaction of the ostreiculturists. They went to the laboratory and sacked it, breaking all its windows, smashing its equipment and distributing its filing system to the four winds. It is difficult to understand why such a peace-loving animal as the inoffensive frog has been adopted as the symbol of Frenchness, when one sees the vigour with which the far from froglike Frenchman reacts to any threat to his livelihood.

So the conchyliculturists decided to teach the government scientists a thing or two about salmonella, and though they smashed up the lab they did not kill nor even injure anyone, and they managed to get the sympathy of the French public: how, we do not know, but they did. Perhaps it was the shock of being deprived of their Christmas oysters. There was a government enquiry about the vandalism which has never produced a report.

At first no oysterman had believed the test. Oysters are obviously good for you. The growers were filmed tucking into them noisily and wetly (it is difficult to eat an oyster elegantly) and with great gusto, putting their mouth where their money is, so to speak. It is worth noting that none of them was stricken with any ill. They were thus convinced that it was all a conspiracy, this was an act of deliberate sabotage by the Breton or Arcachon oystermen on the Atlantic coast who wished to corner the market. When it was reasonably pointed out to them that it was government scientists who had certified their oysters as contaminated they replied that the Bretons had bribed the scientists.

The government responded by sending samples to foreign laboratories for unbiased opinions, and at last the oystermen were convinced and made their appeal for help.

It appeared that there had been a very violent rainstorm in late summer which had flushed through the local sewage treatment works and caused a fair amount of untreated sewage to overflow into the lagoon.

One of the features of life in this part of the world is the need to replace inadequate old sewage works with new ones capable of absorbing the huge loads of the summertime tourist population. Communities put this off repeatedly because of the cost, and are perpetually surprised when things go wrong. The Etang de Thau is surrounded by growing seaside resorts and camping sites. Embarrassing effluent will escalate in the Etang unless ecological efforts are effective.

And the oysters? They were soon passed fit and well

again, though the Christmas and New Year sales had been lost. They cost 15 francs a kilo nowadays, about three dozen oysters. There are fierce supporters of the Atlantic oyster who say that the Mediterranean oyster is too salty. It is a matter of taste.

Bill has to eat them alone, or await a conchyliverous guest. The last time we had a guest, the two of them ate their way through a 3 kilo box. The pigs. Laurel cannot eat oysters.

On Christmas Eve Francine and Boubou called in, and we gave them Muscat and peanuts. They brought with them the best Christmas present they could have had: Cathy their daughter had just arrived back from Australia. It was a complete surprise, as she had been unsure of her flight till the last minute. It was a happy and warming beginning to the festivities.

Down in the Camargue at Le Sambuc, the Camarguais prepared for the midnight mass, the Mass of the Shepherds. It blew a violent mistral. The mass is held outside the Church of Notre Dame du Monde Entière (Our Lady of the Whole World) because the shepherds bring their sheep to the altar, and the *gardians* attend on horseback. (Somewhere in the congregation there are undoubtedly bulls.) The faithful were wrapped in coats, cloaks and scarves, the *gardians* turned up their collars against the screaming wind, and the little leaves that blew past them caught silver from the arc lights and turned to snow. The poor Arlésiennes, dressed in their elegant long-skirted silks, their lace shawls hugged across their shivering bosoms and their 1880 coiffures baring their little pink ears to the merciless wind, looked frozen to death. The only creatures who looked warm were the sheep, wrapped in wool as thick as a crop of cauliflowers. As everyone in the Camargue knows, animals have the gift of speech at midnight on Christmas Eve. We guessed what the bulls would be saying to each other, before giving thanks to the Creator for the birth of The Child. '*Tu sais*, you know when they drive you down towards the canal at Aigues-Mortes? They want you to swim! In October! I would have caught my death. Just take a quick right and head for the vineyards.'

The entire congregation, despite their discomfort, were truly happy. The mistral was for once a blessing, since it had kept away both the tourists and the mosquitoes.

At a quarter to midnight we, in Aigues-Mortes, were blown through the Porte de la Gardette as if pushed by an express train, and hurled down the street to Notre Dame des Sablons, where a large number of people were also trying to get through a small door and out of the wind as quickly as possible. The church was already full, but we found a seat in the last pew at the back. When that was full, it was standing room only, and part of that was occupied by half a hundred children dressed as *santons*, giggling and excited, high on Christmas, dressing up, and the lateness of the hour. Bossy mums twitched costumes into place, the fisherboy's net was rearranged, the sweep's brush disentangled from his miniature ladder, the wood gatherer's bundle of faggots placed at a better angle, and a pipe placed in the mouth of one of the black-hatted shepherds. Another shepherd, in sheepskin waistcoat and black beret, was having his moustache more carefully drawn, after which he became the spitting image of his father. The girls' baskets, containing fruit, the little goat cheeses called *pelardons*, bunches of lavender, all these were carefully checked, along with the bakerboy's bread. While the Mayor coached the choir and congregation in the sung responses loud whispers behind us regulated matters. 'And St Jean Baptiste? He is where? Ah, *le voilà*. And the sheep?' A chorus of quiet baa-ing formed a descant to the Mayor's encouraging baritone.

It was a joyous service. We knew only two of the tunes,

Silent Night and Adeste Fidelis, but with the help of the Mayor we joined in the others right merrily. The *santons* acted and sang out the Christmas story at the front of the church, the priest preached exactly the same sort of sermon as we would have had on Christmas Day at home ('Peace and Goodwill, this Holy Child, born in a stable, shepherds the first to be told etc.'). One small shepherd was overcome by sleep and fell over. Two chattering women behind us, who gossipped and giggled all through the solemn part of the mass, far worse than the excited children who hushed when told, were finally silenced by an angry male whisper: the French equivalent of 'Belt up, you two!'.

The mass ended with the priest explaining the Provençal Christmas custom of the Thirteen Desserts, one for each of the Apostles, that the children would be offering at the church door; baskets of figs, dates, fruit, nuts and sweets, from which we were invited to help ourselves, a charming and friendly gesture, which warmed our hearts as we bent into the bitter wind to return home.

On Christmas morning we emerged after breakfast to sniff the air, enjoy the sun, and admire the fir tree hoisted to the top of our mast, as nautical tradition dictates. Sitting on a post near to the road was a sparrowhawk, something we did not often see close to the river, doing a bit of Christmas hunting. We called the cats in, just in case.

'They don't seem to want their food today,' said Laurel.

'Do they really like peanuts?' asked Bill, interested.

Laurel threw a horrified look into the cats' dish. 'I thought it was crokkies,' she said. 'I shall have to stop keeping everything in Nescafé jars.'

There was a market in town, and an astonished gentleman from up-country asked Laurel: 'Madame! where are the oysters from the Etang de Thau?' and she had to explain that they were *sinistré* and could not be sold. He was shattered. Christmas without the mince pies.

Since there were no oysters, we had *foie gras* to start our

Christmas dinner. Mindful of Sidney Smith's definition of heaven, we put on a cassette of one of Haydn's Concerti and ate our *foie gras* appropriately to the sound of trumpets.

We followed local custom in having on the table the *treize desserts*, an assortment of dried fruit and nuts, marzipan, nougat and glacé fruits.

As we were having a holiday from building, writing or almost any kind of work except cooking and wood-chopping, Bill was watching television. He does not much approve of French television, considering it rather worse than British ITV with a foreign accent, but he makes a point of watching the weather and the news that goes with it. Among other reasons he finds that it helps improve his French.

There are three different *prévisions météo* at about the same time, and he likes to have a choice of weather. If TF1's moustachioed and over-buttonholed extrovert is promising us that there will be overcast skies and some drops of rain, and he finds that Le Cinq's dead-pan presenter on the other hand opts for bright intervals and improvement, he prefers to stay with Le Cinq. Another extrovert on Antenne Deux angers him by standing in front of the map he is trying to explain.

Bill maintains a running commentary on the forecasts to Laurel who is usually cooking at the time, and it is no doubt these aromas that lead him to alimentary metaphors. All the channels use little symbols for their weather maps and his commentary goes something like this: 'There are fried eggs all over western France, and some eggs florentine further east. Antenne Deux has some oranges in the Midi, while further north it's Yorkshire pudding with depending spaghetti. There's a big red carrot going up the Loire, and some artichokes in Corsica.' Very often there is a grand pertubation over les Iles Britanniques, and the afore-mentioned large man with a walrus moustache and a big flower in his buttonhole rrrolls his rrrrs with rrrelish clearly blaming the English for the terrible weather. But on the whole the presentation, with the exception of the sillier symbols and a tendency for some presenters to stand in front of their maps, is very good; no television company ever manages to avoid these daft symbols and we have to ask why even the supposedly cultural channels in Britain broadcast their weather forecasts with a puerility that would be offensive to a batch of five year olds? The French do avoid that at any rate. The umbrella and snowmen no longer appear.

The French television news has much the same faults as that of Britain: no matter how important the news, if there are no pictures it gets no mention; conversely if there are good pictures the most ridiculous triviality is featured. The news is not to inform, but to entertain. Of course like every country the TV news is nationally oriented – they have to pay for imported footage, so anything from abroad has to be very worthwhile. One channel regularly brings in a 'personality' to sit with the news-reader and he is invited to give off the cuff comments on the news items. We can think of nothing less informative to the viewer, for most of the 'personalities', being either actors or politicians (and is there any real difference?) have little to say about anything except themselves.

After the news most channels seem to broadcast old films all evening, mostly dubbed into French by the same small company of actors. One comes to recognise the voices: the same one for Donald Duck, Deputy Dawg, Bugs Bunny and three of the Seven Dwarfs, the same old lady does Edith Evans, Celia Johnson or Peggy Ashcroft, and the same young man does Errol Flynn, John Wayne, Richard Burton and God help us, Jimmy Stewart. The monotony of these old films is relieved from time to time by variety shows of indescribable banality featuring more 'personalities' who interview each other in intimate and adulatory tones.

There is also a series which might be called the 'Worst of Benny Hill' but that supposes that there is a 'Best of Benny

Hill', and we have not seen it yet. If you ask any Frenchman what English TV he has seen, all he can remember is Benny Hill. Almost all the British imports come from ITV, God help the French, but at least some of them are better quality offerings from Channel Four. There is much transatlantic soap, westerns, and cops and robbers.

An almost unique feature of the entertainment side of things in France is the number of singers who go on performing well into their second childhood. Where England specialises in revered elderly actors, France reveres its singers, who are either extremely young, or extremely old, with a scattering of ageing rock stars somewhere in the middle. It sometimes seems that French TV exists almost as a *maison de retraite* for ancient variety artists. With the exception of a few children, no one gets a look in unless they are over eighty. And how the French love these old fogies! And how they mourn them when they die, which they frequently do, leading to hushed flashes at news time, all channels cancelling programmes for the evening in order to do a retrospective. Ah! we say to ourselves, that's one more gone; but no, another one will cross the seventy line and emerge as a star. France seems to produce singers who are already senile.

Two ageing stars we do make a point of watching are Gaby Ney, her jowls strained up by repeated 'liftings' into her red curls. She is, one might say, the pits, but her presence is good, she wears deep black with shoulders padded three feet wide, the magnificent legs revealed from the point where they are still magnificent, and mimes to her records of fifty years ago; and Zizi Branleur, brown wrinkles, white curls, and white moustache, who sings casual witty incomprehensible little songs to the guitar. He always performs solo.

Any good stuff comes very late in the evening. There is some conspiracy among the world's TV companies to deprive intelligent people of their sleep so that hoi polloi can take over. Usually the intelligent just switch off and go to bed, so that they never see anything much worth watching. One thing the French TV does offer, weekly, and at peak viewing time is the best regular programme on nautical subjects that we know of. Called 'Thalassa', it sets out to cover all aspects of anything connected with the sea. The studio bits are hearty and Blue Peterish, and the OBs from boat shows worse, and it is inclined to chauvinism, but one can forgive it because of the outstanding excellence of the specially made films they include. (BBC please note.) Another good series is 'Apostrophe', when a group of authors, who have all written books on subjects that are related, are gathered in to talk not only about their own books, but also about the books of the others. This gives rise to some very lively and intelligent television; but this programme has recently been taken off: it was too good perhaps.

French television is extremely keen about sporting events, and the commentaries on rugby matches, which is the only sport Bill watches, are remarkably free from bias.

French radio has two features that appeal to us, and only two. There is a 24-hour news service to which one can refer in times of crisis, and which is very quick off the mark, often reporting important world events (such as the assassination of the Indian Prime Minister) a very long while (hours in this case) before the BBC Overseas Service. The other is the classical music programme France Musique which has very little to fault apart from a tendency to go on talking about music instead of playing it, a fault which it shares with the BBC third programme.

All in all cultural life in France is more widespread than in Britain, and concerts in the provinces are frequent and well attended. It is obvious that more public money is spent in this way than in England, and everyone accepts that this is good. We hear no complaints about it, and even that extraordinary pyramid in the grounds of the Louvre excited little comment, but then they have not got a Prince of Wales, have they?

19

Epiphany and good resolutions

'Quand leis amendié flourissoun en janvié
Foou ni acanadouiro ni panié.'
....
'When almonds flower in January's
cold,
You won't be needing trug nor pole.'

We greeted the New Year with the firm resolution that this year, come what may, we would get *Hosanna* to sea for the summer. To that end we went to Arles in early January to discuss slipping the boat in March. Laurel was intrigued to discover that Arles was twenty-six hawks from Aigues-Mortes, since that was the number she counted as we crossed the Camargue. They were sitting on posts or fences or a tree branch, one or two casting over the stubble fields, at the rate of one hawk to every two kilometres.

In spite of the New Year holiday season, we found our enthusiasm for voyaging got us working again. There was a tremendous amount to do before *Hosanna* was fit for sea, and we put on our overalls and set to. The roef, or cuddy, had to be cleared of its contents before we went to Arles, as work was to be done on that end of the boat. It was a heavy lifting job moving everything out and finding a place for it elsewhere.

Francine called by with the bread. Nicholas had arrived to spend New Year with his family. In answer to our questions, she said 'Oh, he is much better, but how thin he has become!'

Never mind, we said, you will feed him up while he is with you.

'Certainly, yes,' said Francine, 'I shall give him horse-meat. There is nothing better for strengthening the blood, you know.'

By the end of the day we were both very tired. 'What's for dinner?' said Bill. 'Horsemeat? Or shall we go out?'

'I ought to use up the *lotte*,' said Laurel.

Said Bill: 'You got a lot of *lotte*? Let's pretend it's lobster then, and have it thermidor. I'll get out the sherry. Are you OK to cook a *lotte* thermidor?'

'Give me a slug of the sherry and then I might be,' said Laurel. The *lotte*, or angler fish, has flesh so firm that it can easily pass for lobster, and in some English restaurants it often does, especially if put into a convenient re-usable shell.

The cream sauce was simmering happily on the hob. The rice was cooking on the back burner. Laurel had put in the mustard, and added a generous slug of sherry to the sauce. Whether it was the sherry she had drunk or the fact that she was tired, or both, cannot be determined, but when her hand caught against the wooden spoon in the saucepan it sent the whole thing onto the floor. Her wail of dismay brought her knight to the rescue. 'I can't make it again, all the fish stock is in that sauce!' she howled. Some of it had gone over her hand which she had plunged immediately into the washing up basin. At least she had had enough presence of mind to avoid a scald.

'When did you last wash the floor?' asked Bill practically.

'This morning,' sniffed Laurel. As we have written elsewhere:

> Wash with care your galley floors,
> The portion dropped there might be yours.

'Then we'll scrape it up and boil it again,' said Bill. 'Quick, before the cats find it.' So we did.

As she served the dish on a bed of rice Laurel said, 'I've rechristened it. This is *lotte* thermifloor.'

The following day no ill effects had accrued from eating floored rather than planked *lotte*, but Bill would not allow her to cook the trout that they had bought in that morning's market. 'Sit down!' he commanded, 'and rest.'

It was easier to sit than repose, as the galley became wreathed in blue smoke. Bill popped his head round the door once, to say that the back burner was too hot, and the bottom of her frying pan was not flat.

'There!' he said triumphantly, putting a plate of trout, decorated with lemon, before his love with a flourish.

'I was worried,' she said, 'I thought I smelled burning.'

'No, they're not burned. The skins are hand-crisped by a master-craftsman.'

They tasted marvellous.

In England as soon as Christmas (now elided with New Year, it seems) is over, the sales begin and the shop-windows that were so beautiful ten days before are overcrowded with cheap goods and showcards covered with typographical screams and exclamation marks, not to mention the misplaced apostrophe. Every heap of broken boxes and bulging black sacks that stands in the street awaiting the dustbin men is topped by a withered Christmas tree, a few bits of artificial snow and tinsel still adhering. In England the decorations disappear with unseemly haste, like the best tea service after the funeral.

In the Midi the festive season begins a bit later, at the very end of November, not immediately after Guy Fawkes as in England; and after Christmas it lasts a bit longer, since Epiphany on 6th January is a popular feast commemorating the visit of the Three Kings to the newborn Jesus. Every group or society likes to have a '*tirage des rois*' party with the not very marvellous (but *traditionel*) *gâteau des rois*, or Kings' cake. This cake contains a bean, and whoso receives it in his or her portion becomes King or Queen for the evening, and has their picture in the local paper wearing the gilt cardboard crown that comes with every *gâteau*. That is the fun bit. Here in Aigues-Mortes the cake itself is dry and rather tasteless, and requires washing down with a good deal of rosé wine.

The bean (*fève*, or *fava*) is a very ancient token of good luck (the Greeks used them to cast votes in an election); in Provençal *'estre fave'* means to be lucky: 'favoured' in fact. At one time the cake contained an ordinary bean; the custom has grown to use decorative ceramic 'beans' which take many different forms, some quite beautiful and valuable.

Well-known *patissiers* commission their own, a different one every year, and these are ardently collected. Your down-market *gâteau des rois* will contain a plastic bean, just as the cheaper Christmas puddings contain plastic 'silver' tokens if anything at all; *peuchère*, as they say round here, it would have been a poor pudding without its silver three-penny bit in our childhood.

We motored down the North of France one snowy Epiphany and stopped for the night, rather late, at St-Quentin, booking in to the Hotel de la Gare. Our meal was good, but the huge restaurant was deserted except for us and our waiter, and quiet as the tomb. A sense of correctness led us to choose the *gâteau des rois* for dessert, and a huge cake was wheeled in; it would have fed thirty people. The waiter affected pleased astonishment when Laurel found the bean in her portion, and crowned her with great solemnity and the cardboard crown.

The *patissier* in Aigues-Mortes, M. Poitavin, participates in a scheme whereby each *gâteau (grande modèle)* contains a thin plaque of gold, in the shape of a *département* of France. If you can eat enough *gâteaux*, and are lucky enough to collect the whole set, forming a map of France, you win a holiday in Martinique. You would need it to recover from the *gâteau*.

The French *départements* are an extra link in the bureaucratic chain: state, region, *département*, and municipality or commune. They date from the revolution and point out the lesson that republicans always over-organise everything because they do it by logic. If you are governed by aristocrats things have to stay simple because aristocrats have not the mental capacity to deal with complications. The *départements* are all of roughly equal geographic, rather than demographic size because they were designed so that all parts were within one day's horse ride of the seat of local power, the Prefect. The original concept was disciplinary rather than administrative and it is as well to bear in mind that not all Frenchmen at that time were reliable supporters of the revolution.

Through early January the shop windows in Aigues-Mortes were full of wishes for the New Year. Mme Poitavin let herself go with bottles of champagne, and top hats and chocolates disguised as champagne corks. The strings of lights forming stars across the streets and in the trees outside the ramparts would probably stay till after Carnival. In *Hosanna*, very British, we took the evergreen down from our masthead, and cleared away our decorations on Twelfth Night after our lunch party. They went back under the floorboards till next Christmas.

The weather was not so good and if we wanted a post-market coffee at the Express Bar we had to brave the atmosphere inside, which was not exactly pure. Everyone seemed to be smoking, some were playing cards, while the rest were reading *Midi Libre*, some for the racing results, some for the local news, some for the winning lottery number: hope is the bread of the poor, and why not me the *milliardaire* this week, *pardi*?

French newspapers are not organised into a national press of mass circulation as in Britain. Mostly they are of regional orientation and have incorporated supplements giving detailed local news within their region. Inside this geographical framework each paper carries items varying between the very cultural and very banal, and are written in part in language of great prose and in other parts like a junior school magazine. Thus each paper contains elements of *The Times*, the *Daily Mail*, the *Eastern Daily Press* and the *Lowestoft Journal* (which latter is, by one of those journalistic abuses of our own language, published weekly). There is no equivalent in France to the *Sun* and such papers.

We enjoy the local news, not that there is much from Aigues-Mortes. Sometimes it appears there is a sentry at the gates to stop any news getting out into the wide world (and vice versa), but one does get some fascinating insights into Midi life from the villages and towns about us.

Recently two *gendarmes* of the neighbourhood out on patrol came upon a pool of blood in the road. There is nothing like blood to excite the sleuth lying hidden in us all, and our two policemen, having communed with things rural and met nature face to face quite a lot, set off on what was clearly a hot trail, the blood being if not actually warm, at least newly spilt.

They followed the trail of spattered blood which entered a tall block of flats and continued ominously up the stairs. Surely, they asked each other, an injured person would have gone up in the lift? Was he then already defunct? With mounting excitement they climbed the stairs, where marks on the wall told of a heavy body having been dragged past. They beat on the door of the flat to which the trail led. 'Open in the name of the Law!'

Inside they found a family of Algerians in flagrante delicto. They were cutting up a corpse with a cleaver and several sinister looking knives. The corpse, however, was that of a stolen cow, and the Algerians were obviously not expert in butchery. There was blood everywhere. They were caught red-handed, you might say.

It can be said that the local criminals have a tendency to leave the *flics* a clear trail. Down in Grau-du-Roi a gang broke into a house, having heard that the elderly occupiers had a safe full of money on the premises. The miscreants hid in the loft to await the right moment. The pensioner householders, hearing inexplicable noises above their heads, sent for the police. The burglars were discovered snoring, fast asleep with their skeleton keys on them.

Another pair of Algerians broke into a photographer's shop and stole a lot of expensive equipment. While they were going through the stock they found a polaroid camera. Chortling happily, they could not resist the temptation to take each other's photographs. They left the prints behind, and the police had no difficulty tracing them, they just made use of the convenient mugshots.

The French press are under no restraint in printing the racial origins of criminals, and it is undeniable that there is an amazing preponderance of North Africans among them. The official statistics are quite clear on this. What is not so well publicised is that a large proportion of the Arab population is young, unemployed, and hard-up, three of the most common identifiers in crime statistics regardless of race. Question: would there be so many Arab criminals if the Arab population were predominantly middle-aged and well-off? Whatever the answer, the French tend to regard their Arabs as undesirable immigrants, though before we condemn them for it we must remember that in many towns the proportion of immigrants is extremely high, much higher than we are used to in England. It is this that explains the electoral successes of the Front National; just up the road is St Gilles, a town with a very heavy Arab population and a Front National mayor.

Last year at this time we were eating out of doors on the Association picnic table. This year with a sharp frost, we were thankful to eat lunch in the wheelhouse, admiring our geraniums and watching the world outside.

Everyone in the Sunday market was complaining about the cold. A black-haired marketwoman with mittened hands dropped Laurel's change as she handed it back, losing coins deep among the cabbages, complaining that she could hold nothing, her hands were so cold: *'Je ne tieng rieng den les mengs!'* with the accent that changes 'dimanche' to 'dimentch'. The cheese man was leaning despondently on his counter, murmuring: 'It's a disaster.'

We had another sharp frost overnight; the reeds were feathered and crackly with it, but now the sun was sparkling in and showing all the dust, just as Laurel wanted the saloon to look nice for lunch: two Americans, two French, and us.

We had used up the last of the Bramleys (brought from England in mid November) in an English apple tart. They were among the things we miss in France, together with cheddar cheese, and strong, bitter orange marmalade. Laurel used to make marmalade at this time of year, and has even managed to do so in Florida, Turkey, and southern Italy, with the bitter oranges from trees planted, one to each grove, to fertilise the sweet oranges. She was given as many kilos (or pounds in Florida) as she wished for nothing, and was clearly considered batty. In Spain we could never find Seville oranges even in Seville (but it was in July). They were all sent to the UK. In France they grow no oranges, and do not understand marmalade.

The Reine de Reinettes is queen of apples here in France, and is the one used to make the *tarte au pommes* that is found in all *patisseries*. It is crisp and well flavoured, but to our palates it lacks the tartness of a Cox or a Laxton, and there is absolutely no equivalent to the English cooking apple.

> Quan la Candelour lucerna
> Quaranto jou aprés hiverna
>
> When the sun shines bright at Candlemas
> Forty more winter days will pass

Here in the Camargue, as in all Provence, this is the day to dismantle the Christmas *crèche*. The small ones with a rough stable and perhaps ten or a dozen *santons*, are quickly wrapped and put away in a box till next year; but in some households this is as big a task as taking down a good-sized model railway, as the *crèche* will have occupied quite as much space, and succeeding generations having added to the collection.

In a number of churches the *crèche* is almost an architectural feature, built of stone and occupying an entire chapel. Here the *santons* are put away, but the setting remains all the year. In some Provençal villages a white *crèche* appears at Candlemas, containing a cage with two turtle doves, representing the arrival of Mary and Joseph in Jerusalem to lead the Infant Jesus to the temple.

It had rained hard the day before Candlemas, and continued raining until the next afternoon, when it suddenly got out fine and warm. Last year an immense stable anticyclone had held sway over western Europe from the beginning of December, giving Northern France freezing fog, no rain anywhere, and a desperate shortage of snow at the ski resorts. It brought us in the Camargue a mild dry winter, until it broke up at the end of February in a series of vigorous depressions, bringing March in like a lion with rain and gales. This year the nights were often below freezing, but the days were sufficiently warm by lunchtime to eat out of doors.

We began a social week or two, as many yachts come down the canals in early spring leaving behind the frost from all stations to Ultima Thule. Old and new friends stopped by to make or renew acquaintance. We had a cheerful combined labour-saving lunch party, where everyone brings something and the hostess is not left to do the washing up. Laurel made chicken vol-au-vents, the easy way with bought flaky pastry. One of the yachts was from America. The American lady was used to France, her brother had been at the 'Sawbone' University in Paris.

'Studying medicine?' asked Laurel with a straight face.

February can be a very cold month even in these lands on the very edge of the sunny Mediterranean. Bill, breath steaming as he split large oak logs, recalled the old Lowestoft adage that wood that you chop yourself warms you twice (Lowestofians are not noted for spending money unnecessarily). The canal bore a thin film of ice which disappeared as the big barges ploughed their way through. In the closed Canal du Bourgidou the ice was thick enough for the moorhens to slither on it.

Laurel grumbled about the smuts from the central heating boiler, and Bill grumbled about the boiler as an entity. There was something not quite right about it; it was in that condition where it worked well enough to avoid being thrown out, but not well enough to be relied upon.

Bruno was overhauling his eel sett (locally called a *trabaque*) which remained in place all winter. From medieval times the eelmen have laid their nets in the *étangs* of the region, and when the canal was built it passed through some of these *étangs*. With commendable logic, the eelmen therefore claimed the right to lay their nets in the canal as well, and despite many disputes with other canal users they stick firmly to their *patrimoine*. At cold first light the fifty horsepower outboard on a simple old-fashioned skiff roared up from the seaport four kilometres away and rent our sleep to the point where we would sometimes sigh and rise for breakfast, and watch the eelman working in the wreathing mists of a winter dawn. He was one of several eel fishermen who worked the *trabaques*, wrapped to the eyeballs in gloves and mufflers, topped by a yellow oilskin. The tubular nets were laid along the canal and held in place by stakes, marked according to imagination or ingenuity with bits of coloured rag, dustbin liners, or empty plastic bottles, in the hope of preventing boats from hitting them. The open end of the net faced the current, which usually flows out to sea.

Often his catch was meagre, but at the end of February the eels are more numerous; those of them who buried themselves in the mud of the *étangs* to escape the cold now reappeared. They are thought hereabouts to wander over the damp fields between the *roubines* or dykes, and pause in the kitchen gardens for a nibble of *petit pois*, for which, it is said, they have a predilection. Their elvers arrive at the end of February and beginning of March at the mouth of the Rhône, where in globular masses of transparent vermicelli they mount the river, keeping close to the banks where the contraflow is weaker, and peeling off into the *roubines*, small canals, and *étangs* to continue growing.

Fed up with varnishing, we cleaned up and drove the few kilometres over to the marina at Port Camarge to see our American friends Jane and Clyde in *Audacious*. They had berthed near to the chandlery and workshops as they had work to do on board, as we all do from time to time. It was a corner which was in winter a little more animated than the rest of the complex, which at this season was a vast expanse of four thousand empty boats all with their halyards tinkling against the mast whenever the wind blew, which was often. It was a sound of desolation. The bigger boats produced a slow 'dong!' a passing bell for summer long gone, and the whole orchestra accompanied the winter months, fortissimo in a mistral.

A fine weekend, however, brought the land-bound populace out for jaunts, joggings and bike rides with dogs of all shapes and sizes, mostly large to giant. It was a good day for *bricolage* – that expressive word that the French use for DIY.

Clyde could be detected on the quay at a considerable distance doing something with fibreglass, partly because of the smell of chemicals and partly because the booming 'Hi there!' that emerged from his enormous frame caused folk up to a kilometre away to turn their heads.

For company at Port Camargue there were one or two people spending the winter in their boats, and one or two more in flats ashore. But it was a little mournful during the week, as few of the bars and restaurants and none of the summer grocery stores were open. Jane rode her bike into Grau-du-Roi to do her shopping. Here, where a hundred years ago there were ten sheds and a lighthouse, was a busy little fishing port and enough beach for a summer season. The boutiques and souvenir shops had closed for the winter, but the bakers and grocers and other food stores were as busy as ever.

We invited Jane and Clyde to take a break and come with us to Sommières if the morrow was fine.

It was. Bright and sunny, which took the chill out of our hearts, and lead to thoughts of picnics, fairly easily quashed in favour of a bistro lunch.

Sommières was about twenty-six kms away inland up the river Vidourle, which crosses the Canal du Rhône à Sète a little way away from our mooring on its way out to sea at Grau-du-Roi.

The town is picturesquely set among trees, the houses heaped up a hillside above the Roman bridge, where the river runs, shallow and lazy and treacherous.

The centre of the town is built on vaulted arches, through which the river runs when, swollen with the melting snows of the Cévennes, it overflows its banks and roars through the town.

We sat, ever fascinated by water, and drank at a riverside café, watching the slow trail of weed twist in an eddy, and the froth and bubble of the trickle going over the weir, and the occasional flash of silver among the weedy green as the winter sun caught a bright whisk of fin or fishflank. Lunch was not easy to find on a Monday out of season. The palatial establishment named after the Roman bridge would have been too royal for our purses, even if it had been open. We settled for a little *crèperie* under the vaulted edge of the market square (named after *two* doctors just to make sure) and had an imaginative lunch entirely of pancakes, savoury and sweet.

We then went to a pottery in a village close by, since Clyde was a keen and accomplished amateur potter.

The first time we had visited Micot had been last summer, on firing day when the huge woodburning kiln in the garden had been stoked and fired since five in the morning, and at four in the afternoon she was just finishing. Wood ash covered Micot from head to toe, and her face was white with fatigue, under the smears of ash and smoke.

She left us in her showroom to look at her work while she showered and changed. Dominique, the Aigues-Mortes librarian, had brought us here, and when Micot emerged cool and refreshed in clean jeans, they cooked together a peach pie for tea.

We loved Micot's blue glazes, and had bought a bowl glazed with beautiful blues and purples and lavenders that seemed to shift and change as you looked at them. We determined then and there never to fill it with rubber bands or olive pits – bowls on our boat do tend to house nasty little gatherings of biro tops, wine corks, a small screwdriver, a twist of useful string, bus tickets, paper clips, and a sock. We resolved to keep this one empty so that it would always be a pleasure to the eye.

Now that it was winter Micot was having a good rest, no firing today. Summer was exhausting, she ran holiday pottery courses with marvellous food (her husband Jacques did the cooking) as well as the daily throwing of pots and a weekly firing. Jacques started adult life as a monk, and is now an expert in computer maladies, and it was he who greeted us on this occasion. Now, with no courses to run and students to feed, life was much quieter, and Micot had time to make preparations for exhibitions, and work at her own pots.

After our day out we returned to Aigues-Mortes just at sunset; one of those lovely lemon and thunder skies that winter breeds in the Camargue.

20

Hard times for everyone

*'Foou saupre si plagne
L'on oouten toujours qu'auquaren.'*

....

'Know how to complain
There is always some gain.'

There were no gifts of fresh asparagus this year. The asparagus crop was *sinistré*. The extreme heat and dryness of the previous summer caused a plague of insects out of season. The tender plants were ravaged throughout the *département* of the Gard. A catastrophe. It is not certain that the farmers will get compensation. New crowns are planted in March, and only after three years can you begin to harvest. The plants will live for ten years if you treat them gently and harvest only for six weeks. But to be commercial a farmer must harvest for three months to get a return for his money, and these plants will be exhausted after three years. To replace the ravaged plants with new crowns and then wait three years for the first harvest is a big investment. Jeannot may not replant.

As March progressed the weather became pleasantly warm, the tamarisk was veiled in dusky pink, and strong green shoots appeared among the reeds.

Three of our saloon windows faced the canal. The opposite three gave on to the canal bank. The canal windows were everchanging, the light on the canal itself altered with the weather, the state of the sky and wind. Horses and riders used the towpath on the opposite side, and barges and boats of all kinds passed by. These windows were our television, there was usually something going on; but if Laurel wanted to switch off, or look at the interval signal for a sense of peace and continuity, she sat facing the other three windows, which reminded her of Chinese brush paintings.

All you could see in any of the three windows was sky, and the silhouettes of reeds. Simple, but satisfying. In winter the few reeds remaining were dry and angular, and the colours austere, shades of parchment and whatever hue the sky was. Here the stalk altered direction, there several leaves extended in subtle arabesques, each in complete harmony with the other. Here a stem crossed another at the golden section, there two stiff reeds might be joined by the exquisitely sparing curve of a spider's web. Nothing jarred, everything was perfect. Visitors placed where they could see these windows had been known gradually to cease chatting and go off into a trance.

Sometimes the pictures were in movement, as the wind shivered the reeds. In summer the growth was high and vigorous, the curves of the reeds voluptuous, and arabesques in every shade of green filled the windows, and when the wind blew they roiled like the surging sea. In March there was an extra delight, as in the foremost window appeared the green lances of the water iris, soon to burst forth like handfuls of sunshine. Laurel defended these from all comers, it hurt her to see straggling bunches of them pulled up by the roots and stuffed into jars on the hire boats, now beginning to come past in numbers.

The hireboat industry was started here by the British with out-dated boats from the Broads, but the French have caught up with us now and are developing it further. There are cruisers of many different designs, with varying standards of comfort and elegance. Under French law, seaworthiness no longer imposes a discipline on the designer, for strict separation is maintained: a boat designed for the rivers is forbidden to go to sea (though not vice versa). Some firms have produced nice-looking elegant boats like miniature barges (*les pénichettes*), while others have veered towards pseudo-modernism producing a floating gazebo like the Festival of Britain gone mad. It is remarkable that the French, so artistic in many ways, manage to produce undoubtedly awful designs of both cars and boats. They go well mechanically, but often they offend the eye.

Boat hiring is a growing business, and whether on our native Broads or here in France it makes a popular holiday. Little danger of *mal-de-mer*, and plenty of places to stop for a meal or drink in a café close to the water. At least in summer. In winter most of these attractive little spots are closed. If you hire a boat out of season you must expect a more spartan holiday. In recompense the cost is lower, the countryside more visible, and the sights more accessible. Local people complain that in high summer one cannot see anything for Germans with cameras, but they exaggerate a little. The tourists, both on water and on land, are not all German; there are Italians, Swiss, Belgians and Japanese as well, though it is rare to see the Japanese in a boat.

Many of the boats passing our doors betray their foreign ownership by having mis-spelt French names, just as false red ensigns often have English names that are not quite right. Example. An English company names their boats 'Connoisseur', which you might think was a French word, but the French spell it 'Connaisseur'.

In France one normally needs formal qualification to drive any boat of more than ten horse-power. In the case of the hireboats, this rule is ignored by the authorities so that tourism may prosper, and all the boats, some of which are very large, are inscribed 'No permit required'.

This led to an ironic article in the inland waters magazine, *Fluviale*, envisaging an enthusiastic rookie *gendarme*, unaware of the necessary blind eye, boarding a boat full of tourists and asking to see a licence to drive their craft.

'What? you have no *permis*?' says the gendarme, opening his notebook and licking his pencil. '*Alors, nom de votre mère*?' ('Your mother's maiden name?' equivalent to 'Name and address?' is the first, and apparently the most important, of your particulars to be demanded in France.)

Such would be the howl from the boating tourist industry that the *gendarme* would soon find himself on duty at the far end of Devil's Island, wondering why he had not been commended for his initiative.

Mario and Martine, experienced *mariniers*, were working on *Massilia*, their new acquisition. Since the *Isles de Stel* had been sold to the proprietor of one of Aigues-Mortes' better restaurants, he no longer had to worry about her maintenance, though it had been agreed that he would continue to captain her for the coming summer. Mario was reshaping the bow of his new boat, and had already put there a decorative shield containing his initials. He liked to sign his work. She would be called *La Licorne*, the Unicorn. Both he and Martine were in filthy overalls covered in rust and paint. They were happy as larks.

Serge was getting *Pescalune* ready for the season, smartening up the paint. Power failures were the order of the day again, the new cable was *impeccable*, but at times Mario's massive shipwrighting overloaded it, and it blew. Everything was normal. There was a buzz of contented activity on the peninsula, as of bees in the sunshine.

Bill was mending electric wires in our after-cabins. Sometime last spring, when we had no cats, an alleged rat got into the spare-cabin ceiling space. Until all the electrics fused at that end of the boat we did not realise that we had a lodger, but as Bill traced the wires and found lumps of the surrounding plastic enthusiastically chewed, all became clear. He had put back the ceiling panel with pretty packets of pink poison resting on it, and monitored them at intervals. They were dragged away, whole.

All through May and June there had been a nasty smell at that end of the boat, and when we returned in late July after a month in England the wheelhouse was full of enormous dead bluebottles. It all added up to the demise of the rat, though we never found a corpse.

Bill had cobbled something together at the time to give light, but was now doing a proper repair to the main damage, which was extensive: a good hard chew every metre or so along several metres of the electric cables serving the after-cabin, the after-bathroom and the engine room. None of it was fit to re-use, so he stripped it all out and replaced it.

A good deal of March was occupied with slipping the boat at Arles. A messy, noisy, disruptive, and expensive fortnight; the baths and loo not to be used, buckets and kitty litter standing substitute, a long ladder to be negotiated down to the mud of the yard below, and the dead feeling as you trod the deck of a boat out of its element. However, *Hosanna* finished up in very good shape, and with her bottom newly painted and protected from all evil. The journey back to Aigues-Mortes was pleasant, as our boat, feeling alive under our feet again, chugged through the greening country, and we felt one step nearer our summer at sea.

We were back just in time for Palm Sunday. The church of Notre Dame des Sablons, Our Lady of the Dunes, was full. Just inside the door was an enormous pile of green branches, a mixture of bay and olive. If you had not brought your own branch, you might help yourself. As in all continental churches, people came and went, and shuffled about during the service, but quietly, and no one seemed to mind.

At the high point of the ceremony, after we had sung some slightly wavery hymns, encouraged by the strong baritone of our Mayor who was enthusiastically conducting the music, the children processed down the aisle towards the altar, holding up their branches. Theirs were a sight to see. No simple olive twig or sprig of bay for them. They struggled under veritable Christmas trees, for the palm in Provence is decorated (for children at any rate) with packets of bonbons and macaroons, sugared almonds, crystallised fruit, and chocolate rabbits (for is not next Sunday Easter?) all lovingly tied with ribbons and tinsel.

We held our branches up to be blessed, and several of the smaller children jumped up and down to raise theirs a little higher. How tragic it would be if owing to their shortness of stature the magic passed over their heads and missed them. Laurel has much sympathy with small people, and had to suppress an undignified desire to follow suit, being hemmed behind a couple of six foot *gardians* and an even taller Scandinavian lady. We then all sang quite long and loudly 'Hosanna, Hosanna'. This was because the Mayor had coached us in this three or four times before the start of the ceremony, and we therefore had confidence. He really is a pretty good Mayor.

Laurel emerged with her blessed sprig of bayleaves, with the added attribute, we hoped, of keeping the thunder away, and crossed the square to the Express Bar, where Bill was drinking his *demi* and reading *Midi Libre*. He has found it hard to discover why a quarter of a litre of beer was called a *demi*, meaning a half. It is of course approximately half a pint, and he felt that a pint is so much the obvious natural measure of a beer that even the devisers of the devilish metric system have had to ackowledge this. If the quarter litre is called a *demi*, the half litre is called a *'raisonnable'*, while a litre is called a *'sérieux'*. This denoted a suitably respectful attitude towards beer consumption, and it must also be born in mind that French beer is stronger than the typical English brew, perhaps explaining why so many of our young come unstuck at Calais.

Jeannot the farmer was at the Express. How were his vines, we asked, not daring to mention asparagus. 'Oh, it is a busy time,' he said. 'We have begun to spray against the odium.' We were fascinated by the odium, a disease we had not heard of, and a word which was not in our dictionary. In spring the vines began to bud, and there were treatments to be given against mildew, odium, and various insects.

This began as the first leaves put forth, and would continue every ten days according to the weather. It did not seem that being owner of a vineyard was a quiet number.

One vineyard plague that the local people do not have, it seems, is *court-noué*, which deforms the shoots, but which is put off by a light sandy soil. (It is a wonder we ever get any wine at all.) It is apparently gaining ground elsewhere in France. Perhaps the Camargue wines will have a second chance. Never mind the odium.

Then we ran up against our own attack of odium. Out of a clear spring sky, disaster struck us. Driving into town later that week Bill was disturbed by a brilliant flash in the corner of his left eye, rather as if someone had taken a close-up flash photo of us as we passed. It disturbed and shocked him, but he did nothing until we got home, by which time he had some worrying flecks in his vision.

We consulted the *Ship Captain's Medical Guide*, the renowned tome that helps captains far from professional help sort out the minor and major health problems of their crews. It has changed a lot since the first edition which is reported to have come with a medicine chest of four bottles, the labels of which classified the human body as follows: top half or bottom half, and inside or outside.

Nowadays, apart from a morbid obsession with sexually transmitted diseases, the book has colour photographs of bloody bits of humans, and a do-it-yourself step-by-step guide to amputations and brain surgery. It was no help to us at all. British seamen can clearly be left to finish their voyages without benefit of sight.

We found helpful counsel in another reference book: flashes in the eye, see an ophthalmologist without delay. This might have posed problems at sea, but, thank God, we were well made fast to the canal bank. As it was by now late on Good Friday night we left it until tomorrow.

In France, unlike Britain, medical specialists are accessible to patients without the time-consuming nonsense of having to be referred by a general practitioner. So they are in most countries. Thank God again. We found from the yellow pages that there was an ophthalmologist in the nearby village of Vauvert. It seemed too good to be true. Laurel phoned. As we mentioned in connection with the wood, this is her job. Laurel is quite good at telephones now.

As she described the symptoms to the ophthalmologist she was cut short. 'Come immediately,' he said. 'You can drive, Madame? Excellent, it will be necessary.' Within ten minutes of arrival at his superbly equipped surgery Bill had drops in the eye and was being posed in front of a frightening framework of apertures.

'You have fallen well,' said the young doctor, artistic and wildly bearded. 'This is a retina problem, and I am a retina specialist.'

'Left or right eye specialist?' Bill asked, trying to keep cheerful. He was ignored, the doctor was busy telephoning.

A few minutes later we were driving in the doctor's car to Nîmes where he shared a clinic with other ophthalmologists in the neighbourhood. As he drove he told us that the retina had torn in two places, that the tears must be welded back into place with a laser beam, and that the quicker it was done the better chance of a successful operation.

At Nîmes Bill found himself sitting under a poster asking the French if they wanted a health service '*A l'Anglaise*', where one could wait, sometimes for years, for an operation. He took the point, remembering appalling waits, lasting all day, at the Maidstone Eye Hospital. After waiting fully five minutes in the foyer on this Easter Saturday morning while the machine and surgery were prepared, Bill was in the ops room and his eye was being lasered. 380 times. It was less than half an hour since we had met the doctor, in a village of 6,000 inhabitants.*

We will not go into the operation. Men do not talk about their operations, Bill says while telling everyone about it.

By lunchtime Laurel had driven him home, both of us in a mild state of shock, since we had had no time to absorb the information, or even react to it. Each of us had plenty of time now to reflect on the enormity of the occurrence, and its probable implications. Each of us tried not to think of the worst scenario. Tacitly, the future was not discussed. In any case work was out of the question till the lesions had healed.

If they healed. On doctor's orders Bill was to do nothing that caused physical shock, and no heavy lifting. 'Don't complain,' said the *docteur*. 'Before lasers you would be now in strict bed for six weeks with bandaged eyes, and a very uncertain outcome.' We did not complain. The eye was not even bandaged, and if Bill occasionally wore a piratical patch it was to keep the sun out of his tender eye. 'You may read, write, use the computer, use your brain all you like, but no woodwork or hammering.' said Dr Romano.

We had paid some 870 francs for the treatment, all of which was subsequently refunded. The cost of the drugs was partially refunded. Getting the money back afterwards was not difficult. It took a little longer than the surgery, and needed more persistence. But we got it.

The whole episode was efficiently and quickly handled and we were very impressed. Docteur Romano told us that for the same population there are four times as many ophthalmic surgeons in France as in Britain. 'It is because in your country one has to be accredited to a hospital to be able to specialise,' he said. Apparently this does not apply in France. This young surgeon was trained in nearby Montpellier, one of the oldest and best medical schools in Europe.

Bill, shaken, went into playing chess, writing articles, and reading, often pinned to his chair by the cat Blue, who had adopted him, while Tansy, once so much the smaller of the two, was now a huge plump and lazy cat, puzzled by the way she now overlapped Laurel's knees, and hung down on each side like an altar cloth. Bill did not find reading easy as his left eye was full of flecks and spots. Gradually he learnt how to make them move over out of his immediate field of vision. Laurel, also shaken, vented her feelings by going into painting mode and got coats of paint on various bits of deck and superstructure. As the weather was pleasantly sunny, she rigged up the awning over the poop, which is our sitting out place, and got out the deck chairs. One might as well recuperate in comfort.

A check a few days later showed that the lesions were holding. The spots and flecks would take a while to go, maybe weeks. In the meantime, no physical shocks for at least three weeks. So no building.

March had gone out, unproverbially, like a lion, and April came in like another. The mistral fought the traders next market day, and won. At the early hour of eleven-fifteen the metallic crash of stalls being unmade and loaded back into their trailers blended with the curses of the stall holders and the howling of the wind. They had had enough. That is to say the foodstalls were hanging on, their goods protected largely by their own weight or glass counters, but Clothing and Knicknackeries, tired of chasing flying tee shirts or errant knickers, not to mention a flight of small wicker baskets like straw ducks on the wing, were packing up to go. The ramparts, in whose beetling shadow the market is held twice a week, have the effect of stirring up *tourbillons*, whirlwinds of sometimes quite vicious power. The places where this effect is worst are well-known, and are left unoccupied, or to some unfortunate newcomer who does not understand a market day mistral under the ramparts of Aigues-Mortes.

For there is more to it than the wind, at this time of year. The plane trees that would bring welcome shade to the market in the sweltering days of July were showering down little feathered seeds. These lay in drifts a foot deep in every windshadow, and every gust of wind brought down more seeds to mix with those stirred up from the drifts. The seeds clung to everything on sale. They penetrated the hearts of lettuce, the scales of globe artichokes, they settled in neat rows between the clumps of asparagus. You bought them willy nilly weighed out with your beans or your early strawberries. The fabric seller gave up trying to brush them off the bales of jersey and velour, they did not stick so much to cottons. The undie man shook pairs of socks despairingly, but without success, since the seeds clung. Another puff brought a whirl of them to nestle coyly in among his bras, and the next powerful gust, accompanied by crashes and angry shrieks from every direction, carried away two nightdresses complete with hangers. They landed across the basins of olives on the opposite stall, and were retrieved, with additional trimming in the shape of chopped chilli and damp herbs. The undie man cast his eyes to heaven, and began to stack his goods.

Even this was not all. For these seeds are one of the great plagues of Aigues-Mortes. Even to the resolutely unallergic came a dripping nose and stinging eyes. The business of buying and selling had to be done with purse in one hand and handkerchief in the other, between snorts and sneezes. Those who were really sensitive went home with streaming eyes and rough grating throats, and shut the windows and doors against the twin enemies of mistral and plane seeds. The rest of us completed our shopping faster than usual, counted our change with a little more care (since distracted traders make more mistakes) and dodged flying objects such as plastic bags, lettuce leaves, a parachuting skirt, and the hats of the tourists.

In the Place St Louis Bill, with a patch over one eye, derived much simple amusement over his *demi* by watching the effects of this scourge, well-known to the waiters, but unsuspected by tourists. As the great plane trees, so beloved and cool in summer, now sifting the spring sunlight through a tracery of buds and young green leaves, shook with every gust of wind another million seeds came whirling down, on to café tables, the stacked plates, the folded napkins (the glasses are sensibly upside down, except for that new restaurant over there which has placed elegant waterlily napkins inside the glasses, now filled to the brim with plane seeds). We placed beermats over our drinks, and stayed under the awning of the Express, and watched the tourists shuffle ankle deep through the fluff, watched the brims of their hats fill up, watched them peering down their camcorders while their pint of beer collected a froth that had nothing to do with brewing.

Come lunchtime the Place beckoned one to eat.

Even into your oysters, your champagne bucket, and your *panaché de poissons sauce oseille*, came drifting down Aigues-Mortes' special April garnish: a sprinkle of fluffy plane seeds.

'Let's go home,' said Laurel. 'I think I'm getting a sore throat.'

We got away both from the plane tree seeds and the work screaming to be done on board by going down to the Bird Reserve. There were almost no trees down there in the true Camargue, nothing larger than a tamarisk and thickets of stunted bushes which could tolerate the salt. Everything was bursting into green. The low tussocks of salt-tolerating plants were coming into flower.

One could get to the edge of the Reserve by car, but to go any further into it meant taking the rough paths on horseback, bicycle, or shanks' pony. Out of the tourist season, when the perimeter road is quiet, there were plenty of birds visible close to the road, enough for people like us: not very knowledgeable but interested. Only later as the tourist buses and caravans came would the birds become more shy and retreat further into the Reserve.

The migrating birds flew overhead, some of them too high to be seen; geese for instance often fly above 8,000 metres. The starlings, warblers and thrushes had already passed on their way north. The migrating larks had collected their fellows who wintered here, and went their way. Now the voyaging intensified as Europe warmed up, wagtails, house martins and the hoopoes appeared.

It was nesting time down on the Vaccarès. Among the cushions of marsh grass partridges ran in pairs, and small birds could be heard crooning, but not seen. The mallards had been nesting since March at the edge of the *étang*, away from the trodden paths. The ducks, sensibly, drive their husbands off during nesting, and the drakes go to other *étangs*, for a game of cards and a whisky and cigar with the chaps. We could see sandpipers, oystercatchers, lapwings, and the teals and ducks which were passing at this time and would not return till autumn. The unmistakable flight of a heron caught our eye.

There were of course some flamingoes, but not as many as the birdmen had hoped.

In the old days the Rhône flooded this delta at random and provided the water for the few crops that were grown, mostly round the edges of the Camargue. Later when the Rhône's banks had been levéed and the flood waters passed quickly out to sea, the land came to be irrigated by specially dug canals and *roubines*. Gradually more and more of the salt was leached out of the soil and the character of a large part of the Camargue began to change.

It is one of the paradoxes of life that as the area round the Etang de Vaccarès (the biggest *étang*) was made into a nature reserve for the ornithologists to play in, the pink flamingoes that were one of the deciding factors in the establishment of the park, this being the only place in Europe where they breed in numbers, have gradually left the Reserve to feed, though they still breed there. They have moved west into the *étangs* at the edge of the Petite Camargue, which is not a nature reserve, and which they seem to prefer to the places that are. They are to be found in ever increasing numbers alongside the main road, much to the delight of the tourist authorities of that region (Palavas), and much to the chagrin of the professional bird-men.

The locals tell of the Swiss ornithologists who tried to

ring the baby flamingoes, whose legs are as fragile as a thread of glass. In one year they destroyed more flamingoes than the poachers of Saintes-Maries throughout history. In many of the more beautiful places of the world there is to be found an aristocracy, self-elected, who may enjoy the facilities and beauty of the country at public expense while limiting or even excluding all access to the public. They call these aristocrats ornithologists.

The principal factor that led to the relocation of the flamingo was undoubtedly the gradual de-salination of the *étangs* as land was reclaimed for agriculture, and irrigated scientifically from the Rhône. We cannot altogether blame the ham-fisted Swiss. The birds feed on a sort of krill of minute crustaceans, and these are very sensitive to the salinity of the water. Once upon a time the Etang de Vaccarès had deposits of salt round the edges after a hot summer, and these were a major source of revenue to the poor people of the region, salt being a highly taxed government monopoly, and therefore very profitable to smuggle. There is no longer salt caked round the edges, and the krill, and therefore the flamingoes who feed on them, have moved to the saltier *étangs*.

Probably the survival of large flocks of these flying flowers, as local poet and folklorist Baroncelli called them, has been due to the fact that they are not good to eat, rather than to any work of ornithologists. Many older Camargue people tried to eat them during the war when food was very scarce. The meat is generally reported as stringy, and tasting strongly of sardines, which is not surprising as the sardines, too, eat krill. It is an interesting thought that if the flamingo had tasted as good as pheasant it would not have stood a chance, protected or not. There are not many swans about, for example. Laurel has a recipe for heron pudding, which is interesting, but she would never use it.

Nevertheless there were enough flamingoes to satisfy us that day. They are astonishing birds. They spend much of the time with their heads under water, looking like pink plastic hoovers. Their delicate skulls are built with strainers behind the enormous boatshaped beak, flakes of fine bone, pierced with little holes like a lace fan. The flamingo trails its head upside down under the water, and takes in a large gulp. The krill is filtered out by these strainers and sent to the gullet. Their legs are so long and fine that they do not look strong enough to support the large body and particularly the heavy beak. Their performance on land and water is ungainly.

But when it flies: it is Baroncelli's flower, it is poetry, it is colour in flight, because the pink of the flamingo is not baby pink, or underwear pink, or tinned salmon pink, or the pink of the chairs at the Express Bar. It is a heavenly pink, quite literally, because its wings are the pink of the clouds at sunset in the Camargue, barred with black, the colour of the coming night.

> Almond petals
> Scraps of sunset
> Fly above the lake
> Birds? or flowers?

In our own little nature reserve at Le Bourgidou, at this time, if we ventured outside in the evening after dark to look at the moon, an immense chorus of frogs from the pond under the bridge entertained us. It was more musical than disturbing, so many little voices lifted to salute the night. By day they were shy, we saw one occasionally, still very small, a flash of green under the duckweed in the pond.

By mid April Dr Romano's patient had ceased to be patient. We were beginning to talk of the coming months. 'I suppose this fog in my eye might stop us going to sea,' said Bill tersely. At last the dreadful thought was voiced. 'We'd have to do a canal cruise, like last year,' said Laurel, trying to sound comforting. 'We could do that all right.'

'Mmm,' was all Bill would say.

In another week, when Dr Romano had said there was no need to see him for a month, nothing could stop the convalescent clearing out the forepeak and installing shelves, a necessary step to take before seagoing, as everything had to be securely held in place. When remonstrated with he merely said: 'It's all right, I'm not hammering anything.'

It was hard to watch other boats down at Port Camargue preparing to leave for the summer. When asked what our plans were, we had to say: 'We don't know.' It would soon be the end of April.

Our arch serenader arrived, the nightingale. We noticed him first in the daytime, for he sang a good part of the day at the top of his voice from the top of the fig tree, and his song dominated that of the other birds. It was louder and more confident, a practised soloist well able to overtop a run-of-the-mill opera chorus. At night he sang *a capella*, unaccompanied by rivals, and his sweet true notes brought us up on deck to listen.

At the beginning of May his song was answered by another from across the canal. 'Come, live with me and be my love,' he carolled, pleading, coaxing, irresistible. She was coy. The duet went on every night. 'Cross over the water to my aspen tree,' she seemed to sing in reply. She held out for a week, but he was too strong for her, and they both ended up in the fig tree on our side, to our delight and solace.

21

The gypsy festival

'Que siés tu, santo saro, de toujour coume
vuei,
Siés l'estello que briho, nous moustrant
lou camin,
E de nosto patrio, Sas, soulo, li counfin.'
. . . .
'For 'tis you, Sant Sara, today as in
time long gone,
You are the star that shines to show
the road,
You alone know the bounds of our
land.'

Marquis Folco de Baroncelli-Javon

The sun shone, it was warm, it was May, jackets, coats and
macs had long been put away, and shorts and sunhats dug
out from winter storage. It was safe enough to leave the
deckchairs out, and all doors and windows open, though
the morning dew could be heavy. We were eating all our
meals out of doors.

'Are we going to the duck race today?' asked Laurel one
morning. Bill sighed. Laurel had been quite unable to stop
him working, so she had tried the different and more subtle
tack of getting him away from the boat, to visit friends, go
for drives, or attend happenings.

There had been a poster in the butcher's window
announcing the event. The English occasionally occupy
themselves in racing obscure fauna, snails for example, and
Bill has memories of racing caterpillars along the pews of
his prep-school chapel during the interminable compulsory

services then current. But ducks? There would be difficulties keeping such birds on course, we thought, were they specially trained? We knew plenty of duck eaters, but no duck trainers.

We went down to the Bassin d'Evolution just outside the ramparts near the main Porte de la Gardette. As we have seen, this is where the canal both turns sharply and broadens out so that long barges can turn round. There was a large gathering sitting on the grass under the trees or on the waterside benches (the Mayor's gardeners had been busy here too). The crowd were chiefly Aigues-Mortais for the event had not been much publicised other than in local café-bars. A few tourists were there by accident, attracted by the excitement.

There was an air of expectancy, but as yet no sign of ducks. A couple of dinghies rowed about in aimless fashion, but the officials contained therein mostly rested on their oars.

Then the man in the sternsheets of one dinghy opened a wicker crate and threw overboard the first duck, a mallard, followed immediately by about half a dozen others. The crowd stirred, and from it emerged a dozen or so young men in bathing slips or shorts, who dived into the water and swam towards the ducks.

It was less of a duck race than a duck chase, giving the birds a sporting chance by pursuing them in their own element, or rather one of their elements, since they had had their wings unsportingly clipped so that they could just fly over the water with their feet treading on the surface but could not quite manage a proper take-off to fly out of reach.

The ducks had naïvely gathered together in the centre of the Bassin, and clearly looked upon the approaching swimmers with some concern. As they got near, the ducks dispersed, quacking agitatedly. They had to land on the water surface now and then, and so started the chase. The boys collaborated with each other, the ducks did not. They were fragmented, separated, cornered. More ducks were released, adding to the confusion in the water. Some ducks had had their wings overclipped and were easily caught, while other luckier ducks managed to get airborne and flew away under either the rail or road bridges which constituted safe haven not only for the fliers, but also for any ducks that could swim there: that was considered sanctuary and they were allowed to go.

When a duck was caught it would be brought ashore and *maman* or *papa* would hold it by its pinioned wings while its catcher returned once more to the chase. In all some forty ducks were released, and about half of them escaped capture. Those that were caught became the property of the catcher; some proud mums were happily staggering under four or five ducks. Some would be eaten beyond doubt, this is France where anything that moves (and several things that do not) gets eaten. But others were taken off to nearby farms to join their fellows for rearing.

'What's for lunch?' said Bill as we sat at the Express afterwards. 'Cold duck salad, what else?' said Laurel.

Serge-the-brother-in-law-of-Jeannot came over to say *bonjour*. We told him that we had been reading a mocking account written just after the war, in which a Camarguais was poking tremendous fun at the American scientists at 'Cornhill' University, who were recording the noises of female mosquitoes to attract the males and destroy them. *Quel stupidité*! How could such a thing work? was the opinion in 1945.

'I will tell you something,' said Serge. 'At this very moment we watch for the flight of a minuscule grey butterfly. If she is allowed to lay eggs on the vines, the worm that emerges later burrows into the grape and bursts it. To prevent this catastrophe we watch for the mating flight, and trap the males. With what? Ah!!! With female hormones. Not so stupid, the Americans. We shall probably do this three times before the last flight in August.'

Doctor Romano had checked that the eye had healed well, and passed Bill fit. Bill complained that there was still a screen of wriggly black blobs like tadpoles floating in his left eye, but was told that that was normal and that it would disappear with time. Bill did not believe him. He is suspicious of doctors making reassuring comments. But he said nothing. He remembered his mother-in-law's motto: after the age of sixty, live dangerously and expect the worst.

Nevertheless, he was adapting quite well to seeing things through a fog of tadpoles, he felt otherwise extremely fit after his enforced rest, and it looked as if we might get to sea after all, though time was getting on.

So Bill put the masts up.

Stepping the masts for the first time on a big boat is not only a very satisfying experience but gives one the feeling of having finished a complex job. Something of the original pleasure is always to be had every time the sticks go up in those boats equipped to raise or lower their masts by their own gear and effort. There is little pleasure in lowering them; that is to remove the very essence of seaworthiness from the hapless boat and to sentence her to a period of being out of her proper trim, like an athlete who has over-indulged in pudding.

Re-masting after such a pause in a ship's life is exhilarating, an act of restoration that does wonders for the morale. The boat is back in training, ready to go to sea and fulfil her destiny. The process is not without its trials and perils when the masts are heavy and the rigging is in proportion, and there are only two of you.

On *Hosanna* we had three masts and each was stepped in what is called a tabernacle. Do not ask how it got its name. It is a sort of horizontally hinged pivot and the heel of the mast has a hole to take the hinge pin and when the mast is down it rests on this pin at one end and on gallows at the other. (Do not ask about that either.) It needed both of us to get the masts up. That is to say Bill could do it alone, but it would take three times as long and six times as many swearwords, and Laurel was still being a little nannyish over his left eye.

We chose a windless day, early before the sea-breeze began. We first erected and stayed an intermediate pole near the tabernacle of the foremast and used this as a lever to hoist the mast itself, which with its wire rigging weighed eight hundred pounds, though by means of the science of statics we calculate that there was nearly a ton of strain in the rope used for hoisting. Up went the mast, using the anchor windlass for power with cries of 'STOPPP' every now and then as a trailing piece of rigging, usually the shrouds, got snagged round something and we had to lower a bit and free them. As the mast got nearly upright its moment about the fulcrum decreased and the angle of pull improved, and it finished the process at speed so that one had to be careful not to pull it too far forwards. That is why boats are fun, one is forever on the edge of disaster and trying to fight it off by foresight, like a very physical chess game.

Once the first mast was raised it could be used to hoist the other two, and the anxiety level went down a little. After a morning's work, finishing with tightening up the rigging so that all was held firmly against the rising sea-breeze, and then a good lunch in the open air, there was a great feeling of well-being, ending in an amorous siesta.

What an intriguing etymology there is for all those nautical words. What an odd collection of associations! Shrouds, tabernacles, gallows, cross-trees, trucks, heels, booms, gaffs, jaws and goosenecks. How did all those names originate, and from how many different languages? In truth no one knows (though some have self-explanatory similarities with everyday objects) for they are the product of generations of the spoken word in a craft where the craftsmen were always unlettered. It is not amazing that seamen should have borrowed the odd word from everyday use; what is astounding is that sea-words should be such a part of our normal language, filtering through our lexicons in the same way that a red handkerchief amongst the white linen in the wash leaves its trace; it is everywhere and can never be totally eliminated.

With all this wealth of metaphor one cannot be surprised that no British politician can string a sentence together without a nautical analogy, ever since someone coined the majestic phrase 'The Ship of State'. If the politicians knew how to use the nautical expressions they dote on, they would not give the impression to those who do that their ability and leadership is proportionate to the horlicks they make of our language. It is no good steering a straight course if you are heading for the rocks.

The French do not have this odd obsession with a nautical history, though their politicans, too, get carried away by inappropriate metaphors from time to time. They have managed to keep the sea separate from their everyday vocabulary probably because their authority on language is the Academie Française, forty grandly uniformed, be-sworded, and fairly senile literati deliberating under their cupola in Paris with barely a whiff of seaweed or common-sense in the air. A refreshing sea breeze blew in recently when pioneering senior diver, Captain Cousteau, was called to membership, a lively and fascinating character, if not noted for his literary inventiveness. Until he got there, our French literary friends tell us, the chief qualification for membership was to be pretty old and write books that nobody, other than the thirty-nine other Academicians, ever read. They keep the French Language pure. They also keep it boringly static.

In late May the gypsies, far from static, gather from far and wide to make their pilgrimage to the saint of their adoption at Saintes-Maries-de-la-Mer. On the journey they turn up everywhere.

On one riotous night a dozen of them camped on the knuckle opposite our boat, lit a fire, and while the women in bright headscarves cooked supper, their golden earrings winking in the firelight, the men got out a fiddle and a guitar, and began to play. They sang and danced half the night, but by early morning they had gone, hurrying down to Les-Saintes-Maries.

Later in the week we followed them.

The legend goes that the fortified church at Les-Saintes-Maries-de-la-Mer, a little town near the mouth of the Petit Rhône, known as the capital of the Camargue, marks the spot where a whole raft of saints, particularly Mary Jacoby, sister of the Virgin, and Mary Salome, mother of Apostles James and John, were miraculously washed ashore after being set adrift by the wicked Israelites from that well-known seaport, Jerusalem.

They were cast into the sea in a little boat with no sails, no oars and no victuals, and, almost worse, no little servant girl, who had been left on shore. With great presence of mind one of the saints threw her cloak to their little black handmaiden Sara, who was able to use it as a raft and join them in the boat. It is Sara with whom the gypsies identify, and to whom they pray in extravagant and colourful rituals, coming to do so on the feast of either of the Saintes Maries in May or October, to which they attach their Saint Sara, thus getting two festivals a year. These saints are intimately linked with the town named after them, Les-Saintes-Maries, since the Saintes remained there and built an oratory where they were interred when they died. Other members of the Holy Family, Sainted All-sorts, accompanied them in the boat, but went further into Provence, Saint Martha to Tarascon where she tamed the dreaded Tarasque which terrorised the town, Saint Mary Magdalen to continue her penitence at Sainte-Baume (The Holy Balm), Saint Lazarus to Marseille where judging by the crime rate today he was not very successful, and Maximin and Sidoine to Aix-en-Provence.

We imagine that the boat must have been a good deal larger then legend suggests, since how else did all those others arrive; St Tropez, St Raphael, and St Jean Cap Ferrat?

To this day fishermen who see a line of white streaks off the Camargue coast call it Lou Camin di Saint Mario, the path of the Saintes-Maries, and say that it marks the route followed by the Holy Barque.

The little town was already occupied by gypsies when we arrived on the Friday. It seemed best to buy the little medallion of Ste Sara offered by the first bright-skirted black-haired lady that accosted us with a practised spiel about bringing us good luck for the coming festival. Like Lifeboat Day one pinned it on a conspicuous place and it kept flagsellers away, unless they decided that you positively *must* have your fortune told. However, the gypsies know by long experience the sort of 'face' that goes with the personality who yearns to be told its fortune. Bill is not only too big, but was taught in India how to give the impression of having the evil eye by staring fixedly into the eyes of the approaching importunate so that he tends to be left alone. Laurel has the wrong face, she is too cheerful.

Parking was even more chaotic than normal, since every open space was occupied by caravans and *vardos*, cooking fires, horses, tethered goats, the odd chicken scratching about, and trestle tables full of convivial gypsy families meeting relatives for the first time in months. If our only experience of gypsies before this had been a lay-by full of layabouts, fringed by rusty old cars, dusty old washing, and busty old ladies, this made a pleasant change. There were some very beautiful antique caravans, and even the new ones, doors wide open to the May sunshine, revealed exuberant interiors with a fancy for lace and brocade, fringing, pokerwork, crochet, gleaming brass and polished crystal. In contrast, one or two families seemed to be living in a bare lorry with a tarpaulin over it, and little inside but a mattress and a chair or two. It seemed as if this acted as a spare room, where friends and relatives could be housed for the festival.

After the troubled times a thousand and odd years ago, when Saracen raids on the coast had made it prudent to hide the remains of saints, the whereabouts of the Saintes' bones became uncertain, though it was thought that they were in the choir of the twelfth-century fortified church which replaced the original oratory.

In the fifteenth century King Réné's excavations found there three bodies. They were lovingly placed in decorated coffins, or *chasses*, and at a ceremony attended by crowned heads and high church dignitaries, these were placed in the High Chapel over the choir, where they remain to this day. ('One does not visit the High Chapel,' says the guide book firmly.)

Science acknowledges the remains to be female, of middle eastern race, and of the first century AD. The cult today is strong and emotional. The gypsies' traditional pilgrimage is of long standing, their version of the story tells that the Camargue was the cradle of their race, and that Sara reigned over them here before the Holy Barque arrived in Provence. She is fiercely *theirs*. History, boringly, documents the arrival of *tziganes* in France at the beginning of the fifteenth century.

On previous occasions when we had visited the church it was always out of season and quiet. One entered from the bright winter sun into chill and dark; these Romanesque churches were built with small high windows, not only to keep out the heat of summer, but the arrows of the Saracens. When the raiders were seen out to sea the villagers would crowd into the fortified church, with their beasts and cattle if they could, bar the door, and pray for deliverance. The stone known as the Pillow of the Saintes, where their Holy Heads were resting when they were rediscovered by King Réné, is worn by centuries of such physical prayer, stroked and caressed into folds of stone.

We loved the wooden sculpture of the two Saintes Maries in their *barque* bringing with them their jars of ointment. We loved also the small ex-voto paintings, charmingly naïve, of terrible accidents avoided or illnesses recovered from, thanks to the intervention of the Saintes. Here a man is saved from shipwreck, there a child miraculously plucked from a well. Here a carriage and horses has turned over with none hurt, there a bolt of lightning missed a shepherd by centimetres, and, of course, in one picture someone is saved from the horns of a bull. In most of these pictures the little *barque* containing the two Saintes is painted in the top corner, up in heaven on pink clouds. When we first went these paintings were everywhere in the church, now they are collected together and placed behind protective glass. Some date back to the eighteenth century, and while we regret that their former informality has gone, we are glad that their enormous value both as paintings and documents has been recognised.

Having passed the statue of the *barque* on one's left, and the fresh water well to the right, the entrance to the crypt was before you, down the steps, into a flickering cavern where there was no need for other light than that of the hundreds of votive candles.

Here is Sara's effigy. Alone. There are so many candles that in winter the place is pleasantly warm, in summer stifling. Her statue appears conical, her little black face is scarcely visible, and her body not at all under the layers of gowns given her by the faithful: gypsy colours, pink and lavender and hot orange, blue, and violet, trimmed with froths of lace and bunches of ribbon. Round her neck are gold chains, and brooches are pinned to her robes, and the walls are hung with little silver plaques recording favours received under her aegis.

On the day of the Festival we went into the Church early, and it was well we did, for it filled up fast and soon there was little space. We hitched along the benches to make room for as many faithful behinds as possible, then the standing room was taken, until only the centre aisle was left free.

We looked again at the *barque*, and checked that there were just the two Maries in it. We had begun to doubt our memory, since wherever the *barque* is drawn on a programme, or leaflet or poster, it always contains *three* figures. Sara is there as well.

We then went headlong into a service that was a completely new experience for a couple of cold-blooded protestant English (though we discovered afterwards that it had shaken some Parisians out of their normal *sang-froid* too).

It got straight to the point, the first hymn made it absolutely clear that these were Provençal saints we were greeting, specifically Languedoc and Provence; that their loving care was reserved exclusively for the people of the *terroir*, which included the *gitans*, the gypsies. Having reminded the saints of their duties, and the territorial limits thereof, we roared our appreciation in many refrains, which we learnt fairly quickly as the words were simple phrases of homage, and came after every verse or sentence; indeed the priests had very little to say, it was not so much audience participation as a complete takeover.

We welcomed the saints. We praised them. We asked them to intercede. We invoked. The invocation was lovely:

O Sainte Marie Jacobé
O Sainte Marie Salomé
Saintes Maries, servants of the Lord,
Saintes Maries, faithful of Jesus,
Saintes Maries, present at the tomb,
Saintes Maries, messengers of Easter,
Saintes Maries, abandoned at sea,
Saintes Maries, missionaries to the heathen,
Saintes Maries, the pattern of mothers,
Saintes Maries, valiant to the task,
Saintes Maries, apostles of Provence,
Saintes Maries, guardians of the sea,
Saintes Maries, who reign over the plains,
Saintes Maries, hope of the sick. . . .

Intercede for us, Pray for us.

It was hypnotic.

The emotion was strong about us. Every face was upturned to the portal of the High Chapel (which one does not visit) above our heads from where, slowly, the *chasses* containing the bodies of the Saintes descended, one by one. Every metre the descent stopped in order to attach bouquets to the wires on which they were suspended, bouquets offered by the pilgrims. Hands from below lifted toward the *chasses* in greeting and supplication, the next hymn, an Allelluia, was sung fervently in Provençal, and the feeling seemed one of a family rejoicing in having absent members visiting. Here were their very own saints, down among them again.

The refrain now became 'Viva les Saintes Maries! Viva Sainte Sara!' and for the first time in the service Sara was mentioned by name. The hymnsheet did not mention her. The acclaim redoubled now, as the gypsies really let go. The noise bounded off the four feet thick, old stone walls, as *roms*, *manouches*, *tziganes*, all the tribes, felt their hour had come. They sang, they sobbed, they roared. Two worlds, two faiths, one ceremony, but probably not honouring the same Gods.

It was an exhausting service, and was followed by the procession. Sainte Sara's effigy emerged from her crypt, and was raised high above our heads. She was preceded by a man in a white suit, dark-faced, dark-eyed and regal. He could have been the king of gypsies, had not one of them told us that the idea of a king is an exaggeration of the media, and not their way. A tribal elder then, perhaps. After the Sainte came the gypsy families, smartly dressed, Father in front, and so on in order till Mother brought up the rear with the youngest in her arms.

All processions at Saintes-Maries lead down to the sea, and then back to the church. The gypsies are commemorating the arrival of the *barque* containing the Saintes Maries to the shores of the Camargue, where, they say, Sara was already there, to welcome them.

All are accompanied by horsemen, *gardians* and *manadiers* on the white horses of the Camargue. This alone makes the procession worth seeing, but when in addition the gypsies are there, it is unforgettable. As well as the swaying effigy of Sainte Sara, there were gypsy banners, festooned with flowers and ribbons, and music: accordions, guitars, fiddles and drums. They seemed untiring; we, however, after a refreshing cool drink, retreated into the quiet Relais Culturel, where an exhibition told us something of the history of the gypsies, and where we were able to talk to them. Always before we had failed to divert them from a well-rehearsed sales-pitch – medallions, shawls, basket-ware. Here at last we got answers to our questions.

'Is Sara officially a saint of the Catholic Church?' we asked a priest whose father was a gypsy. We had been unable to find her name in the Calendar.

'She is a saint by popular acclaim,' he told us, firmly, smiling. We had just discovered how many gypsies had been wiped out during the war, as deliberate Nazi policy, and tried to convey to him our horror. In some countries, Holland for example, it had been a hundred percent and there is no doubt they suffered far more (proportionately) than the Jews. We have to ask whether this was due to their fragmentation and lack of tribal cohesiveness, their lack of formal culture? One thing is certain: the Jewish people have been far more successful at reminding us all of those dreadful days. Who, nowadays, thinks of the gypsies in the concentration camps?

Perhaps one of the factors leading to our forgetting the plight of the gypsy people is their lack of a lasting art form. Whereas Jews are accomplished in all the arts, the gypsy is a musician and a dancer, but he does not paint, he does not write books or poetry. The hands that are skilled in plucking the strings of a guitar, such as those of Manitas de Plata (Little Silver Hands, the famous guitarist of the Camargue), take ill to brush or pen. They do not even make something practical and beautiful, like the carpets of the

Middle Eastern nomadic tribes. The gypsy's art is ephemeral, they leave nothing behind them that we can admire.

The priest discovered that we lived in a boat, and that we were, in some sort, nomadic. 'Why, you are Travellers too,' he said warmly. 'Come with me,' and that was how we found ourselves taken through to a churchyard where the sun danced down through the leaves of the acacia trees, and a welcome party was in progress. He introduced us, we felt with a liberal application of the term, as Travellers from England. We were given wine and sweet cakes, and were able to watch as gypsy musicians arrived; the young fiddler was blind, and carefully guided by his companions. The assembly, a convivial mixture of priests, gypsies, Arlésiennes in local costume, *manadiers* and *gardians* in their best cord trousers with the stripe down the leg, velvet jackets and black felt hats, drank and danced and chatted. One of the most eager dancers was a gypsy, her hair caught back Spanish style, her satin blouse pinned with gold brooches, and her earrings twinkling. She was probably well into her eighties.

A young girl danced for us all, in swirling gypsy skirt, proud, graceful, and gay. Her shoes were worn, and as the night went on she would dance through these and need another pair, as the rejoicing continued. Groups of musicians would cluster in the streets, in the carparks, on the beach, and the dancing and music would go on untiring for most of the night.

Not for us though. It was a lovely party but we took our leave at sunset with warmest thanks, and went to look for some dinner.

In the church, the beloved Saintes would not be left alone. All night a vigil would be kept by the pilgrims, a night of quiet friendly companionship, lit by the candles held in the pilgrim's hands.

Bill, who is a religious sceptic a good deal of the time and who only fervently believes when he is caught at sea in a bad gale, was quite moved by the service. Call it superstition, idolatry, any patronising term you will, one can be quite overcome by so much emotion in a confined space. 'These people really believe,' he said. 'It must be a great comfort to them, and it is very impressive.' It was a comfort to Laurel, who has a hotline to the Lord that she uses frequently.

The following day there were early solemn masses for Sainte Marie Jacobé, whose feast it was, and then the wooden *barque*, containing the statues of the two Maries, also processed down to the beach, for the Benediction of the sea itself, presumably for bringing the saints to these shores. Great numbers of people after this ceremony were wet to the knees, having followed their saints into the sea in their fervour, with no thought for their shoes and socks. Old dames with their skirts kilted up revealed kneelength black stockings. The Arlésiennes, in their beautiful full-length silk dresses, took care to keep well back from the sea's edge.

After the return to the church, amid emotional farewells,

the *chasses* were slowly lifted back to the High Chapel, where, since one does not visit, they would remain in peace but no great excitement until October.

On our way home Bill was thoughtful. 'How many people realise that the Holy Family had servants?' he asked.

There were gypsies around Aigues-Mortes for a week or so after the ceremony as they gradually dispersed to the four corners of Europe. Having an evening drink at the Express Bar our continuum was rudely disturbed by an urchin of about seven, with shaggy black hair and his big brother's guitar, who placed his foot on a chair far too high for him, threw his nails across the guitar strings with no attempt to shape a chord, and yelled quaveringly at a hundred decibels (falsetto) something he obviously believed to be flamenco. The effect was wondrously dreadful.

Bill hates even good flamenco; in restaurants he gets very fidgetty when gypsies with guitars are seen approaching, in case they put their behinds on the table where he is eating or drinking and explode in his ear. His expression usually warns them off. The urchin took him by surprise. Not until an (almost) empty ashtray was banged on to our table, making the beerglass jump, and the residual ash fly into our non-smoking lungs, an ashtray that demanded that we cross its palm with silver, did Bill's wrath erupt. The urchin crept off a couple of tables, scowling and making the sign against the evil eye. Bill's eyes get very blue when they are angry, and are thought to bring very bad luck indeed.

The urchin went the rounds of the square and ended up at the Perroquet Bar, where we had the pleasure of seeing a waiter lift him under the armpits, deposit him with a deplorable lack of gentleness in the street, and say: 'One more time, and I fetch the *gendarmes*.'

22

Sailors' farewell

'*Gen de marino*
Toquo li la man viro-li l'esquino.'
. . . .
'Sailor Jack:
Touch his hand, then turn your back.'

It seemed as if everyone was restless, wanting to be on the move, itching to get away. We watched the yachts sweep past on the way to their summer in the Mediterranean, and longed to join them. Most of our itinerant friends were long gone, and sending us postcards which made us green with envy.

It is no small job to get a big boat fit for sea, even if we had not lost a couple of months' serious preparation. We had to scamp some things which had to do with comfort or beauty, but we could not ignore any job that bore on our safety at sea. The galley was at last marinised, or marinaded, which we thought was a better word. That is to say the fronts of the shelves were fitted with varnished lips to prevent the contents falling off, and the pressure cooker was given a safe stowage. Ingenious little holders were devised for the wooden spoon jar and the salt pot, and fiddles were fixed to the hob to prevent that bane of seacooks, errant saucepans.

We went round the inside of the boat screwing everything down. In the saloon we bolted the table and the sofa down and anchored the chairs to the walls with cords going through brass eyes. Laurel packed away breakables that had no safe home, and anything else that was not necessary; life would be simplified now. She put the First Aid in a more accessible place, and bought a pot of dried flowers to replace the real ones that usually stood on the table.

On windless days it began to get unbearably hot in the canal, and we prayed for a mistral or the fortunately almost diurnal sea-breeze to cool us down.

The insect life on the bank was teeming. Huge and lovely demoiselles, dragonflies with lace wings and emerald necklaces darted and swooped over the reeds. The spiders came out at twilight and we watched them as they industriously stitched one part of our boat to another.

The cats occasionally brought in a praying mantis, known here as the *prego diou*. The children of the Camargue used to hold the mantis between finger and thumb, and say: '*Prego Diou! Diguo mi mounto es Marsille?*' and the insect would point in the direction of Marseille, as requested.

The biters and stingers stepped up their campaign to eliminate human beings from the canal bank. Unfortunately said insects made it uncomfortable even to go outdoors. There is a little fly, so small that you can barely see it, probably the same beast that the Bahamians call 'No-see-um', a name far better than anything Linnaeus might have given it. They bite. Ferociously. They are supposed to live near the ground and in times past made the vineyard workers' lives a misery; but they bite not only ankles, they get in one's hair where they seem to use the follicles as footholds to get a better grip and bite deeper. The bites itch like mad, and after about twenty-four hours raise a secretion of a gummy fluid that hardens into a crust. They are disgusting. The local people call them either *arabiques* or *alambiques*, the word varying from place to place. They are immune to all repellents, though one would not credit this to see the preventive nostrums for sale in the market. They appear only between Easter and the middle of June, and only near vegetation. Unfortunately we are moored alongside a grassy quay with reeds, flowers and wild fennel. Very pretty, but harbouring what Francine calls '*bestioles*'. When the *alambiques* have gone the mosquitoes arrive, and if you wish to eat outdoors (and who does not in summer?) the meal must be over before the wind drops at sunset not to be completely disrupted. These are not your namby-pamby little British gnats. These in the Camargue could be harnessed to draw a cart. The smaller ones bite, the larger take you off and lodge you in a tree to consume at their leisure. This feeding frenzy goes on for about an hour, then as the night wind begins to blow, and the stars come out, the mosquitoes disappear, and you are again free to sit out of doors and enjoy the evening. One mosquito, always, will be waiting quietly in the bedroom until you are asleep, when it will float down from the ceiling, and zing in your ear. There follows a room-wide battle with damp flannels, that being the most ecologically sound method of disposal, though as it necessitates leaping over the bed and up on benches it is very disturbing to the sleep pattern. Having stopped the mosquito's *chanson* dead in a damp flannel and composed oneself again for sleep, what happens? Zing! Her sister comes down to see what all the excitement was about. Yes, we have screens in the open portholes, but the doors are also open all day, and we suppose that is when they come in. Docteur Courant assures us that there is no longer any malaria here in the Camargue, *Dieu merci*.

What with the heat and the insects and a bad attack of wanderlust, we could not wait to get away.

Laurel's shopping lists covered almost every available sheet of paper. Catfood, kitchen rolls, long life milk, stores of food and drink, charcoal for the barbecue. One would have thought we were going on an expedition into the desert.

In a way we were. Seldom would we be going into marinas where you can step ashore to the supermarket. We would either be cruising at sea, or moored in anchorages where it could be a long row to the shops, and in any case we preferred to be as self-sufficient as possible. One good store-up a week for the perishables is ideal for our kind of cruising.

In Bill's notebook of 'Things to Do in the Engine Room' more and more items were ticked off, but we were waiting for Bernard to bring back a water pump he was repairing.

We took the books back to the library.

We wormed the cats.

We tidied up the quay, removing all our building rubbish down to the tip. Anything that would burn we put onto a bonfire, on which we barbecued the viands at the farewell party we threw for the whole peninsula. Bernard turned up with the water pump, and was regaled with rosé and hamburgers, and finally there was nothing to stop us going, except unimportant details like the telephone which we remembered just in time. We detached the telephone wire from the wheelhouse, wrapped the business end carefully in plastic, and left it in a box on the bank at the bottom of the pole.

We enticed the cats back on board with crokkies, shut them in the bathroom, and left the quay amid the good wishes and wavings of the neighbours. As we were pointing up-canal, we had to turn round. This is done at a spot between our berth and *Massabielle*, where the canal widens. The dry season had lowered the level of the canal, however, and we stuck fast half way round, right across the canal, which somewhat spoilt the dramatic effect of our departure, as it took a good quarter of an hour to unstick. Luckily no vessel came in sight while we blocked the channel.

At last we came free, and waving our goodbyes all over again we headed seawards, past the cemetery, under the first bridge, past L'Escale (we could see their gay sunblind behind the municipal toilets), through the turning basin at the Porte de La Gardette, through the open railway bridge, and under the third bridge where we made fast alongside the barge *Lormont*, under the Tower of Constance. There were now no more fixed bridges between us and the sea, and it was here we planned to put up the masts and set up all our rigging. We expected this to take three or four days.

Lormont is Patrice's *bateau brocante*, a barge in which he buys and sells nautical antiques and nautical junk, all mixed higgledy-piggledy in the hold of the old barge, which the *mairie* want him to take away. They have classified it as a passenger boat, because customers go into it, and insist on him conforming to all the passenger carrying regulations that would apply to a ferry. Ways and means could be found round this problem but they will not be found. Being a Breton, Patrice has no local pull. That matters down here, so he will lose in the end. But the main loser will be the town for people come from far and wide to visit his *bateau brocante*. Unlike Britain, the French do not have much second-hand nautical hardware, and *Lormont* is almost unique and very well frequented.

We had many visitors, being much more in the public eye than we were at Le Bourgidou, only a kilometre away up the canal. One was a representative of the Harbour-Master at Port Camargue, who manages the port at Aigues-Mortes. He objected to our mooring, outside *Lormont*.

'Where do you want us to go?' asked Bill reasonably.

'Here, alongside the quay.' It was the only vacant berth.

'What is the *fond*, the depth of water there?'

'I do not know.'

'This device is a lead-line,' Bill explained patiently. 'It is used to measure the depth. Please to measure it.'

The representative did so. 'One metre twenty,' he announced.

'If you will look on our stern,' said Bill, 'you will see that the water reaches a painted mark which reads one metre fifty. Will you have the berth dredged or shall we fly?'

He left us in peace, but we were interrogated by other people, tremendously intrigued by the masts and rigging that were going up. The French could not believe it. 'You will go to *sea*? In a *péniche*? How is this possible? It is not allowed!'

One French yachtsman was particularly and persistently

disapproving. Wearily we explained for the seventh or eighth time that only for French *péniches* was it not allowed, biting back the temptation to say: 'and just as well!' Maritime nations like Holland and England, we pointed out, made no distinction between canals, estuaries, the coastal trade, and the open sea. A boat was either seaworthy or it was not, British and Dutch barges were used for both canal work and coasting, *Hosanna* had already crossed the North Sea in bad winter weather, and come down channel to the Baie de la Somme. We considered ourselves seaworthy, which was the only thing that mattered, *et alors*? (so what?). He wondered, with round eyes, what the Bureau d'Affaires Maritime would have to say. 'Nothing,' said Bill shortly. 'We are a British ship, answerable to our own Department of Transport and International Maritime Law, all the rules of which we conform to.' It sounded impressive. Our tormentor disappeared, muttering and shaking his head. The English were mad, it was well known. Your thoroughly reasonable and totally sane Frenchman went racing single-handed in enormous multihulls too light for the weather, breaking down or breaking up, losing their floats, their masts or even their lives; or else they rowed across the Pacific, or windsurfed across the Johore straits; but this, of course, could all be explained and excused by the magic words *sport*, or *défi* (challenge). If we had told our interrogator that we were going to be the first grandparents to row our barge three times round Corsica backwards, he would have understood completely, shaken our hands and wished us luck, but we were not interested in *le sport*, engaged on no *défi*, just a quiet summer cruise, not looking for drama, in a well-found boat. The French find this hard to understand.

We had ascertained in advance that the oil station at Le-Grau-du-Roi closed at the weekend, and that if no one nipped in ahead of us we could occupy that berth while prudently awaiting a weather forecast. So it was at the weekend that, watered, stored, masts up, and in all respects ready for sea, we chugged the remaining four kilometres down the Chenal Maritime to Le-Grau-du-Roi at crack of dawn to catch the opening of the pair of bridges operated by the reputedly bad-tempered bridge-master (who was polite and pleasant to us), and moored along-side the fuelling quay, flushing out several weekend fishermen, to whom we apologised. '*Pas grave,*' they said cheerfully.

We bought a baguette and had breakfast, watching the sea. Everything felt different from the canals. The sea smelt different. The noises of a busy little port in high summer were different. The feeling of the swell and surge of the sea, now only fifty yards away, felt different. And after the punishing heat of the last week, it was blessedly cooler, here by the sea.

We were disturbed, quite happily, by the fishing boats, the tourist day-trip boats and hundreds of anglers on the quay. Serge, the owner of the three-legged dog, looking ten times healthier and happier than when he waited at the Express Bar, waved to us from a little fishing boat. 'You made it then!' he grinned. Everyone including ourselves was good-natured. Later in the day we bought a hugely indecent amount of fresh-caught shell-fish to make up our own *plateau de fruits de mer* (what a nice expression it is: 'fruits of the sea'!), bought our last baguette and some *pain de campagne* for keeping. The weather forecast that evening was excellent.

So on Monday morning early, before the fuelling quay reopened, we cast off the mooring ropes, and sailed out to sea. We turned eastwards, and passed close along the coast in very shallow water, seeing the Camargue from the other angle, from the sea. A low strip of land, a sandy beach with a green line of vegetation above it, then the golden line of Les-Saintes-Maries, and then nothing except an enormous blue sky. Bill was content, he does not like hills and mountains much: they get in between him and the view, he says.

We watched the coast glide past for some time, entirely happy.

'By the way, how is your eye?' asked Laurel rather belatedly.

'Can't see a thing,' said Bill cheerfully. Then he said quietly, 'For Pete's sake, look back. Do you see what I see?'

Behind us, honey-coloured in the sun, was Les-Saintes-Maries-de-la-Mer, shimmering above a turquoise band of sea, the church the highest point by far. Mirrored in the sky above was a second Saintes-Maries, wavering, shifting in the air, a fainter shade of honey, and upside down.

La vieilo danso.

Hosanna is over sixty years old, and she danced on the little waves of the open sea. Laurel is as young as she feels, but she is a grandmother. She spread her arms wide in sheer delight, and danced a step or two in the wheelhouse.

As the last landmark, the lighthouse of Faraman, fell astern of us, there were three old ladies dancing.

Appendix 1

A taste of wild France

We have been blessed with the produce of this region. A bounty of fruit and vegetables grows in the Gard, from early baby artichokes (*les gallices*) to the famous celery from Fourques through all the cherries and peaches and strawberries of summer. Herbs are fresh almost all the year round. The olive oil of Uzès and St Gervasy perfume the frying pans of the Gard. The *charcuteries* of Arles and the Cévennes, the fish from Grau-du-Roi, mussels and oysters from the Etang de Thau, *foie gras* from the Etang d'Or, the chestnuts, mushrooms, honey and goat's cheese from the mountains, the rabbits herb-fed from the Garrigues north of Nîmes, all these things enrich our dinners, and all of it costs a good deal less than it does on the Côte d'Azur. From the Petite Camargue come asparagus and melons, the Vins des Sables, which is cheap and cheerful if drunk young enough and well chilled, rice, salt, and farmed trout and gambas.

With it all, the bread: the French loaf that makes almost any food into a feast. The loaf *artisanal*, vaunted by your local baker, who says that 250 grams of bread per person per day is good for you (250 grams is half a *gros pain*, which does the two of us for lunch and next day's breakfast). The baker also informs his customers, in a printed poster on the door, that the supermarket bread which smells so good in the *hypermarché* has come frozen in tons from the factory, to be baked on site at the last minute, and cheats you into buying an inferior product. Whereas he, *peuchère*, has been up half the night baking your loaf, *madame*, and *voilà*! How good it is.

It would be hard to eat badly at home, in Wild France. Recipes serve four unless otherwise indicated.

Winter

We have to begin with *bœuf gardian*. It has developed, one supposes, from Camargue cowboy food. You carved a chunk of bull, chucked in a good dollop of the *rouge* that you were drinking, threw in a handful of herbs that grew nearby, and put it to stew until you were ready for dinner.

It is a little more sophisticated now. After discussing with the butcher the relative merits of wild bull meat and Corrida bull meat, it appears that the wild bull is better flavoured, and not so tough. 'Look how he has run about, the Corrida bull, before he dies. Much chemistry occurs within the working muscles. Of course he will be tough, like an old horse. One kilo, you said, *madame*? Of *taureau sauvage*? *Impeccable.*'

This recipe is from Vauvert:

Boeuf gardian: Cowboy beef

One kilo of wild bull	One large onion, sliced
Three carrots	Two sticks of celery
A good chunk of fennel stalk	150 grams smoked lardons
¾ of a litre of red wine	2 cloves garlic
A bouquet garni	2 tablespoons tomato paste
Zest of orange	150 grams black olives

You will probably have to do a little substitution here. Instead of *taureau sauvage* you can use skirt or shin of beef. The lardons can be replaced by cubes of thick smoked bacon, or chunks of smoked hock. The rest is easy.

Fry the cubed meat in olive oil until it begins to gild. Add the onion, the lardons, and the carrots, fennel, and celery suitably chopped, and turn it all over till golden. Sprinkle with a little flour and brown everything nicely. Then add the wine, the bouquet garni, the zest of an orange, two crushed cloves of garlic, and the tomato paste. Cover and simmer for three hours, adding water if necessary as it reduces. At the end of the cooking add the stoned olives and cook for another fifteen minutes.

The gravy should be finished with a fillet of mashed anchovy and a spoonful of *pastis*.

Even if you cannot persuade the children that this is wild bull cowboy style, it is an excellent beef stew.

It should be served with *riz camarguais* (Camargue rice).

Cook 200 grams of long-grain Camargue rice, which you have previously washed well, in an enormous amount of salted water. It needs longer cooking than some kinds, so try twenty minutes. Drain, rinse well, and serve.

Beanpot

Call this what you will, it comes down to pork and beans. If you added a morsel of *confit* (goose or duck) or even stirred in a tablespoon of goose or duck fat, we could dignify it with the name of *cassoulet*, provided that you have used good quality beans.

A knuckle of ham	4 slices of pork belly
200 grams of haricot beans	A large onion
1 tbsp tomato paste	A stick of celery
	A bouquet garni

Cover the beans with boiling water and leave for at least an hour, preferably overnight. Turn the slices of pork quickly in a hot pan till each side is just coloured, and a little fat has melted. Set aside the slices, use the fat to fry the chopped onion, and when it is gilded, stir in the tomato paste. Put the soaked beans, the knuckle, the pork slices, onions and the bouquet garni in a casserole, add a stick of celery to the contents, and cover with water. Add pepper but no salt at this stage. Simmer for hours on the hob or in the oven, watching that the bottom does not catch. After three hours test the beans, they should be tender but still whole, and season them if necessary.

One need not be too fussy what meat goes in with the beans. It can be a piece of salt pork, or a smoked hock. You can add at the beginning, with great benefit, a pig's trotter cut in halves, and towards the end of the cooking, chunks of smoked sausage, such as *montbéliard*, or *saucisson à l'ail*. The important thing is to balance the salty meats with the unsalted, and use the very spicy sausages as a grace note. As far as seasoning goes, some like a teaspoon of paprika, some like a dash or two of Worcestershire Sauce, some like mustard, or more tomato, or a shake of Tabasco. It is an infinitely variable dish, always good, sometimes memorable. Good beans soak up the flavours, blend with the spices and seasonings, and absorb the unctuous sauce, but remain a delicious background accompaniment for the pork.

What you can *not* do is throw a tin of baked beans in tomato sauce into a pan with some pallid chainstore sausages made of plastic protein and chemical flavours, and expect the same results.

Spring

In spring we think of young lamb, and asparagus. The first strawberries come in, and we eat them till the season is over, because they are cheaper than *patisseries*. Wild leeks, as thin as spring onions, come into the market, they grow in the vineyards. One market lady warned me to be careful where they were picked, she ate some that had been sprayed along with the vines, and '*Booou Diouuu*! I was very ill with a crisis of the liver afterwards.'

The shellfish are good and plentiful, so I had a go at the crab mousse we ate at the Quatre Vents:

Terrine of crab

200 grams crab meat
25 grams butter
80 ml milk or milk and
   stock
1 tbsp chopped shallots

1 egg yolk
40 grams flour
1 egg white
1 tbsp chopped parsley

It turned out a coarser texture, but excellent in taste. In the restaurant they turned it out of ramekins, a little flower pot shape for each person, and surrounded it with a pretty pool of russet-coloured sauce. I found it easier to cook in a terrine, and that sauce was not needed. A crab weighing 650 grams gave me more than enough meat, and the *court-bouillon* it was cooked in, reduced a little more, provided plenty of stock.

Make a panada by whisking together the melted butter, the flour and the egg yolk, over gentle heat. Remove the pan from the heat and add the boiling milk, or milk and stock gradually, stirring until the mixture forms a dough and leaves the sides of the pan (you may not need all the liquid). When the panada has cooled, pound it with the crab meat, adding it gradually at the same time as you dribble in the unbeaten white of egg. Season the mixture and add the shallot and chopped parsley. If you added fish stock to the panada, you will need only a little salt and pepper and a shake of nutmeg. Butter a glass terrine, line it with clingfilm, and press the mixture well down into it, smoothing the top. Cover with clingfilm and cook in the microwave oven for six minutes. This is good either hot or cold.

Fougasse **with pears**

Fougasse is a square of sponge with a sugary top, a speciality of Aigues-Mortes. It goes dry quickly, like a sponge. I found that when it did this, it made a very good dessert.

Quantities are hard to specify, as it depends on how much cake you have, and how big the dish is.

Stale sponge cake	Butter
Demerara sugar	Orange flower water
Small cooking pears	

Lay the sponge cake in a glass dish and sprinkle the top with orange flower water. (This makes it taste more like real *fougasse*.) Peel, core, and halve the pears, strew them with demerara sugar and dot with butter, cover with clingfilm and cook them gently in the microwave oven for a minute or so, until the juice runs and the butter and sugar make a sauce. The advantage of the micro here is that you get only the fruit juice, no extra water. You then simply upend the pears and the sauce over the sponge. It can go in the oven for half an hour with the rest of your dinner, when the top should brown nicely, or can be finished off in the microwave oven.

Summer

It is too hot to eat much at midday. One needs cold appetising food in small quantities, and plenty of 'summer wine'.

In the evening we cook outdoors if we can, barbecuing, or making *paella*.

Cold duck salad

1 chopped stick of celery	1 chopped crisp apple
2 inches cucumber, diced	4 dried apricots, diced
A handful of quartered walnuts	Diced green pepper

Mix with good mayonnaise or, if you like it a little sharper, with a cole slaw dressing. Add this to the remains of your sliced cold duck, and if it still won't go round four people, add more of any or all of the salad ingredients. DO NOT soak the apricots, the textures of nut and dried fruit and crunchy vegetables are part of the charm of this salad.

Summer wine

This is Bill's speciality.

> ½ bottle cold red or rosé Vin des Sables
> 1 tin of fizzy Orangina
> An egg-cupful of ginger ale essence (Sodastream)
> Several shakes of Angostura Bitters
> One tray of ice cubes

Mix together and keep it cool. You can float some fruit and cucumber slices on the top if you feel festive.

Paella for two

The Camargue has borrowed two dishes and absorbed them into their culture, one is the *couscous* of North Africa, and the other is *paella* from Spain. *Couscous* is a restaurant dish, but *paella* can be made in quantity, in the open air, in pans three feet across, at *fiestas*, *ferrades*, or *fêtes*. We love it, and have developed a smallscale *paellita*, just for us two.

1 chicken leg	1 slice of salt pork
100 grams peeled shrimps	½ kilo of mussels
1 small onion	1 tbsp chopped green pepper
120 grams rice	1 clove of garlic
100 grams cooked peas	A pinch of saffron
salt and pepper	Olive oil

Crush the garlic clove and fry in olive oil. When well browned, discard it. It will have done its job and flavoured the oil. Chop the chicken leg through the bone into bite-size pieces with a cleaver. An even number of pieces prevents quarrelling. Cut the salt pork into squares of about two centimetres. Fry the chicken and pork gently in oil, adding the chopped onion and green pepper, and turning it all over well. Clean and cook the mussels, they need no extra water but their own, and when the steam blows under the lid of the saucepan count sixty and take them off the fire. Decant the mussel juice into a transparent jug, so that you can watch it settle. When the meat has been frying (very gently) for about ten minutes add the rice, and turn it in the oil till it is transparent. Then add about three-quarters of a litre of chicken stock, and a little mussel juice (it may be salty) a bit at a time, stir everything, bring to a boil, then turn down the heat and cook gently for about another fifteen minutes. Towards the end of the cooking you put in the shrimps, the mussels (shelled or not as you wish), the peas, and the saffron, which is essential for *paella* but must not be cooked too long or the delicate flavour becomes bitter.

If you feel really festive now would be the moment to tip in that tin of little octopus you bought on holiday last year and don't know what to do with.

The *paella* looks much nicer if the shrimps are unpeeled and the mussels are in their shells. The colour is Mediterranean, the green of peas and peppers, the saffron of the rice, the blue-black musselshells and their orange inhabitants, and the sharp pink of shrimps. Alas, in the real world, men will not shell their own shrimps, and are even a bit startled if they have to fork a mussel off the half shell. Beauty gives way to peace in the home.

But if you have a party and give them enough to drink first you can coerce them into peeling at least *one* shrimp.

The recipe multiplies up for parties.

Anchoiade

Take some of the following *crudités*, as in season: baby artichokes, sticks of carrot, sticks of celery, radishes, cucumber, fennel stalk, baby tomatoes, strips of green and red pepper, peeled broad beans.

Add a hard-boiled egg or two, and display artistically. Crush a clove of garlic and then add four crushed anchovies, which you have blotted with kitchen paper. To this add two tablespoons of good olive oil. Increase the quantities according to the number of lunchers, and eat in the shade on a hot day, dipping the vegetables in the *anchoiade*. Accompanied with crusty French bread and a bottle of *gris de gris* from the dunes of the Camargue. Excellent summer food.

Autumn

As the leaves turn and the vintage is over, hot suppers beckon again, as twilight falls earlier and earlier. There should be a proverb:

When weather turns chilly
More time spent in galley

Oreillettes

½ kilo flour
4 eggs
Rose or orange flower
water

50 grams unsalted butter
Icing sugar

Soften the butter and beat the eggs. Blend all together to make a dough, and let it rest a few hours in the fridge. Take a ball of dough the size of a walnut and roll into a cylinder. Stand it on end and flatten it with the palm of the hand, then roll it out as thin as you can. Then by teasing gently with the floured hands you make it even thinner. When it is paper thin lay it on a lightly floured cloth, and proceed with the rest of the dough.

The *oreillettes* are then deep fried, one at a time. They cook very quickly, take them out when they puff up and are golden. Sprinkle with orange or rose water, and dredge with icing sugar.

Soupe de poissons façon Isles de Stel

1 kilo soup fish	200 grams little green crabs
1 litre water	
1 carrot	1 leek, 1 onion
1 small potato	2 cloves garlic
400 gram tin of tomatoes	Salt and pepper
2 tbsp tomato paste	Saffron

Put the crabs in boiling water to cover with salt and a sprig of thyme and simmer for about ten minutes. Clean the fish, and put them whole in the frying pan with a little oil. Stir until the fish are well oiled. Add the cut up vegetables and continue frying gently. Since it is unlikely that you will have a crab crusher, pound the crabs as best you can, with a pestle and mortar for example. Some mixers might cope, but I doubt it. Tip everything, with the cooking water, and the fish and vegmix, which by now should be nicely fried and smelling very good, into a large saucepan. Add the tomatoes, the tomato paste, and a litre of water. Season with salt, and plenty of freshly ground pepper, as it needs to be quite spicy. Simmer, stirring now and then, for twenty minutes to half an hour.

Now comes the hard bit. The soup must go through a fine sieve, helped by a wooden spoon. This is a labour of love, and you should make sure your family know this, and comfort you with a sustaining glass of something. While they are there they can make the croutons by rusking slices of french bread in the oven. When you have as few remains in the sieve as will serve to quieten your conscience (we are all different here, and some of us tire before others) reheat the soup, add a good pinch of saffron, and serve with croutons, grated *gruyère*, and *rouille*.

Mushrooms

The *cèpes* which arrive in autumn are delicious, either in an omelette, or with chicken. The dried ones are very good if you cannot get fresh, and can be mixed with ordinary mushrooms, to which they give extra flavour.

Chicken with *cèpes*

1 farm chicken	10 cl cream
300 grams *cèpes*	2 glasses white wine
(or 20g dried *cèpes* and	
150g mushrooms)	

If you are using dried mushrooms, cut a couple of them just as they are into tiny pieces and shake into the interior of the chicken with some salt and pepper. If they are fresh, chop the stalks and use them in the same way. This perfumes the inside. Keep back about half the remaining dried *cèpes*, and soak them according to instructions, then blot them dry with tissues. If they are fresh, cut them into chunks. In either case, sweat the mushrooms in butter, and set aside.

Turn the chicken over in a frying pan containing a mixture of hot oil and butter until it is golden, then place it in a lidded casserole with the wine and three glasses of water, and the dried *cèpes* that you did not soak, again cut into little pieces to flavour the sauce, or if using fresh ones, throw in a handful. Cover and cook for forty-five minutes to an hour, basting occasionally. When the chicken is done, remove it onto a dish and keep it warm. Reduce the cooking juices rapidly, add the cream and the mushrooms, check the seasoning, pour round your chicken and serve with pride.

Heron pudding

This recipe is for historical interest only. The heron is a protected bird.

'Before cooking it must be ascertained that no bone of the

heron is broken. These bones are filled with a fishy fluid, which, if allowed to come into contact with the flesh, makes the whole bird taste of fish. This fluid, however, should always be extracted from the bones, and kept in the medicine cupboard for it is excellent for applying to all sorts of cuts and cracks. The heron is first picked and flayed, then slices are cut from the breast and legs to make the pudding. The crust is made exactly like that of a meat pudding, and the slices of heron put in and seasoned exactly as meat would be. The pudding is boiled for several hours according to its size. (I have been told that, as a matter of fact, it tastes very much like a nice meat pudding.)'

Pot Luck, Mary Byron, 1932

In the sixteenth century you were advised to drink plenty of good, strong, old, wine with 'herons, bitterns, shovellers, and all such weather-sore birds.' There are some wines around here that, while neither very good nor old, would certainly be strong enough.

Les treize desserts

These are the thirteen traditional desserts to be placed on the Christmas table in Provence.

Dried figs	Dates
Walnuts	Almonds
Raisins	*Calissons*
Nougat	*Papillotes*
Pompe à l'huile	Melon and apricots,
Clementines	crystallised
Grapes	Stuffed dates and
	walnuts

A dish of nuts and dried fruit is often called Les Mendiants (The Mendicant Friars) because of the sober colours. *Calissons* are little oval shapes made of almond paste. The *pompe* (does it really translate as 'the oil pump'?) is a flat sweet cake made as its name suggests with plenty of olive oil. The *papillotes* are rather like little crackers, each with a *bonbon* inside.

BOUENO ANNADO

Appendix 2

Visiting the Camargue

With the exception of Port Camargue (heaven preserve us) there is no mass tourism and anyone wishing to stay in the Camargue must make their own arrangements. Hotels are small and all the better for it. Restaurants are not all that good, but we have enjoyed eating in some of them. We can recommend:

Aigues-Mortes:
Les Arcades, Boulevard Gambetta. Good class accommodation and the best restaurant in town, though it does occasionally slip up. Expensive. Wine list unreliable.

L'Escale, just outside the main gate. Cheaper rooms. The restaurant has the cheapest menu, and is good for the price. Simple wines.

Abaca, Rte d'Arles on the outskirts. Above average cooking, reasonable prices and talkative chef.

Les Quatre Vents, a motel on the route de Nîmes. The restaurant is fairly priced and not bad. Wine list adequate.

Les-Saintes-Maries-de-la-Mer:
Hotel les Amphores, Ave G Leroy. Hospitable, near centre of town. Processions pass the door. We do not recommend the restaurant attached (under different management), where the prices outreach the quality.

Pont-de-Gau:
The restaurant is the best we found in the Camargue region, and not over-priced. There are rooms. It is next to the Bird Park. Excellent wine list.

Château D'Avignon (close to):
Restaurant La Gasconne. No Gascon dishes, there is another reason for the name. Not bad, and a fair wine list. The Château is in the middle of the Camargue and is nowhere near Avignon city.

Arles:
There are plenty of hotels, but try the Restaurant Gueule du Loup, Rue des Arènes. Good cooking at a fair price and very well chosen wines. The chef's wife is Australian and the welcome something special.